THE
LINGUISTIC
INDIVIDUAL

THE
LINGUISTIC
INDIVIDUAL

*Self-Expression in
Language and Linguistics*

Barbara Johnstone

New York   Oxford

OXFORD UNIVERSITY PRESS

1996

Oxford University Press

Oxford   New York
Athens   Auckland   Bangkok   Bogota   Bombay
Buenos Aires   Calcutta   Cape Town   Dar es Salaam
Delhi   Florence   Hong Kong   Istanbul   Karachi
Kuala Lumpur   Madras   Madrid   Melbourne
Mexico City   Nairobi   Paris   Singapore
Taipei   Tokyo   Toronto

and associated companies in
Berlin   Ibadan

Copyright © 1996 by Barbara Johnstone

Published by Oxford University Press, Inc.
198 Madison Avenue, New York, New York 10016

Oxford is a registered trademark of Oxford University Press, Inc.

Library of Congress Cataloging-in-Publication Data
Johnstone, Barbara.
The linguistic individual : self-expression in language and
linguistics / Barbara Johnstone.
p.   cm.—(Oxford studies in sociolinguistics)
Includes bibliographical references and index.
ISBN 0-19-510184-7.—ISBN 0-19-510185-5 (pbk.)
1. Linguistics   2. Individuality.   3. Language and languages.
4. Sociolinguistics.   5. Self.   I. Title.   II. Series.
P123.J63   1996
306.4'4—dc20   95-21703

The following material in chapter 5 is quoted with permission:

excerpts from the 1974 House Judiciary Committee speech and the 1976 Democratic
Convention keynote address by Barbara Jordan, with the permission of Barbara Jordan; excerpts
from "Kwanzaa," "Gymnastics a Hit in Bryan in the '50s," "Blacks in Focus: Photos Reveal
Slave Descendants' Story" and "On Being Black in Houston" by Sunny Nash, with the
permission of Sunny Nash; excerpt reprinted from *Voices in America: Bicentennial Conversations*
by Bernard Murchland, Prakken Publications, Ann Arbor, Michigan 1987.

1 3 5 7 9 8 6 4 2
Printed in the United States of America
on acid-free paper

032197-3045X5

for Scott

Series Foreword

Sociolinguistics is the study of language in use. With special focus on the relationships between language and society, its principal concerns address the forms and functions of variation across social groups and across the range of communicative situations in which women and men deploy their verbal repertoires. In short, sociolinguistics examines discourse as it is constructed and co-constructed, shaped and reshaped, in the interactions of everyday life and as it reflects and creates the social realities of that life.

While some linguists examine the structure of sentences independent of who is speaking or writing and to whom, independent of what precedes and what follows in a discourse, and independent of setting, topic, and purpose, sociolinguists investigate linguistic expression embedded in its social and situational contexts in everyday life. Interest in linguistic matters among language observers who are *not* professional linguists also focuses on language in use, for it is only there that the intricacies of social structure are reflected and the situational and strategic influences that shape our discourse are mirrored.

Among some sociolinguists it has been a chestnut that an individual's language represents language at the intersection of the various social groups to which that individual belongs and the particularities of the situation. In *The Linguistic Individual* Barbara Johnstone explores a less deterministic hypothesis. She notes that shared norms are a backdrop to individual choices in forging personal linguistic styles, and she attempts to draw individual style within the purview of linguistic theory. With linguistic analysis traditionally focused on the communal and literary analysis on the individual (albeit within a sociopolitical milieu), the analysis presented in *The Linguistic Individual* explores the interface between commonality and individuality, grappling with the challenge of self-expression within shared norms of expressive behavior. Johnstone argues that a linguistics of the community without a linguistics of the individual cannot adequately explain language use.

Offering a platform for studies of language use in communities around the globe, Oxford Studies in Sociolinguistics invites synchronic or diachronic treatments of discourse and of social dialects and registers, whether oral, written, or signed. The series is host to studies that are descriptive or theoretical, interpretive or analytical. While the volumes in the series generally report original research, an occasional one synthesizes or interprets existing knowledge. The series aims for a style that is accessible not only to linguists but to other humanists and social scientists. Some volumes will hold appeal for educated readers keenly interested in the language of human affairs—for example, in the discourse of doctors or lawyers engaging their clients and one another with their specialist registers—or of women and men striving to fathom the sometimes baffling character of their shared interactions. By providing a forum for innovative and valuable studies of language in use, Oxford Studies in Sociolinguistics aims to influence the agenda for linguistic research in the twenty-first century and provide an array of provocative analyses to help launch that agenda. I am pleased to include Barbara Johnstone's innovative study of *The Linguistic Individual* as the latest volume in the series.

Edward Finegan

Preface

I am interested in this book in exploring the individual voice and how individuality and language intersect. Chapter 1 discusses the theoretical possibilities that come to light when linguistics confronts the individual speaker. In chapter 2 I examine narratives of personal experience by a dying African-American woman and a middle-aged white man. Not surprisingly, the two stories are very different. In asking why they are different, I suggest that the traditional explanations—sociolinguistic (class, gender, and race) and rhetorical (purpose and audience)—are descriptively useful but not explanatory. Familiar ways of thinking about variation among speakers do not account for a crucial part of the process by which people decide what to say and how. Though features of people's talk can be correlated with class or audience, the ways people talk about themselves have to do with the particular selves they are creating and expressing in narrative. Individual variation thus has psychological roots. Chapters 3 and 4 describe variations from individual to individual in speech situations in which we might expect to find less variability than we do in spontaneous personal narration. Chapter 3 deals with fairly impersonal academic discourse, and chapter 4 examines the anonymous, information-oriented talk of the telephone survey. It turns out that self-expression is crucial in these sorts of talk, too: articulateness—assuming one is socially positioned so as to be entitled to articulateness in the first place—depends on self-expression, and telephone surveys, even though they are as referential in aim as talk gets, do not work unless interviewers and respondents express individuated personas. There are thus social and rhetorical reasons for which linguistic variation from individual to individual is essential. In Chapter 5 I explore the theoretical assumption that individual speakers display the same linguistic voice across speech situations, despite rhetorical and socio-linguistic pressure to accommodate. I here suggest that there are also moral reasons for individual variation: speakers' choices about how to talk express moral choices about how to act. Chapter 6 discusses idio-syncrasy and its interpretation: how people make sense of linguistic newness. The final chapter summarizes the book's major themes and tries to connect them to the concerns with which I began this investigation: my interest in language, individuality, and artistry.

The texts with which I work are various. The points I make could be illustrated with any bit of language, so I have chosen examples I like or find intriguing. They range from spontaneous narratives of personal experience to scripted interviews. There is talk in this book by women and by men, by Anglo-Americans and by African-Americans; there is narrative talk intended to define lives, academic talk that shares thought and displays articulateness, telephone-survey talk meant to proffer and accept information, and metalinguistic talk about talk.

I use these snippets of language in support of several claims about language. For one thing, I suggest that social facts affect discourse only indirectly. Social influences and linguistic results are mediated by indi-vidual choices. Individual language is, as Friedrich and Redfield put it, "a level of organization with its distinctive processes and complexities" (1976, p. 435). To illustrate this point, it is necessary to rephrase the claims of sociolinguistics in less deterministic terms, to think of a speaker's linguistic system as a repertoire of resources rather than the cause of his or her linguistic behavior.

In recent years linguists have moved from a view of language as a tool for referring to one that stresses the interactive, phatic, socially cohesive functions of language. Many see language as essentially a tool for the expression of relatedness. I here suggest that the self-expressive function of language needs scrutiny, too. I do this, in part, by showing that self-expression is crucial not only in artistic or rapport-building or emotional talk but also in highly referential, anonymous, supposedly disengaged talk. Speakers express their individuality, in other words, not only when one would most expect them to but also when one would least expect them to, and their talk would not succeed if they did not. Speak-ers expect one another to express differentiated human personalities. Another suggestion I make is that models of pragmatic implicature often assume that more about talk is formulaic and conventional than is, in fact, the case. Illustrating this point involves looking carefully at instances of idiosyncracy and newness in discourse and imagining a view of the linguistic process that saw such things as the unmarked case. My examples are of various kinds: the familiar idiosyncracy of children's meanings; the remarkable newness of literary experiments with language; unremarked idiosyncracies in discourse marking and clause combining by which speakers know each other by how they understand each other.

A final theme of the book concerns methodology. Both explicitly and by example I suggest that the close-reading techniques of philologically based discourse analysis are an indispensable tool for linguists. In order to understand how language works on the most concrete level, that is, to understand the mechanisms that influence what real people say in actual situations, we need to study small bits of talk in great detail. As literary linguists have discovered and rediscovered, style is notoriously difficult to describe. Yet we must find ways to understand and talk about particular speakers' styles. It is indisputable that speech is always multivoiced, always drawing on other speech, and that the ways we talk are constrained, shaped, and dictated to us in more ways than we realize (see, e.g., Scollon 1995). But it is also indisputable that no two individuals always speak with the same voice. Creativity is possible, even if it is sometimes difficult; linguistic innovation is crucial for linguistic change and for human social life. Only by complementing the linguistics of language with a linguistics of speakers can we see how the grammatical possibilities examined by syntacticians, the statistical regularities uncovered in sociolinguistic research, and the interpretive conventions described in pragmatics interact with our fundamental need to express ourselves.

This project is the latest step in what has emerged as a career-long series of attempts to answer questions about individual and community, freedom and constraint, posed by A. L. Becker when I was in graduate school. I owe most of my ideas to him, though he is not responsible for what I have done with them. I am also greatly indebted, intellectually and practically, to my other principal mentor, Deborah Tannen, to whom I am more grateful than I am able to express. I started this project while on a faculty development leave from Texas A&M University in 1990–91; that opportunity for uninterrupted reading and thinking was invaluable. Many colleagues at Texas A&M and elsewhere have listened to, discussed, or read parts of this manuscript or earlier versions of it, among them Scott Austin, Ellen Barton, Judith Mattson Bean, A. L. Becker, Jill Brody, Kathleen Ferrara, Dell Hymes, Bob Ivie, Henry and Margery Johnstone (my parents), Jimmie Killingsworth, Shawn Maurer, Chris Menzel, Neal

Norrick, Joel Sherzer, and Deborah Tannen. Companion dog Io provided calm and routine during most of the project; new pup Eddie provided distraction and hope during the final stages. For the last year, Scott's love has given my life and work new texture.

Bryan, TX   *Barbara Johnstone*
March 1995

Postscript

Barbara Jordan died in January 1996, shortly before this book was published but too late in the production process for me to change references to her in chapter 5 to reflect this fact. It was an honor to have met her.

Contents

THE
LINGUISTIC
INDIVIDUAL

— 1 —

Discourse, Society,
and the Individual

*We all have our individual styles in conversation and considered address,
and they are never the arbitrary and casual things we think them to be.
There is always an individual method, however poorly developed, of
arranging words into groups and of working these up into larger units. It
would be a very complicated problem to disentangle the social and
individual determinants of style, but it is a theoretically possible one.*

Edward Sapir, "Speech as a Personality Trait"

This book takes up the problem Sapir describes, namely, that of disen-
tangling the linguistic from the social individual. As Sapir warns, the
problem is complicated; the tangle is not the kind through which one
can simply run a comb but one that takes picking and tugging at strands.
In this chapter I try to straighten out some strands in order to examine
them carefully. My goal is to suggest some of the theoretical and methodological ramifications of thinking about language from the perspective of the individual speaker rather than, as we usually do, from the
perspective of the social aggregate or the abstract linguistic system.

The project has several parts. For one thing, I examine differences
among individual language-knowers and language-users. In part, this
involves demonstrating something we already know: no two people have
the same knowledge of language or the same ways of speaking. But displaying the dimensions along which individuals' languages can differ
requires finding the best methodology for uncovering differences where

3

linguists usually look for similarities; it leads to thinking about what the differences suggest about the interaction between *langue* (language seen as a social fact) and *parole* (actual speech). For another thing, I examine individuals' linguistic consistency across time and situation, calling into question the idea that discourse is completely rhetorical, that is, completely shaped by audience, situation, or purpose. I also examine individual idiosyncrasy, wondering what a model of understanding would be like that took creativity and newness rather than rule and convention as the basic problems for linguistics.

In doing this, I illustrate the need in linguistics for the kind of language study I find most compelling, the work A. L. Becker (1979a) calls "modern philology."[1] As was the traditional philology that gave rise to modern linguistics, modern philology is centered on particular texts. Philologists try to describe what culturally or historically distant texts might mean and why, and how texts mean at all. Their goal, traditionally, is historical or critical: an *explication de texte* or an observation about literary or cultural history. But in the attempt to understand why particular utterances take the shape they do, one also learns things about how language works, things that no complete theory of language can fail to account for. My goal is to suggest that the issues that define linguistics—the nature of language and how it works—can be fully addressed only with reference to the particular. This means recasting questions about the social as questions about the individual, questions about language as questions about speaking, questions about rules and constraints as questions about strategies and resources. I explain in this chapter why all this is necessary.

Aaahh . . .

I once stayed with my sister during a week when, just having moved to a new town, she made a number of phone calls inquiring about goods and services. During one of these conversations, I heard her begin a response with "aaahh," a drawn-out /a/ made lower and further back in her mouth than the /a/ she used in words such as *father* or *hot* and uttered at a low and very slowly falling pitch. I at once thought of our father, who makes exactly the same noise in the same conversational slot in phone conversations of the same sort. *Aaahh* is a small but unmistakable feature of his individual way of sounding. It means "I think I understand what you've just said, and, if I've understood you correctly, I'm disappointed." *Aaahh* is the beginning of a rejoinder to a statement like "We do carry folding directors' chairs, and they're $175 each" or "We'll be able to collect your bulky trash in two weeks or so."

This *aaahh* is so much the property of a single speaker that I heard it as my father's voice coming from my sister's mouth (though I now, of course, think of it as hers, too). *Aaahh* is a characteristic of my father's voice the way that short sentences with stative verbs are characteristic of Hemingway's voice; it is symptomatic of his interactional style the way that balanced two-part sentences are typical of the rhetoric of the eighteenth century. Not only is my father's use of *aaahh* consistent (he has used it as long as I can remember); it is also, as far as I know, idiosyncratic. *Aaahh*, spoken the way he speaks it, is not a member of the conventional set of English lexical possibilities for expressing the meaning it expresses. In fact, *aaahh* expresses a meaning not fully captured in any conventional English word or sound.

We notice linguistic idiosyncrasy of this sort relatively rarely, because people choose ways of conveying meaning that they know others will easily understand more often than they choose to invent new ways of meaning. But no one would deny that no two people talk exactly the same way, even if neither creates new words or structures or pronunciations. Different people have different ways of using language, and the linguistic characteristics by which we know one individual from another appear to us to be more or less consistent over time and situation. Individual voice has to do with our preferring one poet or novelist over another and with our finding some friends easier to listen to than others. It has to do with our ability consciously to mimic salient aspects of others' styles (as people did traditionally in school exercises in style and do now in contests to write the best fake Hemingway or Faulkner) and unconsciously to incorporate features of the way others sound in constructing reported speech for them in spontaneous talk. The fact that no two real people talk alike has to do with our profound irritation with voices that are not individual, such as mechanical voices that give telephone-number information or tape-recorded telephone solicitations, and with voices that sound canned even when they are not, as in restaurants ("Hi, I'm so-and-so, and I'll be your server tonight") or shops ("Have a nice day!"). Institutional attempts to standardize information by reducing variation in its presentation can lead intended audiences to stop listening and intended speakers sometimes nearly to stop speaking. For example, film presentations of airplane safety and emergency procedures are replacing the incomprehensible and un-listened-to mumbling of flight attendants reciting or reading from scripts.

Some societies encourage the linguistic expression of individuality and others discourage it, just as some value other forms of individual expression and some do not. There are speech communities in which predictable, formulaic language is valued more often and ones in which it is more often heard as meaningless. In Bali, for example, individuals are seen as characters playing parts in a "never-changing pageant" (Geertz 1984, p. 128). Individuals are defined by titles and designations, as an actor is defined by a role, and consistent performance of one's role is what matters. Idiosyncracy is shameful, since when people let individuality show they fall out of character.[2] Geertz contrasts the Balinese attitude about individuality with the attitude of Moroccans. In Morocco, individual identity is partly a matter of external attribution; Moroccan Arabs are traditionally known by names morphologically derived from the names or labels of their places of origin, ancestors, offspring, or physical characteristics. But these attributive names are vague and changeable; they do not completely define a person, and in public interaction Moroccans are, according to Geertz, "hyperindividualists." Rosaldo (1984) discusses the chameleon nature of personal identity among the Ilongots, for whom character is seen not as a result of a person's history but as adaptation to the immediate situation. People's names and personal "presentations of self" (Goffman 1959) change as their relationships with others change. In Western belief, people have relatively hidden inner selves, and their public faces are more or less artificial personae. For the Ilongot, Rosaldo says, the public persona is the self.

The history of individualism in the West has been the topic of recurring discussion. Marcel Mauss's (1938) essay on the social history of the person and the self describes the concept of the person as arising in classical Rome, when the "persona"—the social role played by an individual—came to be thought of as a legal entity, a "person." Mauss's student Dumont (1985) traces the subsequent development of the person as the locus of morality. The Stoics of the late Hellenistic period idealized the truly wise person as one who renounced society, discovering the ultimate truths by living as an individual. This ideal, carried into early Christianity, formed the basis for the development of modern individualism. Contemporary individualism, both utilitarian—believing that each person is motivated by his or her own legal and financial interests—and expressive—believing that truth can be ascertained by looking inward and conveyed though speech and imagery that are not bound by social convention—is widely seen as having its origins in the European Renaissance (see, e.g., Greenblatt 1980), though others trace it further back (e.g., Morris 1987). The late-eighteenth-century Romantic movement added the themes of individual difference and the moral importance of self-fulfillment, of acting according to one's own originality (Taylor, 1989); individuals were now valued not only for being legally, economically, and morally autonomous but also for being unique.

While individualism has been seen as a characteristic of Western society in general, Americans have of course long been characterized as even more individualistic than others; the French visitor Alexis de Tocqueville first used the term "individualism" of us in the 1830s. (I discuss American individualism in more detail in chapter 4.) The people whose talk I examine in this study are all Americans. Their beliefs about language and their ways of speaking are greatly influenced by the ideology of individualism that surrounds them. My own beliefs about language are also culturally conditioned. My interest in the linguistic individual and my conviction that this is an important topic have a good deal to do with my own (very self-conscious) individualism. However, when I display and discuss individual variation and voice in the chapters that follow, my suggestions about the fundamentally individual nature of language apply not just to people like me who especially value individuality.

This is so because individuality is a prerequisite for humanity. While ideological *individualism* is not universal, human *individuality* is. There is a great deal that can vary cross-culturally about people's conception of personality, but there are aspects of selfhood that do not vary. As Hallowell points out (1955), self-awareness—a sense of oneself as separate, autonomous, and temporally continuous—is functionally important in the maintenance of social life. If people were not aware of themselves as distinct from others and of other individuals as distinct from each other, they could not function in communities. In one way or another, culture provides individuals with ways of orienting themselves as individuals: ways of identifying themselves and others (such as names and terms for relationships), ways of valuing and evaluating themselves and their actions, ways of displaying the continuity of their memories and physical beings. Through their talk (as well as through other aspects of their behavior), individuals display the fact that they are individuals. To use the common phrase for this, people express themselves with everything they do, whether or not self-expression is at the moment or in the context particularly valued or even thought relevant at all. A society in which everyone always talked alike, in which people were linguistically indistinguishable from one another, would be unthinkable. People *understand* each other because they use familiar sounds, words, and syntactic patterns, for the most part. When speakers do new things they usually suggest what they mean by the newness, but it is part of the case I want to make, as well as part of LePage and Tabouret-Keller's (1985) argument, that "[James] Joyce only provides a somewhat extreme example of what we all do with language" (p. 12). People *know* each other because each has a unique way of sounding, an individual voice.

Nor can it be denied that knowledge of language is fundamentally private and individual. It is not really necessary to demonstrate that no two people do things with language the same way (though I provide evidence to support this claim in later chapters), because it is impossible that two people could do things with language the same way. This is the result of the fact that people are not born knowing how to talk. Though we say that many American children "learn English," in fact no two are learning exactly the same thing. One person's language is different from another's because each individual has a different set of linguistic memories and each makes different generalizations on the basis of what he or she hears. This is obvious in the case of children, whose stores of linguistic memories are limited, and we regularly notice their idiosyncratic generalizations. (For example, a German child who knew only two Barbaras, the other of whom was her mother, once addressed me as "Frau Mama.") But adults' generalizations are idiosyncratic, too.

It is obviously the case that people have different vocabularies and vary in their senses of the nuances of word meaning, but it is equally the case that people have different grammars. Universal grammatical predispositions may lead human beings to make certain kinds of generalizations about linguistic input and not others, but such predispositions do not determine exactly what generalizations people will make. If two language-acquirers hear similar sounds and patterns, they may make similar generalizations, and if the generalizations are similar enough we say that the two speak the same language or set of languages.

Variation in language use is ultimately explicable only at the level of the individual speaker. No matter how refined our models of the various social facts that correlate with patterns of language use—social class, gender, age, ethnic identity, social network, urban versus rural background—we can not predict what a given person will say in a given situation, or how it will be said. The reason for this is that "every use of language is a fresh application, a metaphorical extension of existing systems, made at risk" (LePage and Tabouret-Keller 1985, p. 196). Sociolinguistic research displays patterns of choice, ways of talking that typify social aggregates, but sociolinguistics is predictive only statistically. A theory that claimed to make absolute predictions about a given individual's speech on a given occasion would not be able to account for linguistic change, because change necessarily involves innovation, and although it may be possible to generalize about what sorts of people are most likely to use new forms (J. Milroy 1992, ch. 6), the precise form and timing of an innovation are by definition unpredictable.

The Physical Voice

Before saying more about what I mean by individual voice, let me talk briefly about what I do *not* mean, namely the acoustic differences among speakers that are the result of physical differences among their bodies. Although "voice-prints" are not as individual as fingerprints, people do have fairly consistent and fairly distinct acoustic voices. Infants less than six months old can distinguish their mothers' voices from others' (Friedlander 1970; Mehler, Bertoncini, Barriere, and Jassik-Gerschenfeld 1978), and under ideal circumstances people can do reasonably well at identifying unfamiliar voices they have heard once before (Bull and Clifford 1984).[3] They can do so because the fourth and subsequent acoustic formants in vowels and the higher formants in nasal consonants reflect physical characteristics of the speaker's vocal tract. In addition, there is variation from individual to individual in the length and type of aspiration after initial voiceless stops and in the rate of transition of formants after voiced stops (Ladefoged 1975, pp. 188–189).[4] Because of the amount of acoustic variation from individual to individual, voice-prints and earwitness testimony have proved useful in the courtroom (Ash 1988; Hollien 1990).

Individual variation in physical voice is rooted in biology. Women's voices are typically pitched higher than men's, for example, for physical reasons having to do with the size and shape of the vocal apparatus and with hormonal activity. But the pitch ranges that can be produced by women and by men overlap; some women have voices low enough to sound male, while some men have high, female-sounding voices. There is evidence that vocal pitch varies cross-culturally (Majewski, Hollien, and Zalewski 1972) and that prepubescent boys and girls learn to adjust their vocal musculature so as to produce lower and higher voices respectively (Sachs, Lieberman, and Erickson 1973). This suggests that the acoustic voice is in some respects a learned trait.[5] To the extent that a person's acoustic voice is potentially self-expressive, it is part of what I am concerned with in this book. To the extent that the acoustic voice is physically determined, I am not concerned with it here.

Linguistics and the Individual

In most contemporary approaches to language, the individual figures hardly or not at all. Under the influence of Saussure's (1916) distinction between social *langue* (seen as the object of study for linguistics) and individual *parole*, linguists attempting to provide formal models of native speakers' knowledge of phonology and syntax usually ignore individual differences. Differences among individual speakers may in fact be less obvious in these areas than they are elsewhere. In an experimental study of people attempting to disguise their voices, Ash (1988) found that people from the northern United States appeared to be unable systematically to alter their phonology except to insert one strongly marked southern feature (monophthongal /a/ rather than the diphthong /ay/ in words such as "five" and "night"). Ash claims that individual speakers from the same speech community cannot reliably be distinguished on the basis of phonological variation, because their phonological systems do not vary much. Macaulay (1991) also suggests, on the strength of sociolinguistic fieldwork in Scotland, that phonology may be more "robust"—more consistent, that is, from speaker to speaker and hence less likely to be a resource for the construction of an individual voice— than are other aspects of a person's linguistic knowledge.

But there is evidence of individual variation in phonology. Payne (1980) examined how children moving to Philadelphia from elsewhere acquired regional features of speech and showed that no two ended up with exactly the same system. Ferguson (1979) cites a study by Kunsmann (1976) that described an English-speaking child who for three months expressed negation by means of a phonological transformation reduplicating part of a word. Thus *wati* meant 'water' and *watiti* 'no water'; *up* was 'up' and *upapa* meant 'not up', or 'down'. Ferguson also points out that some English speakers systematically produce velarized pronunciations of /l/ where English phonological rules usually dictate alveolar pronunciations, as in words like *clear*. There are regions of the English-speaking world where /l/ is velarized or vocalized by large groups of speakers (western Scotland and western Pennsylvania are two), but some individuals who would not be expected to velarize for any social or regional reason do so anyway. Ferguson is led to observe, partly on the basis of examples like these, that "THE phonology of a language variety— the normal object of phonologists' study—is a composite of individual phonologies in which the shared structure inevitably has indeterminacies, fuzzy boundaries, and both dialectal and idiosyncratic variation" (pp. 197–198). Few phonologists would dispute this observation, but few take it seriously.

"Idiolectal" variation in syntax has also vexed some linguists. Some such variation can be handled as transitory disorder, as is the case of a child described by Crystal and Fletcher (1979) who graduated from two-word utterances to the insertion of *of* before every noun, or the child described by Wilson and Peters (1988) who produced questions like "What're we cooking on a hot?" that appeared to violate a universal syntactic principle. But the methodology of generative syntax requires reliance on intuitive judgments about syntactic acceptability, and these sometimes vary from individual to individual. This variability calls into question the validity of results based on one analyst's judgments. A fairly casual study of individual variation in acceptability judgments was conducted by Ross (1979), who found that no two of twenty-nine friends of his made exactly the same set of judgments about a set of English constructions. Labov (1972a, pp. 192–199) deals with the matter more systematically. Labov and his coworker Mark Baltin tested people's reactions to sentences like "All the circles don't have dots in them," which can be read two ways (there are no circles with dots or there are some with dots and some without). Previous work on this issue by a syntactician (Carden 1970) had suggested that there are two syntactic "dialects": some speakers interpret the sentences one way and other speakers interpret them the other way. Labov found that any speaker could produce either interpretation if the context was right. Labov claims, on the strength of these results, that there is no such thing as homogeneity in intuitive syntactic judgments. Syntacticians are aware of this, and many regularly exchange anecdotal evidence about their own idiosyncracies. But the issue is rarely dealt with.

The lack of concern in phonology and syntax with issues raised by evidence of individual variation is the result of the fundamental incompatibility of the linguistic individual with Saussurean structuralism (as linguists have interpreted it). Linguists who study *langue* study something that is by definition superindividual and self-replicating. *Langue* is seen as the property of the community, not the individual. The object of study for structuralist linguistics is thus social: societies and social groups, dialects and languages. These are sometimes treated not as convenient abstractions but as real entities.[6] Languages and dialects are often referred to in the discourse of structuralism as agents: languages drop pronouns, for example; dialects influence other dialects.

From an historical perspective, structuralist linguistics is partly rooted in the political realities of the nineteenth century.[7] The ideology of nationalism (which had a great deal to do with the explosion of nineteenth-century interest in historical and comparative linguistics) depended on the notion of autonomous, superindividual language, since a nation was defined, in part, linguistically. Arguments in favor of the nation-states that replaced authoritarian feudal systems were supported by claims of the existence of national groups based on images of sharing;

a nation consisted of people with a shared culture, a shared history, and a shared language.

The metaphor of sharing is ambiguous, however. People can share objects, such as hammers or spoons, by taking turns using them; the objects remain in existence, in drawers or on pegboards, even when they are not in use. Other objects, also with objective existence outside the individual subject, can be shared by being divided, like offices or restaurant desserts. More abstract, currency is shared; two people may never handle the same dollar bill, but they both use and trust the same system. If no one were using a currency system, it would be somewhat difficult to claim that it existed. More abstract yet, people share feelings such as love or distrust, feelings that exist only when they are being "used." For structuralists, language is shared the way a cultural system is, like currency; this seems to have been Saussure's view. But it is also possible to see language as shared the way a feeling is, unimaginable and certainly impossible to study outside a situated personal context.

In the Saussurean view, there are two ways of handling individual variation. One is to treat idiosyncracy as deviance. The other is to see a linguistic individual as constituted by the set of strategic adaptations he or she makes from a closed set of conventional possibilities, in the interactions in which he or she takes part. As Epstein (1978, p. 73) puts it in reference to literary artists, "By combination, anyone may sew himself together a syntactic suit of clothes that expresses his individuality." In this view, individual uniqueness is an artifact of the infinitude of possibilities provided by language. It is theoretically impossible to study the individual in the linguistics of *langue*, since the object of study is the social. This means that studies in this framework that purport to examine individual variation invariably turn out to be studies of the jointly held linguistic competence of socially constituted groups, albeit sometimes relatively small ones.

One study that illustrates this point (Bates, Bretherton, and Snyder 1988), is an interesting and well-argued book entitled *From First Words to Grammar: Individual Differences and Dissociable Mechanisms*. Bates and her coauthors build on research suggesting that there are two styles of language acquisition: some children use language first for referential purposes, others for expressive purposes; the first group tends to use more nouns and the second group more pronouns. Other tendencies appear to vary along with these. Several explanations for the variation, relating to environment, personality, cognitive style, and so on, have been advanced. The authors use correlational statistics to test the hypothesis that there are two clusters of tendencies and to see whether the clusters that emerge from the analysis suggest the existence of linguistic modules such as syntax and semantics or, alternatively, more general cognitive alternatives such as rote versus analytical processing. Their results show that there are in fact more than two clusters and that what separates one from another has to do with general cognitive tendencies rather than with special sensitivity to or facility with one linguistic module or another. They conclude that linguistic modules, for which there *is* psycholinguistic evidence in adults, must develop later.

Despite its title, this work is a study of groups, not of individuals; though the authors show that the groups are smaller than was thought (i.e., there are more than two types of language learners), they are not interested in what characterizes one individual's style as opposed to another individual's. What they are primarily interested in is cognition in the abstract as it relates to language in the abstract. Like most psycholinguistic studies of "individual" differences, the book actually examines how individuals can be grouped, on psychological grounds, into categories.

Most scholarship in sociolinguistics and pragmatics, like the work of Bates and her colleagues, is focused on languages and groups rather than on speakers. A contrasting view underlies recent work, however. Newer approaches to linguistic variation and pragmatic interpretation locate language and dialect in the individual's creative choices for how to talk and understand. These approaches stress the dynamic, changing nature of social groupings, the importance of personal identity and its linguistic expression, and the indeterminacy of meaning.

The sociolinguistic study of variation has its roots in nineteenth-century efforts to systematize the study of language change. A change in the behavior of a group necessarily begins with an innovation by an individual, and the competing perspectives engendered by this fact mark the development of the field. The neogrammarian Hermann Paul stressed the role of the individual in change, remarking that "every linguistic creation is always the work of one single individual only. Several no doubt may create similar products, but neither the act of creation nor the product is affected by that" (Paul 1889, p. xliii). Change spreads through contacts among individuals, too, as "whole new language varieties, many of them eventually spoken by millions of people, grow and develop out of small-scale contacts between individual human beings" (Trudgill 1986, p. 161). In a textbook summary of the goals of sociolinguistics, Hudson (1980, p. 12) claims that "sociolinguists would agree that it is essential to keep the individual firmly in the centre of interest, and to avoid losing sight of him while talking about large-scale abstractions and movements."

But while sociolinguists might indeed agree to this condition in principle, the individual is often anywhere but in the center of interest in practice. Only when an innovation has been partially or fully taken up by a socially delineated group of speakers is it handled as a change in progress, and the group is then identified with the new form. So, for example, Chambers and Trudgill (1980) make the point that "in the progress of any linguistic (or other) change, it is natural that some *element of society* should take the lead" (p. 167; emphasis added). Labov is especially clear on this point:

> What is the origin of a linguistic change? Clearly not the act of some one individual whose tongue slips, or who slips into an odd habit of his own. We define language . . . as an instrument used by the members of the community to communicate with one another. Idiosyncratic habits are not a part of language so conceived, and idiosyncratic changes no more so. Therefore we can say that the language has changed only when a *group* of speakers use a different pattern to communicate with each other.
>
> Let us assume that a certain word or pronunciation was indeed introduced by one individual. It becomes part of the language only when it is adopted by others, i.e., when it is propagated. Therefore the origin of a change *is* its "propagation" or acceptance by others. (1972a, p. 277)

As J. Milroy points out (1992, ch. 6), the "actuation problem"—how linguistic change begins—has in fact been relatively little studied, because the linguistic system, not the individual speaker, is the focus of interest for Labovian sociolinguists, who are interested primarily in the mechanisms of change in language and only secondarily in how individuals' linguistic behavior is socially constrained.

Because quantitative sociolinguists focus on the linguistic system rather than on the individual speaker, they have little to say about individual idiosyncracy. "Idiosyncratic habits are not a part of language so conceived," as Labov puts it in the passage just quoted. This means that when idiosyncracy does intrude, it tends to be handled in somewhat ad hoc ways. Linguistically idiosyncratic individuals are inevitably deviant in this framework. In an article written for a volume about individual differences, for example, Labov (1979) suggests that individual psychological differences can cause deviance in two ways: they can cause an unusual level of conformity, making some speakers particularly clear cases of the group's patterns, or they can cause some individuals' speech to differ from the patterns. Labov cites the case of Nathan B., a New Yorker who would be expected, on the basis of his socioeconomic background, to be able to distinguish [t] from [θ] or [d] from [ð] but did not learn to do so. The speech-behavioral expectations from which speakers such as Nathan B. deviate are statistical norms based on the speech of all members of the community, including ones like Nathan B. Deviant speakers are ones whose speech patterns are toward the ends of the range of figures being averaged, and the speakers whose speech sociolinguistics is best at describing are those whose patterns are closest to the average. The speaker who is best described is thus the one whose speech differs the least from that of his or her fellows. The theoretical idealization on which the model is based is that patterns of variation are homogeneous across individual speakers in a group as well as across groups of speakers.

As a result, the analytical techniques used by quantitative sociolinguists have sometimes made it hard to see the workings of variation and change in individuals' speech. Guy (1980, p. 2) points out, for example, that Labov's early probability studies of variable-rule phenomena lumped together tokens produced by different speakers in such a way that it is impossible to tell whether the phenomena being described represent variation in individuals' speech or variation within the community, with each individual's speech being homogeneous. Suppose, for example, that a certain group is described as deleting consonant-cluster-final /t/ and /d/ 50 percent of the time. This could mean that each speaker behaves exactly the same way, displaying the deletion in exactly 50 percent of his or her consonant clusters. Or it could mean that some speakers delete 25 percent of the time and others 75 percent, the mean being 50 percent.

If individual variation is not described as deviance, it is sometimes described as immaturity. For example, Trudgill (1986, pp. 28–31) holds that there is a fixed way in which speakers come to accommodate their speech to different sociolinguistic norms when they move to a new environment. Trudgill cites a study of English twins learning to adapt to Australian speech patterns. Contrary to Trudgill's hypothesis, the two displayed very different routes of accommodation and accommodated their speech at very different rates. What this means for Trudgill is, however, not that there is indeed individual variation but that the fixed-route theory has to be confined to postadolescents.[8]

The study that could be said to have initiated modern sociolinguistics was Labov's (1972a, pp. 1–42) demonstration, first published in 1963, that linguistic variation on Martha's Vineyard could be correlated with personal identity. Labov and others, in subsequent work, found other, more easily quantifiable variables that correlated with variation: socioeconomic class, gender, and ethnicity. Dialectologists had long been examining the linguistic effects of region and rurality. These more tractable explanatory variables came to be the ones whose effects were most often adduced and examined in later work by sociolinguists. But there is a growing feeling that identity needs to be considered again. Multivariate statistical analyses by C. Bernstein (1993) suggest, for example, that we are not as far along in our understanding of the causes of sociolinguistic variation as we might have thought: a large residue of inter-speaker variability is left even once differences in age, socioeconomic class, region, rurality, gender, and contextual style are carefully considered.

Dorian's (1994) study of "personal pattern variation" shows that among bilingual Gaelic-speaking "fisherfolk" in three villages in East Sutherland, Scotland, there is considerable linguistic variation among people who are, in terms of the usual social parameters, closely associated: siblings, spouses, parents and their children, members of the same social networks, people the same age. Dorian points out that because sociolinguists are not forewarned about the possibility of this sort of variation, they may not notice it. In the East Sutherland communities, according to Dorian, some variation in Gaelic speech simply does not take on social meaning: one form is just as good as another. This means that individuals are freer to speak differently from one another.

Recent models of variation have moved toward providing ways of understanding variation from individual to individual, because sociolinguists are increasingly coming, once again, to see variability as a resource for the expression of an individual's identity. Reviewing this development, L. Milroy (1987, pp. 131–134) points out that social groups are more fluid than models like Labov's require them to be and people's speech less consistent over time and situation. Individuals show that they identify with different groups at different times by varying their speech. Milroy's work focuses on the effects on an individual's speech of the strength of his or her social ties to the community; she finds that differences among individuals are better accounted for in terms of the density and multiplexity of one's relationship to the local community than in terms of social class or status.

In relatively homogeneous societies with relatively clearly defined social norms and much contact among speakers, different people are likely to attribute the same symbolic meanings to linguistic choices. (As J. Milroy points out particularly clearly [1992, pp. 95–109], this does not of course imply that everyone in such a community will actually make the same choices; more solidary communities may in fact display greater variation so that the symbolic meanings of choices are enforced.) These are the ideal speaker-hearers whose behavior is best accounted for in the Labovian model and in other theories of language in which the focus of study is the language, the dialect, or the variety, rather than the speaker. The setting in which such speakers are most likely to be found is a monolingual nation-state on the European model. As LePage and Tabouret-Keller show (1985), individuals' models of linguistic norms are less consistent in more heteroglot, culturally diverse settings, where people are less likely to project linguistic self-images similar to their neighbors'. If culturally fluid contact settings like these are taken as the object of sociolinguistic inquiry, a different concept of linguistic variation emerges. Seeing language as "essentially idiosyncratic" (1985, p. 2), LePage and Tabouret-Keller push the furthest towards a sociolinguistics of the individual. "Language," for them, is the linguistic repertoire of an individual, perhaps all drawn from one conventionally defined "language" such as French or Spanish but perhaps not. Some speakers in any community may use language in relatively conventional ways that are easy to codify, while other speakers may be far more inventive and idiosyncratic. The individual is thus seen by LePage and Tabouret-Keller as "the locus of his language" (p. 116).

Just as sociolinguistics offers two ways of treating how people talk—from the perspective of the linguistic system and from that of the speaker—so linguistic pragmatics offers two ways of conceiving of how people understand talk. Formal pragmatics is analogous to the first approach, as it attempts to model rules for interpretation that reduce the possibility of semantic indeterminacy. A representative study, done in the framework of speech act theory, is Fraser's (1981) extremely lucid analysis of apologizing. Fraser's goal is to specify precisely which English utterances can count as apologies. He first lists four beliefs that an apologizer must hold—some act, A, has been performed before the time of speaking; A has offended the hearer; the speaker, S, is at least partly responsible for the offense; and S regrets A—and two basic conditions for the performance of an apology—S must acknowledge responsibility for the performance of A and S must convey regret for A (pp. 261–262). Fraser then lists nine semantic formulae that can be used to display the apologizer's beliefs about the nature of the situation and to convey responsibility and regret: announce that you are apologizing; state your obligation to apologize; offer to apologize; request the hearer to accept your apology; express regret; request forgiveness; acknowledge responsibility for the offending act; promise forbearance; and offer redress (p. 263). Representative examples of utterances expressing each formula are given. For example, "Let me apologize for . . ." requests that the hearer accept an apology, "I'm sorry" expresses regret, and "I beg your pardon" requests forgiveness. Other attempts to provide complete accounts of what utterances can mean employ other theoretical frameworks. Cheepen (1988), for example, attempts to show that topic, in conversation, is predictable. Like other formalists, Fraser and Cheepen focus on the systemic, aiming at the description of presumably shared rules that account for how individuals are likely to interpret what they hear.

Any theory of pragmatics has at least to suggest an explanation for the interpretation of linguistic newness, since, as Levinson points out, "[an] utterance may have no conventional meaning at all" (1983, p. 17). Relatively unconventional utterances are handled with reference to mutual knowledge, available to speaker and hearer alike, upon which hearers draw to make inferences. Schiffer (1972), for example, discusses the role of precedent in the establishment of conventions (pp. 118–155), prior uses of a nonconventional strategy being an important source of inferences about what a current use of the strategy might be taken to mean. Gumperz and Tannen (1979), in a discussion of individual variation and conversational inference, also point to the role of precedent. Speakers and hearers decide what is meant by what is said on the basis of "habitual use and perception of surface cues which make up discourse strategies" (p. 322). These cues are conventionalized, but they are learned through experience, and since no two speakers have the same set of experiences to draw on, different speakers employ different combinations of strategies. These differences, Gumperz and Tannen suggest, account for variation from individual to individual.

But what of a completely unconventional utterance, the very first time a speaker intends a given proposition to mean a certain thing? About this Schiffer says only that mutual knowledge of other kinds comes into play. In discussing discourse marking, the process of showing how one's contributions are related to the surrounding talk and to the situation at hand, Schiffrin (1987) points out that no particular way of showing how utterances are coherent is ever required; speakers are free, in other words, to choose or even invent strategies. To explain how hearers make sense of unusual or invented discourse-marking strategies, Schiffrin also refers to inferencing but does not elaborate on how it is done.

What could be called "processual" approaches to pragmatics treat the interpretation of newness and idiosyncracy as the model for interpretation in general. Processual pragmatics frames regularities in how people interpret speech as maxims or principles rather than as rules and treats understanding as a hermeneutic, problem-solving procedure. As Leech (1983, p. 21) observes, for example, "Semantics is rule-governed (grammatical); general pragmatics is principle-controlled (rhetorical)." While there are conventions that sometimes relate the sense of an utterance to its force, "the principles of pragmatics are fundamentally non-conventional" (p. 24). Levinson (1983, pp. 112–113) points out that any convention or expectation can be flouted, so that "a full account of the communicative power of language can never be reduced to a set of conventions for the use of language."

The competing approaches to pragmatics I have outlined are not mutually exclusive, of course. No one would argue that the process of interpretation is entirely describable in terms of conventions, because it is clear that people make guesses about what others mean even in the absence of most linguistic and contextual cues—as when one begins to read Joyce, for example. Nor would anyone deny the importance of conventionality. Hearers rarely have to make inferences completely de novo, since in all but the most difficult of situations speakers and hearers share understandings of where important information generally goes in a sentence, and interlocutors expect one another, in one way or another, to be cooperative (Grice 1975) and polite (Brown and Levinson 1987).

Thinking about language from the perspective of the individual requires a pragmatics that deals centrally with newness and idiosyncracy rather than a pragmatics in which conventionality is the focus. I show in chapters to follow that newness and idiosyncracy are more common than linguists' usual analytical techniques have allowed us to see; I suggest that linguistic idiosyncracy is in fact a cultural and psychological requirement for many speakers. I thus argue for a processual approach.

Underlying the work I have described on the expression of identity through variability and the heuristic, rhetorical character of understanding is a refocusing of linguistics. For a growing number of linguists, speakers and their utterances are replacing linguistic systems as the object of study. These linguists see language as residing in talk. Reluctant to abstract away from our actual experience of language—the experience of seeing people, not language, do things and possess linguistic attributes—they ask why actual, situated utterances take the shapes they do, aiming thereby to display the processes by which people create their own identities and communicate with others. In this view, the social is an artifact of the individual. As Hockett (1987) puts it, for example, language is a "social system" only to the extent that individual systems overlap. Individual languages are constantly "intercalibrated" in the process of communication so that "by virtue of these parallels the participants can ordinarily manage to understand one another" (p. 157, note for sec. 8.3). "Language" is, then, the concept that people create when they start thinking about the abstractions they make that enable them to say the same things over again (Love 1990).

A return to individualism in linguistics is in some ways a return to the pre-Saussurean nineteenth-century Romantic view of humanity. The individual voice is valued because it represents autonomous, creative choice in the expression of individual spirit or genius. Among the linguists of the nineteenth century, the "idealist" or "aesthetic" school of linguistics best exemplifies this view (Robins 1979, pp. 189–190). According to linguists such as Humboldt and Vossler, language change originates in conscious, aesthetically motivated creative innovations of the sort made most noticeably (to the literate, at any rate) by poets and novelists.

Among the founders of American linguistics, Edward Sapir was the most adamant about the importance of the individual in language and culture. If one looks at culture from the perspective of a child acquiring it, Sapir notes, one sees that culture is not a unitary whole. Each individual's culture is different ("The Emergence of the Concept of Personality in the Study of Cultures," 1949, pp. 590–597). He wonders elsewhere about the status of a sociologist's generalization about Omaha culture when one Omaha, Two Crows, denied that the generalization was true ("Why Cultural Anthropology Needs the Psychiatrist," 1949, pp. 569–577). In *Language* he defines his topic as "the collective art of expression, a summary of thousands upon thousands of individual intuitions" (1921, p. 231). Sapir argued strongly and explicitly against social realism. In his writings he points out again and again that the abstractions studied by anthropologists and linguists—cultures and languages, in other words—should not be taken as real. In "Cultural Anthropology and Psychiatry" (1949, pp. 509–521) he calls the idea of culture as a superorganic entity "a useful enough methodological principle to begin with" but a "more serious deterrent in the long run to more dynamic study of the genesis and development of cultural patterns" (p. 512). In "Psychiatric and Cultural Pitfalls to the Business of Getting a Living" (pp. 578–589) he is more explicit about the danger:

> In linguistics, abstracted speech sounds, words, and the arrangement of words have come to have so authentic a vitality that one can speak of "regular sound change" and "loss of genders" without knowing or caring who opened their mouths, at what time, to communicate what to whom. (p. 579)

Sapir argued for an approach to culture and language that does not take itself unduly seriously as a science. He argued, in other words (though not in these terms), for a humanistic understanding of humanity, one that does not depersonalize its subject or abstract away from the human spirit. Here he touches on the problem of scientism in linguistics:

> It is not really difficult, then, to see why anyone brought up on the aus-
> terities of a well-defined science of man must, if he is to maintain his
> symbolic self-respect, become more and more estranged from man him-
> self. . . . The laws of syntax acquire a higher reality than the immediate
> reality of the stammerer who is trying to "get himself across." . . . (p. 580)

Sapir by no means abandoned abstractions such as "the laws of syntax."
He wanted linguists and anthropologists only to be able to think both
ways: from the perspective of the social and from the perspective of the
individual. Individual behavior is always socially conditioned, "the complex resultant of an incredibly elaborate cultural history" ("Why Cultural Anthropology Needs the Psychiatrist," 1949, p. 572), but "conversely, no matter how rigorously necessary in practice the analyzed
pattern may seem to be, it is always possible . . . for the lone individual
to effect a transformation of form or meaning which is capable of communication to other individuals" (pp. 572–573). As a result, the only
way to come to a complete understanding of culture is through "a minute
and sympathetic study of individual behavior . . . in a state of society"
(p. 576).

Anthropologists who work with linguistic informants are regularly
faced with individual style and idiosyncracy and led to wonder in what
sense an individual speaker can embody a language or represent its other
speakers.[9] (See Coulmas 1981 and Craig 1979 for discussions of the concept of the representative native speaker.) Dell Hymes, in particular,
has taken up and expanded on Sapir's recurring interest in the linguistic individual. Commenting on Bloomfield's analysis of Menomini, Hymes
(1974) remarks on the absurdity of describing most of the remaining
speakers of a language as incompetent to speak it, noting that such a
case "forces us to face the fact that for both the individual and the community, a language in some sense *is* what those who have it can do with
it—what they have made of it, and do make of it" (p. 72). Hymes
defines linguistic competence as "personal ability (not just grammatical
knowledge, systemic potential of a grammar, superorganic property of a
society, or, indeed, irrelevant to persons in any other way)" (1974,
p. 206). Elsewhere (1979) Hymes suggests that individual differences be
given "foundational status" as a "vantage point from which to consider
questions of method and theory in the study of language in general"
(p. 36). This is the goal of the present study.

Discourse Analysis

The study of individuals' linguistic voices is most often employed as a
critical tool in the study of particular individuals and particular texts.

Students of Flannery O'Connor's style or the style of Faulkner in *As I Lay Dying*, for example, are typically interested in what Flannery O'Connor was like and what she might have meant by her writing or in how Faulkner's novel might most rewardingly be read. Studies of individuals' styles also contribute to practical knowledge about the possibilities for style: people read the orations of Gorgias and Cicero to learn about the language of classical oratory, fiction by Joyce Carol Oates to find out how contemporary English can be crafted. Stylistics, as the term is used by rhetoricians and literary critics, usually means the study of individual voices for critical purposes such as these.

As should be clear by now, my purpose in writing about individual voices is not critical. It is linguistic. I am not interested primarily in how paying attention to individual voice helps us to understand how particular individuals talk and write or to analyze the stylistic possibilities of a language, genre, or literary period. Instead, my purpose is to show how paying attention to individual voice helps us to understand language. I hope to demonstrate that taking this perspective provides useful ways of thinking about some fundamental issues in linguistics. But although the goal of this study is not critical, its methodology borrows from literary criticism, because the linguistically attuned close-reading techniques of discourse analysis, in particular the sort identified at the beginning of this chapter as "modern philology," provide the best way of seeing what is individual about language.

Discourse analysis has been variously and not always clearly defined. In its earliest appearances (Harris 1952; Pike 1967), the term referred to the use of models developed in the analysis of clauses and sentences in the analysis of connected speech or writing, and some still describe discourse analysis as the analysis of units larger than the sentence. Alternatively, discourse analysis is sometimes defined as the analysis of "language in use" (Brown and Yule 1983, p. 1) or "situated speech" (Coulthard 1985, p. 3). Neither way of delimiting the field differentiates it from any other subdiscipline of linguistics except formal grammar, which explicitly studies sentences and smaller units and is explicitly focused on underlying linguistic competence rather than in language in use. Quantitative sociolinguists, for example, analyze actual linguistic performances and students of pragmatics study the role of the situation in the interpretation of utterances. Noting the heterogeneity of data and theory in discourse analysis, Tannen (1989, p. 6) suggests that "the name for the field 'discourse analysis,' then, says nothing more or other than the term 'linguistics': the study of language."

Tannen is right in pointing out that discourse analysts study data of all sorts—transcripts of speech, written texts, hypothetical conversations—and that a variety of theoretical orientations underlies their work. But the work of many discourse analysts is united by a common approach to linguistic research.[10] Discourse analysis is qualitative far more often than quantitative, particularistic rather than generalizing. Discourse analysts study relatively small amounts of data in relatively great detail. Their methods typically involve close reading or listening, reading or listening again and again until patterns emerge. Hymes describes the process as follows:

> In short, a satisfactory solution emerges only after several tries. One plunges *in media*[s] *res*, making a trial segmentation by hand, and reconsiders and adjusts it in the light of the principles of consistent structure and form-meaning covariation. As one gets more deeply into a text, one gains a deeper sense of its inner logic and form, its particular integration of content and expression, and one's sense of inconsistency or arbitrariness of analysis grows finer. (1981, p. 151)

Discourse analysis is like translation. It involves taking foreign texts (whether in a foreign language or not) and making them meaningful in one's own terms. A. L. Becker puts it this way: "The goal of the philologist is to guide outsiders . . . to what might be called an *aesthetic* understanding of a text" (1979b, p. 240). Discourse analysts often work with texts they like and come to love them in the process; they often know their data by heart.

There is nothing about the methodology of discourse analysis that determines what sort of work it can be used for. There is no reason, for example, why discourse analyses cannot be used in inductive support of very general claims. Inductive research is valid if the number of cases in which the researcher's claim is borne out is sufficient by some acknowledged standard of sufficiency. (In the standard research paradigm of experimental psychology, for example, one must show that one's hypothesis has been borne out often enough that there is less than a 5 percent chance that the result could have been random.) It is possible—increasingly so with increasingly accessible computerized data bases of text and software for manipulating them—to perform large numbers of discourse analyses and compare them (e.g., Biber 1988).

But discourse analysis is in essence a very slow procedure and as such is relatively ill suited for large generalizations. Discourse analysis lends itself best to showing other sorts of things. For example, it is well suited for showing that linguistic phenomena are multiply determined. As Becker (1988) points out, the multiple sources of constraint on discourse—the multiple factors delimiting what can be said, by whom, and how—come together only in actual texts, the products or memories of actual discourse. It is only in discourse that we can see how the grammar of a language, the medium, the topic, the genre, the interactants, the background of silence, and perhaps other factors all interact in shaping language (Becker 1983). The question that underlies close reading is always "Why does this text (or transcript, or utterance) take the shape it does?" Even if the immediate question is about a single variable ("In what ways is this text, transcript, or utterance reflective of gender?"; "How is the text, transcript, or utterance a result of its medium of production?"), discourse analysis keeps making it obvious that there are others. Scholarly articles based on discourse analyses almost always end by suggesting that the linguistic phenomena they study are the results of many factors.

Discourse analysis is well suited, too, for uncovering linguistic newness. Like ethnography, it is a science in the "cases-and-interpretations" mode, rather than a science of the "rules-and-instances" sort (Geertz 1980, p. 165). Discourse analysts' goal is to understand their data, rather than to prove or disprove preformulated hypotheses or to create general predictive models. Discourse analysts in the philological mode are not bound by their theoretical goals to notice only what they already think might be there, or only what fits into a list of items they are looking for, or only what can be generalized about. One's text or texts, rather than one's theory, tends to be the source of discipline. As Callow and Callow describe it (1992, pp. 15–16), "The main proviso to be borne in mind is that at all levels surface-structure evidence should be available to support every analytical decision concerning the message." New "lingual strategies" and "lingual categories" (Becker 1983) can be uncovered through discourse analysis: categories and strategies that are new because they are foreign, or new because never before used.

Discourse analysis is also well suited to the study of the individual. It is only, in fact, by looking in depth at every aspect of a text that one can even tell what is individual about it. In writing the results of discourse analysis, one talks (or should talk) about *these* women and men or *this* speaker or *Hiram Smith*'s or *Louis Simpson*'s telling of a myth (Hymes 1981); one describes what one's research subjects *did*, not what they *do*. If discourse analysts are vigilant enough in avoiding the temptation of invalid induction, they describe individual voices. Claims to generality are then based on careful demonstration that these particular voices are representative of larger sets of voices. In showing in what respects a particular voice is representative, the discourse analyst is forced to notice how it is not, too: how it is individual.[11] Discourse analysis should be well suited, then, for the project of looking at language from the perspective of the individual. Conversely, if I can show that fundamental questions about language can be answered only with reference to the individual, I will have provided an argument in favor of discourse analysis as a linguistic research technique.

− 2 −

Resources and Reasons
for Individual Style

*Both the "Cartesian" syntactician, in his chamber with his pencil, and the
"empirical" sociolinguist, in the department store with his tape recorder,
commit what are, strictly, analogous methodological fallacies in moving
directly from the so-called data of intuition or a questionnaire to
generalizations about the "competence" of an ideal speaker-hearer or the
"speech" of a community. Between the data and the generalizations there
exists the variable, the phenomenon of individual language—seen, not
as the "idiolect" of a naive behaviorism, but as a level of organization
with its distinctive processes and complexities. Our models of language
and of linguistics should include individual language and speech as
significant variables.*

   Paul Friedrich and James Redfield, "Speech as a Personality Symbol"

Why does this sentence—the one you are now reading—consist of precisely these twenty-three words, and why are they in this order? There
are many reasons. For one thing, the sentence begins with *why* and not
with *pourquoi* or *warum* or *limaaða* because it is in English, not in French
or German or Arabic. The fact that the sentence is in English means
that it is likely that the sounds and structures of its words will conform
to the conventions of English phonology and morphology and that the
words will be part of the English lexicon (though the Englishness of a
sentence does not make it *necessary* that all its words be English, as my
third sentence shows). Because the sentence is in English, it is also likely
that the words will be in the order typically used in sentences in that

language, that, for example, subjects will follow inflected verbs after *why*, as they do in "why does this sentence" and "why are they." Further, it is likely that syntactic and pragmatic relations among elements in the sentence will need to be understood the way they usually are in English: "the one" heads the restrictive relative clause "you are now reading," which establishes the referent of "the one"; and "the one" refers to the same entity as does "this sentence."

There are other reasons as well for the sentence's being the one it is. The fact that its first element is *why* and not *how come* has something to do with my choice, from among several varieties of English, of a standard, writerly one. My ability to make this choice has to do with the fact that I have learned how to make my writing conform to an educated standard, a result partly of my education, which was affected in many ways by my parents' social class and income and, partly, and probably to a lesser extent, of my native aptitude for language. The wording of the sentence also has to do with the situation, both in general (I was writing a book) and in particular (I was beginning a chapter). Some might claim that the fact that the sentence expresses a question rather than an assertion, and that it refers to you and leads into a discussion of me, has something to do with my being a woman; perhaps my use of a Socratic question has to do with my being part of the broad Western cultural tradition of scholarship and teaching. And so on.

For each of the sources of constraint on the shape a sentence takes, there is a subdiscipline that studies it. Phonologists and syntacticians describe what linguistic structure contributes to the forms of utterances. Sociolinguists correlate pronunciation and syntactic and pragmatic choices with region, ethnicity, urbanity, gender, social network, and so on. Ethnographers of communication examine cultural constraints on what can be said, by whom, and in what order in a given speech situation, and on how it can be said. Rhetoricians talk about how lines of argument are generated and persuasive discourses organized and presented. A person conversant with all these fields could bring many modes of analysis to bear on the question my first sentence poses and could provide many compelling answers. My choices about what to say in the sentence and how to say it were limited, focused, bounded in many ways. If we knew everything there was to know about all these sources of constraint, we could, in theory, ascribe every choice I made in composing the sentence to some combination of linguistic, cultural, rhetorical, social, psychological, and historical facts.[1]

But there is another side to the observation that many factors limit what a particular person can say in a given case and how it can be said.

Each of the sources of constraint on discourse—language, culture, purpose, personality, history, and so on—is also a source of options for discourse. Knowing how to say *why* in German enables me to write *why* in German in an English sentence. I know how to sound informal in English without sounding illiterate, so I can make my academic writing seem relaxed. Because I know how to structure an argument the way Arab writers traditionally have done (Koch 1983a), I can structure an argument that way with an audience of Americans. Knowing that English adjectives usually precede the nouns they modify, I can utter a phrase in which the adjectives follow the nouns. I could even write a sentence that violates the laws of universal grammar. I could talk like a man, assuming I knew how men talk (and that "how men talk" were a viable abstraction); because I know what *y'all* means and what its use represents, I can say *y'all* instead of *you guys*. To do such things is of course to risk being misunderstood or not understood at all, but that does not alter the fact that I can do them. In fact, I must do them in order to express a fully human self. Speakers create distinctive voices by pushing at the boundaries of convention, sometimes breaking through the boundaries. Each potential determinant of the shape of discourse is thus also a resource in the creation of an individual voice.

In this chapter I reformulate the question "What are the sources of constraint on discourse" in the way I have just suggested. Rather than discussing constraints, I want to discuss resources, asking instead "How do speakers draw on their individual repertoires of linguistic resources as they formulate things to say?" I want then to examine one of the things people use their linguistic resources for: as a way to express their autonomous, unique selves. To do this, I will discuss two texts, short discourses by two Americans. The two texts are generically similar, broadly speaking, both being narratives of personal experience, and they are linguistically similar in that both are in English. This is to say that both speakers made choices that made their talk interpretable as being about themselves and about the past, as well as choices that result in English speakers' being able, more or less, to understand them. The stories are also pragmatically similar. Both speakers had to find ways to fit their anecdotes into the context of the ongoing talk, the context of knowledge shared and unshared with their interlocutors, the context of the world at hand. But the two speakers did these things in different ways, and my discussion focuses on the differences and on the reasons for them.

My approach to personal-experience narrative in what follows is not a novel one. It is based on the insights of Labov (1972c) about how such spontaneous stories are structured and why, as well as those of Hymes

(1981) on thematic "acts" and "scenes" in stories and of Chafe (1980, 1994) on more microscopic layers of segmentation. It also draws on uses Polanyi (1985), Young (1987), Linde (1993), and many others have made of these ideas in the analysis of personal-experience stories in many settings, as well as on my own previous work on the subject (1990a). I will not be making new claims about what conversational narrative is like, nor will my analytical techniques be different from those I and others have used in the past. What I will be doing in this chapter that is new is juxtaposing two stories that should be expected to be different in as many ways as possible, rather than—as is the norm in such studies— examining a controlled corpus of narratives that are similar in all but one or two ways. That the two stories do in fact turn out to be very different is not at all surprising. My reason for displaying the differences is not to prove that they exist but to lead to a discussion of *why* they exist.

Since for my purposes in this chapter there is no need to control any variables other than the generic and pragmatic ones I have mentioned, I have chosen to work with two stories I like and about which I have been curious for a long time. They are also both stories I know extremely well, having played them many times for classes and at conferences and studied them repeatedly since collecting them over a decade ago. This should, I hope, add to the sensitivity of my analysis. I begin with the stories; I then discuss them.

Two Stories

Neither of the two stories has a name, of course—people rarely have titles for the anecdotes they tell in conversation—but for ease of reference I have entitled them. The story I call "Sonny" was told by a woman I will call Mattie Blair. Mrs. Blair told her story into a microphone several months before her death of brain cancer. After unsuccessful therapy of various sorts, she had been moved to a church-supported convalescent home in Fort Wayne, Indiana, that accepted indigent patients like her. Mrs. Blair was lonely and at loose ends in the nursing home; glaucoma complicated by the cancer had blinded her, and family members, scattered and in some cases on poor terms with her, visited infrequently and took her out to visit or shop even more rarely. When the home's activities director asked what she would like to do with her time, Mrs. Blair said that she would like to tell her "story" and have someone write it down and publish it, though she had only the vaguest idea of what producing a book would entail. She had led an interesting life, she thought, and people should be interested in knowing about it. Comparing her story to that of the author of the recently televised "Roots" series, she claimed that what she had to say was "as good as anything Alex Haley wrote about. Alex Haley . . . had to go to Africa to get his roots; all mine are right here in Fort Wayne." I was recruited to record Mrs. Blair's story.

The moment I started the tape recorder on our first visit, Mrs. Blair began crisply and chronologically: "Well, as you know, my name is Mattie Margaret Blair, born December the 20th, 1926, in Chester, Georgia. . . . I was born out of wedlock to Sarah Johnson and James Deer."[2] She had obviously planned how she would start. She insisted, especially during the first of our eight meetings, that her story not be interrupted except for relevant reasons; when I asked, for example, whether her mother was living in Fort Wayne, she quickly got me back on task: "Yeah, she was out to visit me I think yesterday. So we're going on to tell the story like I was trying to tell you. . . ." She sometimes referred to the story as a book and gave thought to possible titles. On one occasion she told me, "If I should write a story or anything, I'd call myself 'throwed away'"; at another time she commented, "Whatever I would write, it would be either 'Bastard Child' or 'Threw Away.'"

Typically, a session of Mrs. Blair's story began with an attempt at a chronological summary or with a description of a person, elicited by me. Then Mrs. Blair would tell a string of stories evoked by the memory of a person or a place or a period in her life. (On the basis of the ten or twelve hours of tape recordings I made, I could not provide a complete chronology of Mrs. Blair's life, though I could piece together most of it.) "Sonny" is from the second of our sessions.[3]

> Uh, he was an entertainer. I met him at . . . uh ( ) out there, at Fontana, and uh, his name was Sonny. And him and Doc became good friends. And uh, Sonny was real nice. He had a new car, first car I ever rode in had a record player in it, a tape or whatever. And him and Doc was very good friends.
>
> So he has, he eh, eh got, carried me someplace with him that day, to the insurance company, t- to to take out insurance on his car. And while he was in there, eh the (man) was out, and he tore a bunch of checks out of the back of the checkbook, insurance checks. Well you know those type of checks, it's checks like you can write 'em any amount, like you have an accident.
>
> So uh, he goes around cashing checks, buying me, uh, 'cause I've always I'monna be truthful with you, always been a clothes freak. I *love* pretty clothes, here I am blind. And the first time

he give me a piece of — a dress or something, I bit it! You know, you know how you feel everything? I don't know. I said, "Yeah, this is good material!" And I used to be fond of Lili Ann suits.

But anyway, this Sonny cashed all of them checks, and I found out about it, that he had made about, seven eight hundred dollars, they — I don't never known that, I always been kind of a dummy, 'cause I was brought up that way, old *country*, old dumb country girl. If I hadda been brought up hip like the little city girls, I'd have some sense. But I was raised down there in them cotton fields, you know I ain't had no sense, anybody could use me.

So he goes to work and uh cash them checks that day, and he e- he showed me all this money. And he carried me in the store, and all I got out of it was he said, to cash another check, (I bought) all them groceries see. And (I just got) "Get anything you want. Get anything you want." And I was putting that stuff in the, in the uh, buggy, and he just wrote this check and give it to the woman and she'd give him back the change.

And then uh, so he, I said "What are you — ? Ooo!" And he had wa- *all* that money. And so he told me, "Honey, you be doing that all today with me?" And he said oh we'd buy, oh we would need to buy something, a little something, not too much, and people'd give him back money, and he'd give them a piece of paper. And so I said, "Ohh my God." And he said, "Yeah, you didn't know I was a paperhanger, baby?" I said, "What — who you hang paper for?" I thought he meant hang paper on the walls! I told you I wasn't nothing but a dumb, old *country*, ignorant Georgia girl. And he meant hang paper write checks.

And he said, "Hey." Said he was gonna go with me, to this place, where he was gonna take me, he — he'd give me some money. I said, "Oooh uh-hn, no-oo, uh-hn," I said, "I ain't going noplace with you." And uh, he just caught me by the arm and pushed me and shoved me in the car, said, "Oh yeah, you're going." And they told me, he was smoking marijuana, he was you know he was a dope addict. And I said, "No-oo uh-hn." So he taken me to this here, here, here motel, and I crawled through the window and got out the window and run and went to the motel office. And that's what saved me from him.

So, soon as I got back and could find Doc, I told Doc. So Doc got his gun, and went looking for his rump. And when Doc — uh, uh everybody told Doc, say eh, "I seen him. Over here. I seen him over there." He went to every big tavern in, in, in, in, in, in, San Bernardino. Finally, we didn't find him so we went on home.

So he was so ignorant, he (goes to work) and gets in his pretty car, and come over there and knock on my door, on 30th Street, and say, "Hey, I know that that old — that nigger of yours was looking for me." And here Doc say, "Yeah man, I sure was." I didn't know he was look- listening, I thought he was in there watching television. But he (gon) always peek to see who at the door, don't want nobody come in, think it's some man come looking for me.

And so Doc say, "Yeah, man," say, "I sure was looking for you." And he said "Well here I am, big man, what you want?" And so Doc say he's "Aww, man." And next thing I know *pumm*. Shot him right through the head, right there in my doorway. And I said, "Oh my God," my kids went to running went to hollering went to screaming, I run and went to hollering, run across, uh them old little stickers that (put) in your feet, and went to running went to run — I told you about he hid in the church. You know he hid in the church when he killed that boy.

So he went on to the penitentiary, and uh, they had me accessory to the fact, but he pleaded guilty, you know 'cause I didn't pull no trigger, but you know they had to go through the whole procedure. . . .

The second story I will examine is "I Know When I Bought Mine," told by a man I call Lon Bauer. The story was part of a conversation among three men, Bauer and his friends Norm and Ross. The conversation in which Mr. Bauer's story arose took place one Saturday afternoon in early spring, at Bauer's service station in a small town in northeastern Indiana, during a slow moment. A television was tuned to a baseball game. Bauer was about forty-five years old, a high-school graduate who had lived in the same town all his life and was married to a local woman. Norm, a part-time employee at the gas station, was twenty-five and also a graduate of the local high school. Ross was thirty-seven. He was from the same town, and he and Bauer were old friends. Ross had been a visitor at the gas station since he was a child; this time he brought a tape recorder for the purpose of recording some of the talk that went on for a class assignment for me, but the machine had been running long enough that the men were no longer conscious of its presence.

BAUER: Just about everybody now, like they tell me, when they
          sell you the car, they give you the bill of sale, and it says
          on there, "Bought as is."

NORM: I know. (*chuckles*)

BAUER: I know when I bought mine, Denny said, "Aw we give you thirty days or —" How was that he said? "A thousand miles or thirty days, whichever comes first." And I ended up putting a new battery in it, and a new tire on it.

NORM: What, on your Caddy?

BAUER: Yeah, and I tried — and they were *supposed* to put a tire *on* it for me. They never to- they all they did was put the spare on.

(*two-second pause*)

NORM: Do you know that they never fixed the battery?

BAUER: Huh-uh.

NORM: Why, did it say "As is" when you finally got the final bill?

BAUER: No, he said, aw they'd put one in for *half price*, well I could — I could that — I might as well done that myself, 'cause I could buy it for half price here you know.

(*two-second pause*)

NORM: Yeah, I see what you're saying, plus they'd probably charge you three- or four-tenths labor.

BAUER: Probably. (*two-second pause*) *Tire* I thought they should have, the *tires* — For the price I paid for it, I thought it should have had good tires on it, you know. And the front ones weren't that good. I ended up putting two new tires on it, and putting a new battery in it.

    The night I drove it, when I went to start it, it went "Rr, rr rr rr rr" took off, I, "I don't know what that is for sure, surely it shouldn't be any starter problems, any more miles than it's got on it." Every time after we'd drive it it was warm, it would do that.

    I drove it up to Michigan, was out in the boonies there, when we went canoeing, with the Scouts last, over Labor Day last year. Everybody else left, and we were the last ones there, and I said "*Boy I hope this starts!*" I got in and it went, "Rr." And I said, "*Oh no!*" "Rr rr rr" and it took off. I didn't have any more trouble with it l- till I got home you know.

    Jane went to — The next Saturday Jane went to Fort Wayne, had a meeting up there, the church. She called back on Saturday night, she said, "Uh, car won't start." I says, "What do you mean the car won't start?" She says, "It won't turn over, won't do anything." She said they tried to jump it, and it wouldn't even jump. I said, "Oooh," said, "Unless it's in the starter it should jump." Said, "Got lights and everything?" Yeah she had lights. Just Greg and I was here, and I couldn't — didn't feel as though I could leave, so I sent Greg up. He took the truck, and I gave him a new battery, jumper cables, and a hammer, and stuff. I said, "First thing, try jumping it, and if that doesn't work, jump it, and take and tap on the starter at the same time as you have someone turn it on, maybe — maybe it's out of brushes, I don't know." He went on out and he came home, finally they come back in, said aw he jumped it and it took right off. Put a new battery in it, never had any trouble with it since then.

NORM: No kidding.

BAUER: Just that battery.

ROSS: Yeah.

BAUER: Just "rrr" though is just — Those old good old Delco Freedom Batteries, when they do that, that's the way they go.

Lon Bauer and Mattie Blair both managed to get and hold an audience's attention for several minutes, and both told stories. In order to do these things successfully, Blair and Bauer both had to fulfill certain pragmatic requirements. Most general, they had to make themselves understood and to ensure that they were listened to. More specific, they had to get their stories started, somehow announcing that they had a story to tell and needed time to tell it and shifting into the "storyworld" (Young 1987) of the narrative by introducing time, place, and characters. They had to move along the chronological line of the stories, showing how the events represented in their words were related in time and pacing their talk so that their listeners would understand it and enjoy listening to it. They had to show when they were moving from one episode or scene to another and when they were leaving the story altogether to comment on it. And they had to highlight the key moments, creating suspense and pointing to what made the story worth listening to. By comparing how Mr. Bauer and Mrs. Blair did these things, we can begin to identify the dimensions along which their stories differ.

Creating a Context

Because she was engaged in the preplanned project of telling her life story, and because I was a willing recipient, Mrs. Blair had to do very little to get the "Sonny" story started other than simply begin talking about Sonny. (In order to come closer to displaying how the talk actually sounded, I now switch to a system of transcription in orthographic lines that correspond to "intonation units" [Chafe 1994, pp. 53–70]: groups of words uttered together in a spurt without final-sounding pause or drop in pitch. Commas indicate brief pauses.)

> Uh, he was an entertainer.
> I met him at, uh ( ) out there, at Fontana,
> and uh, his name was Sonny.
> And him and Doc became good friends.
> And uh, Sonny was, real nice.
> He had a, new car, first car I ever rode in had a record player in
>   it, a tape or whatever.
> (BJ: Um-hm)
> And him and Doc was very good friends.

Mrs. Blair had already done most of the work of getting me to listen to her, and we were already in her storyworld, southern California in the 1940s. The topic of Sonny arose chronologically, in Mrs. Blair's narration of a series of vignettes about men she "got together with" in California.

Since I already knew that Doc was the man she had been living with, her talk before this excerpt having been about how she met him, she began the Sonny story by naming him ("and his name was Sonny") and then making a bridge between this new topic and the former one, "him and Doc," who, she says twice, were "good friends." Despite the story's horrific climax, a fatally hostile interaction between Sonny and Doc, the beginning of the story does not foreshadow its development or its ending. The story simply starts at the chronological beginning, describing Sonny as he struck people then: a good friend of Doc's, "real nice" in Mattie's eyes. The story continues to unfold in this way, without hindsight, like play-by-play reportage. Since her audience was both captive and attentive, Mrs. Blair had minimal need to tantalize, to abstract the story's ultimate meaning and suggest it at the beginning.

Lon Bauer's linguistic task was much more difficult in this respect. Competing with two other speakers and a TV ball game, Bauer had to work to get his story started. "I Know When I Bought Mine" began to emerge when a new topic emerged, after a pause. Rhetorically, the snatch of conversation that preceded the story proper is organized much the way the introductory paragraphs of many essays are. Bauer introduced the topic of used cars bought "as is" with a generalization:

BAUER: Just about everybody now,
        like they tell me,
        when they sell you the car,
        they give you the bill of sale,
        and it says on there,
        "Bought as is."
NORM: I know. (*chuckles*)

Then he switched to a specific case, his own, moving from a description of the warranty to more specific details about the car's condition, couched in syntactically parallel phrases

BAUER: I know when I bought mine,
        Denny said, "Aw we give you thirty days or,"
        How was that he said?
        "A thousand miles or thirty days,
        whichever comes first."
        And I ended up putting a new battery in it.
        and a new tire on it.

Bauer's intonation in these last two lines reinforced their grammatical similarity. His delivery of the words "and I ended up" was quick and low-pitched. At "new," he jumped to a higher pitch and slowed down for the rest of the clause, during which the pitch fell. He used the same intonation for the succeeding phrase. The musical effect is suggested in figure 2.1.[4]

Norm's role in this part of the conversation was supportive. He made agreeable comments ("I know"; "I see what you're saying") and asked questions that kept Bauer talking ("What, on your Caddy?"; "Do you know that they never fixed the battery?"). Through his verbal displays of interest, Norm helped Bauer create a conversational situation in which Bauer's story would be appropriate and appreciated.

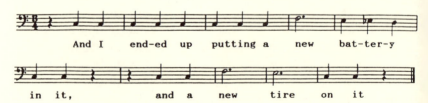

Figure 2.1 "And I ended up . . . ," first variation.
Transcript represents relative rather than absolute pitches.

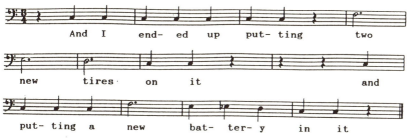

Figure 2.2 "And I ended up . . . ," second variation.

Bauer next presented some more details about the state of the Caddy's tires and battery ("they were *supposed* to put a tire *on* it for me, all they did was put the spare on"; "he said they'd put [a new battery] in for half price"), recreating his frustration with the deal he made. He then repeated his musical refrain, changing the order of its elements, as illustrated in figure 2.2.

The scene was now set for the story. Bauer introduced the topic by moving toward it in increasingly specific steps, from warranties on used cars in general to his used-car deal to what was wrong with his car. By making a verbal refrain, marked with a special musical voice, out of his problems with the car, he underscored the crucial background of his story and provided a clue as to its denouement. Bauer also established that he had a receptive audience. During three long pauses, nobody else offered a new topic; after the first and second, Norm in fact encouraged Bauer to continue.

Mattie Blair's story began smoothly in medias res; Lon Bauer, on the other hand, worked hard to move from two-person chat about his Caddy to the story he decided to tell. This happened because the stories were told in very different situations. But the particular strategies Bauer chose —his stepwise thematic move from general to specific and the parallel syntax and musical shape of his repeated claim to the conversational floor— were not dictated by the situation. These are things American storytellers often do, things Bauer had heard done before and that he had perhaps done himself. They are resources he could choose to use to shape his own story.

Narrating

Once the scene was set and the characters were introduced, both storytellers were obliged to get the action started and to move through it, showing how events were related both chronologically (what happened first, what next, what finally) and thematically (which events formed part of the same scene or episode). Both stories proceed in chronological order, from further in the past to later in the past—there are no flashbacks in either—and both narrators used the past tense far more frequently than the historical present.

The pacing of the stories and the details of the sequencing and dividing up of events are, however, very different. Mr. Bauer's story proceeds, as it began, in relatively small bursts of words. If the number of clauses in the story is divided by the number of intonation-unit lines, the result is 0.8; in other words, Bauer's short lines contain, on the average, fewer than one clause each. (To count clauses, I have counted finite main verbs except those occurring in constructed dialogue introduced with a quotative. "I said, 'Boy I hope this starts'" thus counts as a single clause.) In this fairly typical excerpt, four lines, separated in Bauer's speech by brief pauses and punctuated with falling final intonation, express the meaning of two clauses:

> Jane went to—
> The next Saturday Jane went to Fort Wayne,
> had a meeting up there,
> the church.

Compared to Mattie Blair's talk, Lon Bauer's sounds clipped, like poetry recited a line at a time. Mrs. Blair's speech emerged in longer, more proselike lines of 1.4 clauses on the average:

> And so he told me "Honey, you be doing that all today with me?"
> And he said oh we'd buy, oh we would need to buy something,
>   a little something, not too much,
> and people'd give him back money, and he'd give them a piece
>   of paper.

The long lines of Mrs. Blair's talk make it sound less hurried but also more headlong, ordered and organized as it emerged rather than planned in advance.

The stories are, in fact, organized very differently, and their organization signaled differently. Lon Bauer's story has three episodes,[5] each of which describes a time when the Cadillac made an ominous noise ("rr rrr rrr") and almost or completely failed to start. The first takes place "the night I drove it" and describes the car's first near-failure:

> when I went to start it, it went "Rr, rr rr rr rr" took off I
> *(three-second pause)*
> "I don't know what that is for sure,
>   surely it shouldn't be any starter problems,
>   any more miles than it's got on it."

Bauer set up his audience's expectations for the next episode with a generalization: "Every time after we'd drive it it was warm, it would do that." He illustrated with an episode about a trip to "the boonies" in Michigan, first describing time and place and then action:

> Everybody else left,
> and we were the last ones there,
> and I said "*Boy I hope this starts!*"
> I got in and it went, "Rr."
> And I said "*Oh no!*"
> (*laughter from listeners*)
> "Rr rr rr" and it took off.

Bauer ended this episode as he ended the last, by setting up expectations for the story's next episode: "I didn't have any more trouble with it l- till I got home you know." The last and longest episode describes Jane's trip to Fort Wayne with the car and Greg's subsequent trip in the truck to help her.

The three episodes of the story are parallel in structure and contain repeated elements. Each begins with a line of scene-setting orientation that includes a verb of motion:

> The night I **drove** it (first episode)

> I **drove** it up to Michigan (second episode)

> Jane **went** to— /The next Saturday Jane **went** to Fort Wayne (third episode)

This scene-setting line is followed, in each episode, by some orientational material describing place, time, and actors:

> when I went to start it (first episode)

> was out in the boonies there, when we went canoeing, with the
> Scouts last . . . over Labor Day last year (second episode)

> [Jane] had a meeting up there, the church (third episode)

Then the car acts up. In episodes 1 and 2, the problem is presented in almost identical form:

> . . . it went "Rr, rr rr rr rr" took off (episode 1)

> . . . it went, "Rr."
> "Rr rr rr" and it took off (episode 2)

Episode 3 presents the car trouble in more detail. But when the problem is finally solved, Greg's report echoes the resolutions of episodes 1 and 2:

> said aw he jumped it and it **took right off.**

Episodes 2 and 3 further echo each other in their final lines:

I didn't have any more trouble with it l-
till I got home you know. (episode 2)

never had any trouble with it since then. (episode 3)

The three episodes are followed by a coda that provides a very short summary of the story ("Just that battery") and a more general, humorously moral-sounding observation about batteries:

Just "rrr" though is just —
those old good old Delco Freedom Batteries,
when they do that,
that's the way they go.

The overall structure of this story—three episodes of increasing length, with parallel structure and echoic phrasing—is strongly reminiscent of the structure of many less spontaneous and more consciously performed genres of talk. American jokes, for example, very often have this structure, as do many Euro-American folk tales: there are three main characters, or something happens three times. Nonverbal forms of art such as film also often make use of parallel sets of three. In all these cases, and others, the third episode provides the resolution or completes the pattern. Lon Bauer did not create or present his story as an artistic performance; to him and to the members of his audience, it was a perfectly mundane, forgettable bit of talk. But the story partakes of the conventions of folklore for familiar, predictable structure and borrows such a structure from genres such as jokes.

Mrs. Blair's story does not have so transparent a structure. If Bauer's story is comedy, Blair's is tragedy, and its structure is reminiscent of the conventions of tragedy. As with dramas like *Oedipus Rex* or *Hamlet*, the story involves slowly but inexorably rising tension leading to a tragic climax (the shooting) made inevitable by preordained, inescapable character flaws in the relatively finely drawn protagonists ("ignorance," as Mrs. Blair called it, in this case).

The segments into which Blair divided the events of her story as she told it are separated not by junctures of time but by shifts in character, point of view, and state of knowledge. In the first scene, Mattie and Sonny go to the insurance company:

So he has, he eh, eh got, carried me someplace with him that day,
to the insurance company,
t- to to take out insurance on his car.

And while he was in there,
eh the (man) was out,
and he tore a bunch of checks out of the back of the checkbook,
insurance checks.
Well you know those type of checks,
it's checks like you can write 'em any amount, like you have an
    accident.

Mrs. Blair announced the beginning of the scene with *so*, a discourse marker (Schiffrin 1987) often used for the purpose of showing when a new "paragraph" of spoken discourse starts. *So* has a dual effect. Consistently enough used as a boundary marker to be defined that way in at least one desk dictionary (*Webster's Ninth New Collegiate Dictionary*, 1983, p. 1117), *so* is also a marker of result. Connecting two clauses with *so* is thus ambiguous. To say, as Mrs. Blair did, "so he carried me someplace with him that day" is to raise the possibility that Mattie's going off with Sonny was the inevitable result of knowing him, or of his being Doc's friend. Mrs. Blair's story continues to present new events as being connected to previous ones in this quasi-causal way, and the effect is to suggest that the events of the story flowed inexorably out of one another.

Just as Bauer's "the night I drove it," by locating one event in time, serves to signal that a sequence of events is beginning, so does Blair's "that day." But though Blair's temporal anchor sounds just as specific as Bauer's, it is in fact completely unspecified. She has not said before, and never does, which day "that" day was. The expression thus functions entirely as a discourse marker signaling the start of temporal narration and has no part at all in the orienting of the events in time.

In the next episode, Sonny "goes around cashing checks." Like the first, this episode begins with *so*.

So uh, he goes around cashing checks, buying me, uh,
'cause I've always I'monna be truthful with you,
always been a clothes freak.

Sonny's check-cashing is presented three times in this segment: "So uh, he goes around cashing checks"; "But anyway, this Sonny cashed all of them checks"; "So he goes to work and uh cash them checks that day." In between, Mrs. Blair described her character in the story, telling how Mattie had "always been a clothes freak" and why she didn't understand sooner what Sonny was up to: "I always been kind of a dummy, 'cause I was brought up that way." After the third mention of the only real action in this section, she explained how the scam worked: "And he just wrote this check and give it to the woman and she'd give him back the change." The structure of the narration perfectly fits the Mattie character's developing understanding, first unthinkingly accepting pretty clothes, then wondering why Sonny has so much money but still not hip enough to know why, then finally catching on.

In the third part of the story, Mattie realizes what is happening and finds out exactly what her role is to be. This scene portrays a new state of knowledge. The change of scene is signaled by *then*—here indicating not a temporal shift but rather a rhetorical one—and, again, *so*:

> And then uh, so he, I said "What are you — ? Ooo!"
> And he had wa- aaall that money.
> And so he told me "Honey, you be doing that all today with me?"

An aside in this scene about Mattie—"I told you I wasn't nothing but a dumb old *country* ignorant Georgia girl"—echoes the one in the previous scene, and Mrs. Blair continued to employ linguistically definite but in our universe of discourse indefinite noun phrases: neither "this place" nor "this here motel" were identifiable. As she did the preceding scene, Mrs. Blair ended this one with a summation: "And that's what saved me from him."

The next scene starts, as have previous scenes, with *so*. A new character comes into play here, namely Doc, and the temporal framework changes, the change marked with a subordinate modifying clause:

> So, soon as I got back and could find Doc, I told Doc.
> So Doc got his gun,
> and went looking for his rump.

A summary marks the end of the scene—"Finally, we didn't find him so[6] we went on home"—and character and the point of view shift into the next, the initial *he* now having to be taken as referring to Sonny rather than Doc. The new scene is marked at the beginning (not surprisingly) with *so*:

> So he was so ignorant,
> he (goes to work) and gets in his pretty car,
> and come over there and knock on my door,

As have others, this scene ends with a summation: "he killed that boy." Not having been foreshadowed in any way, this event comes as a surprise. Sonny's "ignorance" leads him blindly into trouble, as Mattie's ignorance did her.

The final segment of the story presents its aftermath in a flat, reportorial way:

So he went on to the penitentiary, and uh,
they had me accessory to the fact, but he pleaded guilty,
you know 'cause I didn't pull no trigger,
but you know they had to go through the whole procedure. . . .

Unlike Mr. Bauer, who concluded his story with a tidy moral about Delco Freedom Batteries, Mrs. Blair ended hers without commenting on its significance in any way. Instead, she simply mentioned the final result, "so he went on to the penitentiary," and the part of it that was most relevant to her: "they had me accessory to the fact." She went on, in subsequent talk, to a different episode of her life involving a different man and a different place.

The outcome of Mrs. Blair's story seems inevitable. She provided no foreshadowing clues about the ending and thus no reason for listeners to think about alternatives to it, so there seem at first to have been no options. In this respect the story contrasts sharply with Mr. Bauer's. Because he presented three increasingly annoying episodes of car trouble in a predictable format, Bauer's audience was far more likely to have been thinking in advance about what the solution to the problem was finally going to be. Mr. Bauer's story is lively and gamelike in a way Mrs. Blair's is not, and Mrs. Blair's (in keeping with her style throughout our sessions) flat and reportorial in a way his is not. This has a lot to do, of course, with what the stories are about. But it also has a lot to do with how the events of the stories are narrated, how the narratives are structured, and what linguistic choices their tellers made for marking this structure. Lon Bauer's quick pacing, his use of a familiar format that makes it possible to second-guess the outcome, and his consistent, melodic parallelism all contribute to the comic effect of his story. Mattie Blair's longer, heavier verbal lines, the less predictable criteria for scene setting that force her hearer simply to follow rather than anticipate, her consistent use of the result-toned transition marker *so*, and her unevaluated, emotionless summaries throughout all contribute to the tragic effect of hers, as unseeing protagonists move inexorably toward an inevitable tragic outcome.

Moving In and Out of the Narrative

The tragic effect of the story about Sonny has also to do, as I have suggested, with the fact that the characters are relatively carefully sketched, people rather than symbols or abstractions. Mrs. Blair brought her characters—the younger Mattie, Doc, and Sonny—to life in several ways: through their actions, through the talk she attributed to them in the narrative, and by leaving the narrative altogether to describe them. Blair shifted on several occasions from portraying the series of events that form the story's foreground to describing states of affairs that obtained in the background and then shifted back to narration again. Almost every time she did this, the departure consisted of details about what one of the characters was like. In most cases the character in question is Mattie, Mrs. Blair's younger self, and in most cases the characterization of Mattie provides an explanation for her susceptibility to Sonny's manipulation. She liked pretty things to wear, for example:

> 'cause I've always I'monna be truthful with you,
> always been a clothes freak.
> I *love* pretty clothes, here I am blind.
> And the first time he give me a piece of — a dress or something,
>   I bit it!
> (BJ: Uh-huh)
> You know, you know how you feel everything? I don't know.
> I said, "Yeah, this is good material!"
> And I used to be fond of Lili Ann suits.

The principal reason for Mattie's youthful encounters with trouble (this being one of many in her life history, most involving men) was, Mrs. Blair claimed, her naiveté. She pointed out over and over, twice in this story alone, that she had been disadvantaged by her rural upbringing in Georgia, with her grandparents, while her mother and a series of stepfathers lived in Indiana and Michigan. Being raised in the South and in the country made her "dumb," she claimed, "ignorant," not "hip like the little city girls."

> I don't never known that, I always been kind of a dummy, 'cause
> I was brought up that way, old *country*, old dumb country girl. If
> I hadda been brought up hip like the little city girls, I'd have some
> sense. But I was raised down there in them cotton fields, you
> know I ain't had no sense, anybody could use me.

Mrs. Blair departed from the narrative line to describe both the other characters in the story, too. Sonny "was real nice. He had a new car, first car I ever rode in had a record player in it, a tape or whatever." Later on, when he gets rough, Sonny is described as "smoking marijuana, he was you know he was a dope addict." Doc is possessive: "he gon always peek to see who at the door, don't want nobody come in, think it's some man come looking for me."

To signal that she was returning from background characterization to foreground action, Mrs. Blair repeated what she had said before the digression. The first characterization of Sonny is surrounded by almost exactly identical clauses:

And him and Doc became good friends.
And uh . . . Sonny was . . . real nice.
He had a . . . new car, first car I ever rode in had a record player
in it, a tape or whatever.
(BJ: Um-hm)
And him and Doc was very good friends.

as is the final characterization of Doc:

And here Doc say "Yeah man, I sure was."
I didn't know he was look- listening, I thought he was in there
     watching television.
But he (gon) always peek to see who at the door, don't want
     nobody come in, think it's some man come looking for me.
**And so Doc say "Yeah, man," say, "I sure was looking for
     you."**

In between, digressions about Mattie's character also end with a near repeat of the line that preceded them or with a paraphrase. Rather than presenting detailed information about the situation, or the time, or the place—aspects of orientation that seem important to many storytellers—Mrs. Blair gave details about her characters. Mr. Bauer did not. This is not because the main character in his story is a car—the car does in fact come to have a personality—but because Bauer acted out his characters, giving them voices rather than describing them. Bauer departed from his narrative line only three times, and each time the digression provides details either about place or about situation. Bauer's digressions explain the actions of the human characters, but only in very practical terms. When Bauer "drove [the Caddy] up to Michigan," for example, he more specifically "was out in the boonies there," and this was because of a Scout trip. When Jane "went to Fort Wayne," it was because of a meeting at the church. Greg rather than Bauer went to help because "Just Greg and I was here, and I couldn't—didn't feel as though I could leave." Two of Bauer's three digressions are marked with syntactic incompleteness: grammatical subjects are missing at the beginning.

was out in the boonies there,
when we went canoeing,
with the Scouts last,
over Labor Day last year.

had a meeting up there,
the church.

Bauer did not use repetition to signal a return to the narrative track the way Blair did.

Marking Key Points

Another favor storytellers must do their audiences, if they are to have audiences at all, is to signal the moments of special tension in their stories, particularly the moments at which matters come to a climax or crux. A narrator who fails to create dramatic suspense leading to a high point will be perceived as not having a point (Polanyi 1979), no matter what the events being recounted may be. (Think, for example, of a five-year-old's breathless but often frustratingly pointless recital of what happened in a movie, or of an eyewitness's ideally neutral, pointless recounting of events to the police.) Mattie Blair and Lon Bauer were both effective storytellers. Both, accordingly, found ways to create dramatic tension at key moments of their narratives.

In each episode of his story, Lon Bauer used dialogue to slow the action and create suspense.[7] The three episodes are like three dramatic acts of increasing length and complexity. Perhaps the most salient bits of "talk" in the story are the "rr rr rr" noises of the car. Bauer's car noises, impossible to do justice to with English orthography,[8] recreate the sound of a car failing to turn over as exactly as is possible with a human voice. The car's sounds are introduced with *go* ("it went"), a verb often used to introduce human speech. This personifies the car and makes it a character in the story.

Each episode of the story also includes dialogue. As he put words in his own and others' mouths, Bauer altered his voice to mimic each speaker's style. In the first episode, he created a mental monologue for himself, using a whiny, questioning voice:

"I don't know what that is for sure,
surely it shouldn't be any starter problems,
any more miles than it's got on it."

Though there are no external signals like "I said to myself" to indicate that these lines are to be taken as a quotation, Bauer's intent is clear from his choice of "I don't know" rather than "I didn't know."

In the second episode, Bauer noted that he had been left alone in "the boonies" as part of the last group to leave and then created anticipatory tension in loud, nervous-sounding dialogue: "*Boy I hope this starts!*" The car begins to make its threatening noise again, and Bauer's character comments on it, again in a loud, worried way: "*Oh no!*"

The third episode is the longest and includes the most dialogue. The first bit recreates Bauer's telephone conversation with his wife:

> She called back on Saturday night,
> she said "Uh,
> car won't start."
> (*laughter*)
> I says, "What do you mean the car won't start?"
> She says, "It won't turn over,
> won't do anything."
> She said they tried to jump it,
> and it wouldn't even jump.
> I said, "Oooh,"
> said, "Unless it's in the starter it should jump."
> Said, "Got lights and everything?"
> Yeah she had lights

As he spoke his wife's lines, Bauer acted out her voice, using conventional strategies for sounding like a stereotypical worried woman such as raised pitch and hesitant intonation. Throughout this dialogue there is a great deal of parallelism and repetition, both within utterances in the dialogue and between them. This transcription technique, borrowed from Tannen (1989), highlights the repetition:

> she said, "Uh,
>   car won't start."
> I says, "What do you mean the car won't start?"
> She says, "It won't turn over,
>   won't do anything."

She said	they tried to	jump it,
and	it wouldn't even	jump.
[I] said, "Unless it's in the starter		
	it should	jump."

Said, "Got	lights and everything?"
Yeah she had	lights . . .

The effect of these repetitions is to slow the dialogue down, creating extra suspense before the problem's resolution. They also create the impression of conversational attunement, as Bauer and his wife borrow each other's words and phrasings.[9]

Additional constructed speech in this episode slowed it down further, when Bauer quoted himself giving instructions to his assistant Greg, in a weary, hassled voice:

> I said, "First thing,
> try jumping it,
> (*one-second pause*)
> and if that doesn't work,
> jump it,
> and take and
> tap on the starter
> at the same time as you have someone turn it on maybe —
> maybe it's out of brushes,
> I don't know."

By inserting this set of instructions in the story, Bauer demonstrated his expertise with cars, at the same time claiming ignorance in this case. This makes the Caddy's problem seem real and mysterious. Note that Greg's report, on his return to the gas station, is phrased indirectly ("said aw he jumped it and it took right off"); Greg is not a major character in the drama, while Bauer is.

In "I Know When I Bought Mine," Lon Bauer captured and created ordinary talk and everyday suspense the way many playwrights try to. Each episode in the story is molded around a core of dialogue, and the characters who speak are given personal voices and moods. The drama evoked laughter from Bauer's original audience and has evoked laughter from subsequent audiences as well; it makes Mr. Bauer's story memorable and enjoyable to listen to.

Mattie Blair's story is also memorable, and her use of dialogue, like Bauer's, is part of what makes it so. The higher the level of dramatic tension in the events Blair recounts, the more dialogue there is. Mattie's discovery about Sonny's scam is marked with dialogue that not only slows the action and thus signals an important moment in it but also reveals a great deal about the characters and their relationship: Sonny speaks decisively and calls Mattie "Honey" and "Baby"; Mattie's utterances are hesitant and questioning.

> And then uh, so he, I said "What are you — ? Ooo!"
> And he had wa- aaall that money.
> And so he told me, "Honey, you be doing that all today with
>   me?" . . .
> And so I said, "Ohh my God." [disbelieving semiwhisper]
> And he said, "Yeah, you didn't know I was a paperhanger, baby?"
> I said "What — who you hang paper for?"
> I thought he meant hang paper on the walls!

When Sonny abducts her to the motel, Mattie protests, and the repetitions of her protests increase the tension:

> I said, "Oooh uh-hn, no-oo, uh-hn,"
> I said, "I ain't going noplace with you."
> And uh, he just caught me by the arm and pushed me and shoved
>   me in the car,
> said, "Oh yeah, you're going."
> And they told me, he was smoking marijuana, he was you know
>   he was a dope addict.
> And I said "No-oo uh-un."

Repeated dialogue also marks the story's climax, the encounter of Sonny and Doc:

> [Sonny] say, "Hey, I know that that old — that nigger of yours
>   was looking for me."
> And here Doc say, "Yeah man, I sure was." . . .
> And so Doc say, "Yeah, man," say, "I sure was looking for you."
>   [mimics high whiny voice]
> And he said "Well here I am, big man, what you want?"
> And so Doc say he's "Aww, man."
> And next thing I know *pumm*

Even the interactional turn during which Doc shoots is represented as speech: "Aww, man."

Dialogue is not the only concomitant of narrative tension in Mrs. Blair's story, however. Another of the variety of techniques she used to build suspense was to portray a single event with a series of verbs or verb phrases, drawing out the event by drawing out its telling: Sonny "**goes around cashing** checks" or "**goes to work** and **cash** them checks," for example. In abducting Mattie, Blair said, "he just **caught** me by the arm and **pushed** me and **shoved** me in the car," and when she escaped, "I **crawled** through the window and **got** out the window and **run** and **went** to the motel office." Sonny "**goes to work** and **gets** in his pretty car and **come** over there and **knock** on my door," and, after the shooting, "my kids **went to running went to hollering went to screaming,** I **run** and **went to hollering, run** across . . . and **went to running went to run-** ." Note, too, how many of these verbs are in the present tense, despite the fact that all the action is in the past. Though there is some debate about the precise roles the historical present can play in narrative (Schiffrin 1981; Wolfson 1982; Johnstone 1987a), there is no question that, when actions are being portrayed in the past tense, a shift to present can alert an audience to key events.

The conventional structure of Lon Bauer's story sets up expectations that do much of the work of helping a listener predict when the story's high point will occur. Though they may not be consciously aware of it, listeners like Bauer's original audience would be surprised and discomfited if the resolution did not come about during the third episode. Mrs. Blair's story is more fluid and less predictable in structure, and there are several climactic moments. As a result, Blair had to be more explicit about marking climaxes in the action. Hence, perhaps, the multiple marking of rising tension in her story, the overlapping ways of slowing action and creating suspense.

Reasons for Variation

"Sonny" and "I Know When I Bought Mine" are very different—different in theme, most apparently, but also different in structure and rhythm, in how digressions are marked and what they are for, in how suspense is created and sustained, in how characters are presented. They are also different in ways I have not yet spotlighted—Bauer's syntax, for example, is on the whole more standard than Blair's and Blair's more varied than Bauer's—and in ways that are almost impossibly hard to capture in transcripts. Blair's voice was that of a black woman; more specifically, it was soft, a little tired, but compelling, the voice of a woman with the large physique she had before her illness. Bauer's voice is that of a mature white man from the Great Lakes region, just slightly slowed and drawled for self-deprecating effect in this performance.

Why did Mattie Blair and Lon Bauer sound so different? The differences can be related to social, rhetorical, and psychological facts, facts ranging from biology to birth order to parents' income level to the nature of the audience, as well as to facts about linguistic background, ethnic and cultural identity, gender, occupation, the tellers' friends and neighbors, the medium of their communication, how they related to the people they were talking to. Let us examine how a few of the best-studied reasons for variation may help account for specific facts about the language of Mattie Blair's and Lon Bauer's stories.

For one thing, Lon Bauer sounded like a northern white and Mattie Blair like a southern black. They drew on resources provided by varieties of American English that had different regional origins in England (and possibly, in the case of African-American English Vernacular, a different ontogeny altogether) and that, for familiar reasons involving social and geographical isolation, eventually diverged even further. Accordingly, they had different ways of pronouncing many words, and there are differences in their morphology and syntax. The complementation pattern in Blair's "I told you about he hid in the church" sounds southern, as does the lack of a relative pronoun before *had* in "[That was the] first car I ever rode in had a record player in it." Bauer's second *any* in "surely shouldn't be any starter problems **any** more miles than it's got on it" sounds northern, as does his use of the demonstrative form *those* ("those old good old Delco Freedom Batteries") and the verb form *took* ("he took the truck"), whereas Blair used *them* ("them checks") and *taken* ("so he taken me to this here motel").

Their regional dialects provided Bauer and Blair with different ways of sounding and meaning in many common and apparently predictable ways, and it is tempting to talk about the relationship between their dialects and their discourses in deterministic ways: being a northerner *made* Bauer do one thing, and speaking a southern variety *caused* Blair to do another. But their regional dialects can also be seen as providing them with different resources for innovation; for example, because *carry* can mean, for speakers of southern varieties, something close to what *take* means, Blair could use *carry* and *take* in a way Bauer could not, to distinguish willing accompaniment from forced. When she wanted to go along, Sonny "carried" her to the insurance company and to the store, but when she was unwilling, he "taken" her to the motel.[10] Her knowledge of southern possibilities provided Blair with a way of creating meaning that someone without her resources would have had to create another way.

Bauer and Blair also had access to different (though overlapping) cultural resources. Both were Americans, but one was of European ancestry and one African-American, and they held some different values and beliefs, both general—ideas about how to behave, what is good, how the world works—and specifically related to language and talk. That "I Know When I Bought Mine" was, once Bauer got the right to tell it, a monologue punctuated only by laughter has to do with the fact that for white midwesterners like him, the responsibility for creating and conveying meaning in a story is mainly its teller's (Johnstone 1990a). Audiences are expected to be quiet, and evaluative interjections from hearers are considered rude. African-Americans like Blair are used to multivoiced, collaborative oral narrative; the fact that Blair's story was monologic had to do with the formality of the situation, with the fact that her hoped-for readership, not I, was the ultimate audience for the story, and with my cultural preference for silent listenership. As a result, Blair was forced to find ways to compensate for the lack of audience participation; this accounts in part, I think, for the number of times she left the narrative line of her story to provide explicit evaluation of her own.

Cultural predilections and possibilities affect how these two voices sound in other ways as well. Bauer's repeated use of specific detail, even when such detail was unnecessary for understanding the story, reflects a white midwestern preference for reportlike, factual-sounding stories (Johnstone 1990c). The pejorative *country* in Blair's descriptions of herself not only reflects regional usage (*country* is often adjectival in the South and often labels perceived quaintness or backwardness; for example, Texans with strong regional accents "sound country" to others) but also identifies an oppressive cultural milieu from which she said she never escaped. This central claim is the key not only to this story but to Blair's whole life history. The legalistic tone of Lon Bauer's story, beginning with talk of contractual obligations concerning used cars and ending with an implied warning to other careless buyers, contrasts with the moralistic tone of Mattie Blair's, in which what is right is clearly more important than what is legal. Culture and ethnicity thus provide many resources for theme and structure, without determining what the nature of either will be.

Blair was a woman and Bauer a man; this difference, too, helps account for the different resources out of which they constructed their stories. The younger self Blair depicted is a naive rural girl, easily and repeatedly victimized by men. It is part of a life history that is a plea for understanding, an attempt to show that her mistakes were not her fault and that she did the best she could with her life. Bauer depicted himself making mistakes, too, but the mistakes resulted only in minor annoyance. By describing them, he presented himself as a genial bumbler for whom things do eventually work out just fine. His story is about an object, the Caddy; Blair's about a person, Sonny, and the development of a relationship. The different experiences that give rise to these thematic choices were shaped, in part, by gender, and the content of the two stories contrasts in ways men's and women's narratives have been found to contrast in other studies (e.g., Johnstone 1993).

Gender has something to do with the language of the stories, too. Bauer's was confidently told; he rarely paused and never filled pauses with hesitant *ums* or *uhs*. The only *uh* in the story was in his depiction of his wife's speech ("Uh, car won't start"). He also represented his wife's voice with tentatively rising final intonation and a whiny high pitch. Blair hesitated somewhat more often, especially at the beginning of the story, as if not sure that she had the right to tell it. Her younger voice is strong and confident ("Oooh uh-hn, no-oo, uh-hn, I ain't going noplace with you") but still ineffective. The gender of their addressees may also have affected Blair's and Bauer's choices; women talk to men differently than to women in some respects (Holmes 1989; Johnstone, Ferrara, and Bean 1992), and men probably do, too.

Mattie Blair's is a story about sexual oppression, and telling it, even to a sympathetic woman, was bold and difficult in a way Lon Bauer's telling of his story was not. She talked graphically about the murder ("*pumm*. Shot him right through the head"), but the purpose of Sonny's taking her to the motel has to be heard between the lines. Even in a story about a near rape, Blair didn't mention rape. An obvious and partially accurate way to explain this omission is to attribute it to constraint, to say that women cannot talk about some of their most terrifying experiences. Note, though, that I understood what she was referring to. The fact that a thing cannot be labeled doesn't mean that it cannot be referred to, and constraints on direct labeling encourage the making of new, maybe innovative, creative forms of reference. (Some of the world's most moving poetry is after all the result of constraints on the direct expression of erotic attraction.)

Mattie Blair's story is about social oppression, too, about the results of poverty, and its telling made a statement about social class that Bauer's telling did not make. Social class, in particular the linguistic choices through which social position is expressed, was a resource in the telling of the stories, too. On the whole, Blair's speech was less standard than Bauer's: she used *ain't*, multiple negatives, verb forms such as *he taken, he cash*, and *he give* in the past tense, *them* as a demonstrative pronoun; she said "him and Doc" while Bauer said "Greg and I." Used by African-Americans and whites alike, these forms are stigmatized by Americans whose repertoires include more standard forms as well. A person with fewer choices along the stylistic continuum of standardness has fewer resources for creativity, but all speakers can vary their speech to some extent, and all accordingly can use standardness and nonstandardness as resources for discourse.[11] Mattie Blair was no exception. She used socially marked, nonstandard forms as a resource in the depiction of herself in the story. Though negative concord is consistent throughout the story and thus may not reflect the result of choice, her use of *ain't* as an equivalent for *did not* in the first person singular was not consistent. Describing herself as an incompetent country girl, she used the lower-status form ("I ain't had no sense"), but, describing herself as being in the right after the murder, she used the higher-status *didn't* ("I didn't pull no trigger"). Blair's use of nonstandardness in the depiction of versions of herself resulted on one occasion in overreaching the mark, in the ungrammatical, hypernonstandard "I don't never known that," which also describes the country girl.

Lon Bauer's story includes an occasional nonstandard verb form, in "Greg and I **was** here" and "they **come** back in," but Bauer's speech was on the whole like that of a white TV announcer. He, too, varied his speech for creative purposes, however, only in the opposite direction on the standardness-nonstandardness scale. Bauer presented himself in the story as a bumbler, a person whose response to trouble is to shout "Oh, no!" and who buys a lemon of a car and can't figure out why it won't start. But he simultaneously managed to present himself as intelligent and informed. He did this through strategic uses of writerly syntactic complexity, editing his phrasing, as he talked, in the direction of carefulness and explicitness. He did this, for example, in introducing his topic, moving from the casually structured "*Tire* I though they should have, the *tires* . . ." to the carefully structured "For the price I paid for it, I thought it should have had good tires on it," and again when he edited "I couldn't [leave]" to "[I] didn't feel as though I could leave." Just as Mattie Blair's strategic style-shifting led on one occasion to ungrammaticality, so did Lon Bauer's, in "I could — I could that — I might as well done that myself." In the attempt to shift from the less elaborated "I could do" to the more elaborated "I might as well have done," he ended up with a nonexistent form, "I might as well done."

The two stories were also shaped by the situations in which they were told. In one case, the audience consisted of familiar peers, in the other of a strange professional; the locale in which one story was told was home, the locale for the other a nursing home room. In Bauer's case, the relationships among participants in the event was relatively clear: they knew one other, and they knew how they were socially arrayed vis-à-vis one

another, in general and in this situation. Norm's being a cooperative listener was, in light of his being Bauer's employee, not surprising, and Bauer
used Norm's interactional helpfulness to aid in getting his story started,
letting Norm ask the right leading questions. Knowing his hearers, and
confident that they would understand him, Bauer almost never checked
for comprehension or listenership; once the story begins, there is only
one "you know." In Blair's case, the social situation was murky. I deferred
to her. As an elderly person and as a dying person, she had, I thought,
the right to be the talker (that, after all, was why I was there), but we
were both aware that I was doing her a favor, too. Blair was never sure
whether I would understand, and sometimes I did not and had to ask
what 1940s African-American slang meant or where places were.
Accordingly, she checked my comprehension often and added information she thought I might need: "You know those type of checks";
"You know how you feel everything?"; "you know, 'cause I didn't pull
no trigger."

Lon Bauer and Mattie Blair were very different people, both in terms
of the social and linguistic categories into which sociolinguists group
people (e.g., race, socioeconomic class, geographic background) and in
terms of individual psychology. They created these stories out of differing personal histories: though Mrs. Blair may well have had a car whose
battery failed at some point, she never had a mechanic in her employ
whom she could send to fix it, and Mr. Bauer never witnessed a murder,
as far as I know, or inadvertently helped pass stolen checks. And they
told the stories to different audiences, in different settings, for reasons
that were at least on the conscious level quite different. Neither the fact
that the stories are different nor the degree of difference between them
should be surprising. But why are the two stories different? What is the
relationship between ethnicity and "Sonny" or between socioeconomic
status and birth order and "I Know When I Bought Mine"? Linguistic
behavior varies statistically with social factors—sociolinguistic research
has made this abundantly clear—and with psychological factors, as well
as with changes in rhetorical situation. But none of these factors *causes*
people to talk one way or another. What, then, is the mechanism by
which facts about people's voices are connected with facts about people?

Narrative and Individuation

The factors I have discussed—language and dialect, culture and ethnicity, gender, social class, situation—all have something to do with the
shape of discourse. So do factors I have not discussed, such as, for

example, whether an utterance is spoken or written and whether the speaker is an extravert or an introvert. When we study people as members of groups and examine their linguistic behavior statistically, and when we concentrate on what happens within a word or a phrase or a sentence, it is tempting to think of and talk about these factors in a predictive way. It is tempting, for example, to think that because a person is African-American and a woman, she will not pronounce certain verb endings and will use tag questions, or that because a person is writing he will use subordinate clauses, or that because a person is from the South she will pronounce *pin* and *pen* the same way. When we study individuals' speech, however, and when we concentrate on what happens in stories or speeches or conversations, it becomes clear that no two people talk alike and that it is more enlightening to think of factors such as gender, ethnicity, and audience as resources that speakers use to create unique voices than as determinants of how they will talk.

That no two people talk exactly alike or say exactly the same thing is especially clear when the texts we look at are narratives. No one would suppose that two different people would ever produce identical stories in identical words. And no one would suppose that the reason for this is simply that there is an infinitely large set of sentences that could possibly be said in a language. The commonsense explanation for the fact that we would never expect two people to produce precisely the same narrative text is that no two people are alike. In fact, it is precisely in narrative that people's individuality is expressed most obviously, because the purpose of narrating is precisely the creation of an autonomous, unique self in discourse.

When people transform personal experience into stories, they create meaning on three levels. In the first place, people tell stories to create and share knowledge about the world. Stories are displays of what goes on in the teller's and the hearers' world. At the same time, stories provide potential storytellers with information about what sorts of events count as reportable ones, what sorts of events are relevant in the local world, and what sorts of knowledge can be conveyed by or gained from stories about these events. Stories are thus referential: they mirror and shape the world they are about.

Second, people tell stories to evoke and create interpersonal relationships. Stories shape, and are shaped by, the interactions in which they occur. Stories reflect and mold the social relationships they tell about, too. People use stories to shape and reshape relations of solidarity, power, and status. Stories also create community identities: in an important sense, communities are groups of people who tell stories the same way (Johnstone 1990a) and who tell the same stories. Stories thus have social meaning.

A third sort of meaning in stories is personal. Stories express people's individuality; "acting yourself" is speaking yourself, telling your own stories. People perform their identities as they act and talk (Goffman 1959), calling attention to who they are as they call attention to the ways they choose for creating meaning and coherence in their stories. This involves showing that one is a person at all, that is, an autonomous member of the species with a temporally continuous history (Hallowell 1955). This, it can be argued, is the primary reason for narrative; it accounts for the "autobiographical impulse" (Rosen 1988). Children differentiate themselves from others when they notice that different things happen to them than to others, that they can, in other words, have a life story different from anyone else's. When there are temporal holes in people's life histories, people can lose their sanity, and sanity can sometimes be regained, in therapy, by constructing a new, complete life narrative (Schafer 1981). Furthermore, speaking oneself involves showing what kind of person one is, both explicitly and implicitly. Speakers create selves in narrative through choices of theme (you are the history you create) and language (you are how you talk). Stories are always covert performances of self, and sometimes overt ones.

This point is clearly illustrated by Charlotte Linde (1993) in a book about oral narratives by American professionals. Linde argues that personal narrative is perceived as coherent if it establishes causality and continuity (or successfully explains accident and discontinuity) in the teller's life. She claims that "narrative is among the most important social resources for creating and maintaining personal identity" (p. 98) because it helps express and maintain three characteristics of the self (pp. 98–126). Through narrative sequencing and the implied or overt causal connections narrators make between events, stories express the continuity of self through time. Through markers of person ("I," "you," "she") and because narrative is told to another, narrative expresses the relation of self to others. And through the retrospective process of creating narratives and in highlighting what was important in their stories, narrators express the reflexivity of self, the ability to treat one's self as an other.

This function of narration accounts for the most basic differences between the two stories we have examined in this chapter, one a comedy and one a tragedy. The themes of the stories, their structures, and their sounds and syntax are all relevant to the selves of their tellers as these selves are created in discourse. Bauer's story is the story of a lighthearted, comfortable life; this is reflected in the familiar three-episode comedic structure of the story. More specifically, Lon also created in the story a competent but modest man who can take a joke on himself. He did this by telling about an embarrassing series of events in such a way that his competence and humor are implicit rather than explicit. This self-image is reflected in the story's understated tone. Mrs. Blair's story is, in contrast, an explicit attempt to create a meaningful life—part of her "book." This is serious business, and the story has the serious structure of tragedy, a structure that allows for reflection and revision and in which the meaning emerges slowly. This accounts, for example, for the digressions about her, which are syntactically more complex than the rest of the story and were uttered in longer intonation units. In creating their lives, Blair and Bauer drew on different linguistic resources, and each used available resources to create new ones.

To summarize, different speakers tell different stories about themselves, and they tell them differently. This is a familiar fact; we would be astonished, in fact, to hear two different people speak with the same narrative voice. Many accounts of the reasons for differences of the sort I have illustrated in this chapter seek to explain them with reference to social, psychological, and rhetorical factors. Such accounts contribute enormously to our understanding of discourse, but they leave out the key part of the process. People narrate differently because they are creating different selves in discourse. To do this, they use the resources available to them. These resources vary, depending on language, dialect, gender, and so on, but a story does not take the shape it does *because* its teller is African-American, poor, or female, because her audience is captive, or because she is uninhibited. The influence of society, situation, and psychology on language is indirect; the role of social, rhetorical, and psychological differences is that they provide differential resources for talk. Social, psychological, and rhetorical facts are mediated by the individual, who selects and combines linguistic resources available in his or her environment to create a voice, not just a voice with which to refer to the world or relate to others but a voice with which to be human.

— 3 —

Individual Voice
and Articulate Speaking

It is believed by speakers of Malagasy, who live in Madagascar, that there are two kinds of talk: everyday talk and *kabary*, or formal oratory (Keenan 1973). A person who can perform *kabary* well is a good speaker, an articulate person. Not everyone is allowed to be an orator; women, for example, who are in general thought to be overly direct and pushy in speech (Keenan 1974), are excluded. And not every man who has learned something about the roundabout "winding words" in which *kabary* must be phrased and the rules for who speaks when in the situations that call for *kabary* is equally good at performing it. Some orators are more articulate than others, in other words, and accordingly in greater demand to speak at marriage-request ceremonies and in other situations in which *kabary* is necessary. Being articulate, for the Malagasy, requires two things: being a member of the category of people who are allowed to perform articulate roles, and, assuming that one is a member of this category, being competent at those roles.

There is even more to it, however. Being an articulate orator sometimes requires strategic *inarticulateness*. When the orator representing a young man's family speaks to request a young woman's hand in marriage, he must symbolize in his speech the inferior role of the petitioner.[1] To do this, he must purposely make errors in delivery and protocol— but not so many that he jeopardizes his reputation as a good speaker. To make matters even more complex, the Malagasy have no canonical set of rules about what makes a good speaker. Whether an orator is being articulate is open to debate, and such debate often takes place during the oration itself. A crucial facet of speaking well is thus the ability to win debates about what constitutes speaking well.

The matter of what it means to be articulate is as complex for others as it is for the Malagasy, if not in exactly the same ways. As it does for the Malagasy, being articulate always requires, first, being allowed to be articulate and, second, being competent at being articulate. Competence at speaking well is not everywhere achieved the same way, though every way of achieving it, I will argue, requires linguistic self-expression.

That not everyone is allowed to be equally articulate is clear to many Americans. Students who go to professors with carefully planned requests sometimes find themselves stammering foolishly, because to speak as confidently as they had planned somehow seems inappropriate. Children were once expected to be silent in adult company, and blacks in the pre–civil rights American South were considered "uppity" if they spoke too much or too clearly to whites. The right to be articulate is a perquisite of power, and the people in an interaction who have the least power are meant to be the least articulate.

Mainstream American ideology does not recognize the sociopolitical dimension of articulateness. It is thought by traditional educators (as well as by Dale Carnegie instructors, members of debate teams and lunchtime public-speaking clubs, and most of the rest of the American public) that anyone can learn to be articulate, articulateness being simply a matter of self-confidence, practice, and energy. Efforts to bestow articulateness on the socially inarticulate—to give speakers of nonstandard varieties a "right to their language" in writing classes, for example, or to include the literature of the socially oppressed with the traditional Greats in English curricula—often founder because they do not address the inequities of power that give rise to this inarticulateness in the first place.

Among the people in a situation who *do* have the right to be articulate, not all are equally good at it. Presidents of the United States who speak in complete sentences are perceived as more articulate, for example, than ones who do not, though all American presidents are powerful and all are carefully listened to. Articulateness traditionally implies, to Americans, matters of delivery, such as syntax that is carefully planned and written-sounding (except for good, consistent reasons), and distinct enunciation, as well as matters of content, such as "logical" organization of one's thoughts and convincing support for them, and clarity in showing how ideas are related to one another. Being articulate also means being heard, "getting one's ideas across," without seeming overbearing or overly obtrusive.

Articulateness and Self-Expression

Throughout its history, discourse theory in the Western tradition has also considered linguistic self-expression a hallmark of articulate speech and writing. For Aristotle, for example, *ethos*, or the presentation of an appealing, morally suasive self, was a critical concomitant in public oratory to *logos* (having good ideas and arguing them well) and *pathos* (appealing to the feelings and desires of one's audience). In contemporary rhetorical pedagogy, the idea that persuasion is in part a matter of the presentation of self in discourse underlies the emphasis on expressive writing as a skill to be learned together with exposition and persuasion.[2] Writers and literary critics speak, similarly though not identically, of "voice," the characteristic, consistent amalgam of theme and style that distinguishes one writer (or in some usages of the term, one narrator) from others.[3]

In this chapter I examine connections between linguistic self-expression and articulateness, in a genre of talk that is unlike oratory or literature in being neither carefully planned in advance nor overtly evaluated according to aesthetic criteria and like oratory and literature in the importance of articulateness to the matter of being heard. The talk I will examine comes from a discussion among eleven people, all advanced graduate students or professors, at a scholarly conference. I look at the contributions to this discussion of two participants in particular, whom I have chosen because they struck me and others as especially articulate people: easy, fluent speakers who had intelligent things to say and got their ideas heard without irritating or intimidating anyone. I try to show how each of the two managed to be articulate.

I have several aims in doing this. A detailed analysis of the concomitants of articulateness shows how the expression of a distinct individual voice crucially enters into the process of being articulate. For Americans, being articulate requires speaking in complete sentences, expressing ideas and relations among them clearly, and supporting one's claims with reasons. But there are different ways to do these things, with different effects, not all of which result in being heard and listened to. To be articulate means to express an articulate persona.

Because the two speakers to be described in this chapter are more similar than the two described in the last, we will also be able to begin thinking about the loci for individual style. When two speakers have equal command of the ways of speaking most appropriate in a situation both are in (here, standard English in academic discourse), on which levels of discourse will their talk vary and on which will it not? Is it more likely, for example, that one will use more embedded nominal or relative clauses than the other, or that one will choose subordinating patterns of conjunction more, or that one will construct larger persuasive "paragraphs" of speech differently than the other? Macaulay (1991) and, less directly, Labov (1972a) suggest that the resources for individual style are to be found mainly on the "higher" levels of the hierarchy, a person's phonology, for example, being relatively static and resistant to stylistic variation, whereas syntax allows for more stylistic choice. I consider this question here in closer focus.

The genre of discourse we looked at in chapter 2—personal narrative—is, as I pointed out, the genre in which individual voice is likely to be the most salient, because creating an autonomous self is precisely what narrative is for. Narrative is performance of self (Goffman 1959) as well as performance of language and culture (Bauman 1977). The genre we look at here—debate about ideas—is less overtly performed. "Showing off" in talk like this is discouraged by community norms (though such discouragement by no means suppresses it). People whose manner in academic disputation strays too far from the average can be ridiculed for having inflated "academic egos" or for "lecturing" or, conversely, for being too quiet, not doing a fair share of the talking. The intellectual ideology underlying academic discussion about ideas is that the ideas, not the people, should prevail, the model being Aristotelian dialectic rather than rhetoric. Despite this, individual voice is crucial in this genre as it is in narrative. Just as it is impossible to create a life history without creating a unique linguistic individual to have experienced it, it is impossible to engage successfully in disputation without expressing a distinct individual way of being articulate.

Two Articulate Voices

The conference at which the people I call Zia Bryant and Leo Stoller (both pseudonyms) spoke was somewhat unusual. It consisted of a relatively small and relatively heterogeneous group of scholars—thirty-five people from a variety of disciplines in the humanities and social sciences, at every level of the academic hierarchy from graduate student to professor emeritus—who came together to discuss a topic on which all had worked. The conference had been designed with an eye to making things as egalitarian and cooperative as possible. There were no keynote speakers, for example, no preacknowledged stars; every participant was given the same amount of time to present his or her work, and all were forced to stick to this limit; and most of the conferees' time was spent in discussion groups of ten or eleven people, working on answers to general questions about the topic, questions that they and the conference organizer had suggested in advance.

Nonetheless, some participants clearly felt excluded from articulateness. The discussions were being tape-recorded, and people were asked to speak their names at the beginning of each workshop so that transcribers would later know what names to put with what voices. One graduate-student conferee, when asked to do this, said, "My name is x, but I'm not going to say anything." Others showed by their silence that they thought they had no claim to articulateness, and others spoke little or hesitantly. And while not all the student participants refused to speak, none of the faculty participants failed to.

But among the people who claimed the right to be articulate—those whose voices can be heard on the tapes and whose contributions are memorable—not all were equally successful at performing this role. Some talked too much or were combative or condescending, irritating other participants. Some mumbled or spoke in disorganized spurts of words that were difficult to understand. Some strayed too far from the topic at hand or appeared not to understand it. In each of the ten taped discussion groups there are perhaps two or three successfully articulate voices. These belong to people whose contributions most closely approximated the dictionary definition of articulateness: people who were, in the words of one dictionary, "ready, clear, and effective" in speech. Let us look now at exactly what this meant in two particular cases.

Zia Bryant and Leo Stoller practiced the same academic discipline and worked with similar data in similar ways, though influenced by different teachers. Bryant was associate professor at a state university; Stoller was professor and department chair at another. Bryant was younger than Stoller and not as well known in the field, and the university where she taught was less prestigious than his. On the basis of these differences (and perhaps the difference in gender as well), we might expect Bryant not to have assumed as articulate a role as Stoller, but she was in fact audible and influential throughout the conference and after, when she sent notes detailing her interpretations of the discussions in which she took part to be used by the organizer in assembling an introduction to the conference proceedings. A joke she made at the beginning of the conference was repeated throughout it and was common knowledge by the end; she herself became known to all the conferees. Stoller was also audible and influential. He was aware of having a hand, indirectly, in the organization of the conference, having encouraged the organizer to proceed with plans and offered the support of his institution if necessary; he also knew that his scholarly work had influenced the organizer's. He spoke a lot throughout the conference and made more, and more detailed, editorial comments on a draft of the proceedings introduction circulated afterward than did anyone else. At a party during the conference, Stoller took it upon himself to call everyone to attention to thank the conference organizer and assistants. He was also, by the end of the conference, known to all.

How did Bryant and Stoller create articulate voices out of the resources available to them? To answer this question, we first need to find an operational way of defining what articulateness consists of.[4] What are the linguistic correlates of "readiness," "clarity," and "effectiveness" in speech? Readiness, or fluency, might display itself on two levels. An articulate person might be fluent within his or her own turns at talk, speaking in syntactically complete units, for example, or using syntactic dysfluency in strategic ways. One might also look for correlates of fluency in conversational interaction: getting turns to talk, setting topics. A good discussant does not get and hold the floor only for his or her own speech, however. People whose only goal is to talk can be perceived as overbearing and selfish. So we might also look for fluency in how articulate people enable others to participate—how they assign turns to talk to other speakers and manage what others say in their turns.

Being clear appears to mean indicating relationships among propositions in explicit ways. Linguistic correlates of clarity might be uses of subordination to express relationships of relative weight and relevance among propositions, uses of conjunctions to express relationships involving time, causality, evidentiality, and so on, and uses of parallelism and other ways of lining up ideas with equal weight. Being effective might mean being explicit and consistent about supporting one's claims with reasons. Being effective also involves drawing others into one's arguments, making them care whether they agree and making them want to agree. In an egalitarian discussion group like this one, this means not setting up an adversarial relationship with one's codiscussants so that one is not perceived (as one conferee widely was) as probably right but irrelevant to the discussion's outcome because he was so obnoxious. Let us look now at correlates of each of these aspects of articulateness in the speech of Bryant and Stoller in one ninety-minute discussion in which both participated.

Readiness

The eleven participants in the discussion took an average of 30.6 turns at talk and uttered 1,239 words on average. Leo Stoller spoke quite a bit more than this, taking 56 turns and uttering 2,381 words. Zia Bryant spoke slightly less than the average, taking 22 turns and speaking 1,188 words. However, Bryant's turns tended to be longer than those of Stoller. When she had the floor, Bryant said, on average, 54 words in 7.2 clauses; Stoller's typical turn involved 45 words in 5.9 clauses. Bryant made far fewer short contributions to the talk than did Stoller. She was less likely than he to join in segments of the conversation in which many people were involved, all taking brief turns, preferring to speak when the conversational coast was clearer and she would be listened to more intently. This had partly to do with the fact that she had volunteered to be the note taker for this group, responsible for summarizing the discussion for others at the end of the conference.

Both Bryant and Stoller almost invariably spoke in complete grammatical clauses, and both sometimes employed complex syntax involving multiple embeddings of clauses within other clauses. Bryant's utterances in particular were characterized by embedding and subordination of various kinds. (The discussion had to do in general with functions of repetition in language; in the following extract Bryant responds to a question from another discussant about simultaneous speech.)

> It happens a lot. Although when I listen to tapes really carefully what seemed to me to be overlap when I was hearing it in real time, on tape what it is is an immediate repetition afterwards. Since you're the one being shadowed upon, you're going to know if somebody's talking at the same time.

There are examples here of clauses within clauses, sometimes doubly embedded (smaller type indicates deeper embedding): "[Although [when I listen to tapes really carefully] what seemed to me to be overlap [when I was hearing it in real time]], on tape [what it is] is an immediate repetition afterwards." Embedded clauses serve as nominals ("what it is"; "if somebody's talking") and as adverbial modifiers ("when I listen"), and conjoined subordinate clauses express quasi-logical relationships ("since you're the one being shadowed upon"). Bryant was this fluent, syntactically, throughout the discussion; only once, in attempting to phrase a claim, did her talk become dysfluent.

Stoller produced four clauses that were incomplete, editing as he spoke without returning afterwards to his initial syntactic pattern. Far more often his words formed complete phrases and clauses, often in complex combinations:

> Both can happen. Both can happen in New York City. But both can happen in the world too. Both can happen in our own society, because there are certain forms of communication where presumably one is not supposed to use repetition—though of course we really haven't quite unpacked what we mean by repetition. But perhaps we can generally say that there are certain kinds in which you are not supposed to. Then there are many different kinds of repetition. One of the reasons that it is interesting to study poetry, oral poetry or written poetry, is because we see pretty formally laid out certain kinds of repetition, meter and rhyme being examples and grammatical and semantic parallelism. People have talked about them for hundreds of years and laid out the principles for them so that they're right there.

Stoller's writing (like Bryant, Stoller is the author of scholarly articles and books) is of course more edited than this. For readers, elliptical references in clauses such as "there are certain kinds in which you are not supposed to" would probably be clarified, and expressions such as "pretty formally" and "they're right there" made less colloquial. Syntactically, though, the passage was spoken in sentences of the length and complexity one would find in a written text.

The two speakers attained interactional fluency—sensitive control over their and others' turns to talk and topics—in different ways: Bryant by asserting herself and ratifying and speaking for others at the beginning of the discussion, Stoller by repeatedly evaluating others' contributions and making suggestions about the group's task, as well as by occasional insistence on having his topics taken up. Bryant claimed a dominant role in the talk at its very beginning. The discussion began with talk about who was to guide the group through the written questions. Another discussant volunteered, and Bryant ratified this person's suggestion, claiming thereby the right to ratify others' contributions and speak for the group in doing so. (Speakers other than Stoller and Bryant are identified by code labels.)

> BEA: Does anyone want to moderate or what?
> BRE: If no one minds, I'll moderate.
> BRYANT: **Absolutely.**

The new moderator then made a claim to control the discussion but hedged the claim immediately and then rejected it:

BRE: Good. My chance to be a dictator. No. I looked at the questions; I assume everyone else did. I'm not sure where to start with them.

Another speaker volunteered a suggestion—

SCH: We could start with individual texts.

—and the moderator paraphrased the first question on the sheet:

BRE: The first question, if we start with that and don't get tied up with whether or not we could come up with a taxonomy or something. But just think about the first question: what appear to be the functions of repetition in the data or texts that we work with? Let's put it that way.

Bryant then took the first substantive turn in the discussion, claiming the floor as explicitly as possible with "I'll start," which she included twice.

I'll start because I think—I am aware that I'm about to make all kinds of disclaimers—but I think I take objection to the presupposition that we can identify functions and put them in a taxonomy to start with. So I'll start at that point and say that I think that what's really interesting about repetition is that the function is always open and, insofar as—at least the conversational texts—insofar as the text is created over time, the way that repetition is interpreted by the next speaker and responded to would determine its function.

Bryant's claim to being listened to was expressed not only in the idea she put forward, a radical objection to the way the discussion question was framed, but also in her repeated references to her own processes of thought: "I think" (three times), "I'm aware," "I take objection." After a question from one of the student participants who had obviously not understood what she meant, Bryant continued:

Yeah. I think that the function is open and, to talk about general function, I think the function in general is to direct, so that— a pointing function—to direct a hearer back to something and say, "Pay attention to this again. This is still salient; this is still— has potential meaning or some kind of potential that can be exploited by us and let's make use of it in some way." So that's my little bit.

Again she repeatedly pointed to herself with "I think," ending with an explicit claim to having a serious contribution to make to the discussion: "So that's my little bit." The diminutive hedge "little" kept her from sounding overbearing or closed-minded. (Another discussant ended a long turn, also in objection to the direction the discussion seemed headed, with "I'm sorry to be so long-winded, but that's one of my pet peeves," a structurally similar way to end a turn but with quite a different rhetorical force.)

Bryant continued to dominate the beginning of the discussion. In her next turn, after three words from another speaker, she began to speak for the others: "But I had a feeling . . . that **we were on our way to saying** . . ." Another discussant then suggested that Bryant might be overstating her case that one can not identify functions of repetition. But Bryant had the last word on her opinion over this objection, responding to it with an ad hominem argument:

> But as you say in your talk, those are patterns created by the interaction.

A third speaker stated a conciliatory opinion: "I think we can identify a range of functions . . . the danger is . . . tying it to one specific kind." Bryant then summed up this speaker's contribution, again speaking for the group:

> So we can say after the fact that repetition's done this work and this work and this work?

All these interactional moves—taking the first turn, deictically pointing to herself, speaking for others, getting the last word on a topic, summarizing others' contributions—helped Bryant express a dominant interactional self at the beginning of the discussion. But throughout the discussion Bryant also took a complementary role, repeatedly enabling others to take the floor. She did this by bringing up others' research topics (discussants had presented summaries of their work earlier on), by sometimes deferring to others' expertise ("you're going to know if somebody's talking at the same time"), and by asking rhetorical questions that encouraged others to begin to speak ("Are you going to clear this up for me?"; "Then that's repetition?"; "How can anyone really know?").

Stoller took a much quieter role at the beginning of the discussion, not speaking until directly asked a question by another discussant. His response was at first hesitant and hedged with "well," "I guess," and "I mean." (The question was about the relationship between repetition and pattern.)

Well, I guess—people have spoken about this in different ways—
but I mean, what kind of pattern is there which doesn't involve
repetition? When you think about it, there probably isn't. So you
know, when you talk about different types of patterns, which in
one way of thinking are different types of repetition. That, of
course, leads us to want to say, "What different types of repetition are there?" Because to simply keep lumping things together
and saying, "Oh that's repetition; that's repetition," then we lose
the fact that the interesting things are the differences.

By the end of his turn, Stoller had begun to speak for the group ("That
leads us to want to say"), making overt suggestions about how they should
proceed ("Because to simply keep lumping things together . . . then we
lose the fact that the interesting things are the differences"). Increasingly as the discussion continued, Stoller phrased his contributions as
assertions about what the group should be doing: "we have to unpack
. . ."; "we'll have to do something about . . ."; "it's our job to say . . .";
"we have to come up with . . ."

Another way in which Stoller created a fluent self in the interaction
was by praising others' contributions to it. When one participant brought
up the image of "repetition glasses" for looking at patterns, Stoller said,
"You see, that's interesting. Why are we—what you are calling a repetition pair of glasses—why do we look at certain types of patterns and
call them repetition and other types are not?" When another proposed
a hypothetical situation for the group to consider, he evaluated it: "That's
why your example is so interesting." Doing this had several effects. For
one thing, Stoller's saying nice things about others' ideas and examples
made them like him, which made them more likely to want to listen to
him. In addition, evaluating what other people said was a way of claiming the right to be an evaluator vis-à-vis the others, someone with supe-
rior knowledge or sensitivity. Praising others' contributions was also one
of Stoller's ways of getting the floor for his own, the first move in connecting his topic with the preceding one.

Stoller also sometimes displayed interactional readiness to speak in
more direct ways. At one point in the discussion he became insistent about
having a topic he thought particularly important—the lack of theoretical
focus in the discussion—taken up. When others at first failed to respond,
he simply kept stating and suggesting his case, refusing to back down where
another speaker might have. Gradually, he moved the talk in the direction of theory, finally getting into position to guide the discussion along a
path he had chosen. Here are the eight moves it took him to do this:

(1) But [x's being an example of repetition is] according to **your theory**.

(2) The point is a good one because it shows how much **we need a theory** here.

(3) Because we can't agree on this, because **we don't have a theory** . . .

(4) Yeah, but that's a very good point though. Because you could turn it on its head and **from another theoretical point of view** say that it's identical repetition.

(5) **There are some theories out there. Many people's different theories of frame** . . .

(6) That's where **different people's theories of frames** . . .

(7) It's a **reframing** of a prior text. In the case that you said was not repetition, it's not a **reframing** of a prior . . .

(8) Okay, **can we be theoretical** and sort of **frame** terms using Becker's notion about what repetition is? Let's see how far we can go if we say that, in picking up on your very interesting example, if we say that in order for us to have a case of repetition, there has to be a prior text. Now what will it work for and what will it not work for?

Having gotten his topic acknowledged, Stoller returned to his usual style, making suggestions to the group ("Let's see how far we can go") and praising other contributors ("your very interesting example").

In sum, both Bryant and Stoller were syntactically fluent speakers once they had the floor (both spoke in complete phrases and clauses), but they had different ways of being constructively audible throughout the interaction. The two styles complemented each other, Bryant taking the major role at the beginning of the discussion—getting it off to a confident start—and Stoller guiding, encouraging, and sometimes insisting on articulate thought during its course.

Clarity

In American folk linguistics, clarity has to do with saying exactly what you mean and showing what your ideas have to do with one other. This is generally understood as mainly a matter of lexical choice—"finding the word that expresses the thought [so that] really no other word would suffice," as one well-known American orator has put it (Jordan 1992). Linguistically speaking, what people refer to as clarity is achieved by expressing propositions in unambiguous words and structures and by overtly displaying the relations among propositions. It is difficult to evaluate lexical and syntactic choices within clauses, since there is no measure against which the "rightness" of words and structures can be compared. (It might be noted that neither Bryant nor Stoller was ever directly asked what she or he meant or requested to repeat.) But it is possible to look at how speakers connect clauses: how often they do, how explicitly they do, and by what means they do. Let us examine three ways of showing relationships among finite clauses (that is, clauses with inflected verbs): embedding, conjoining, and parallelism.

Embedding   Embedding occurs when a clause is used as a constituent of another clause (when a clause functions as a noun phrase, for example). When Bryant said "**what's really interesting about repetition is that the function is always open**," she employed two embedded nominal clauses, one as subject and one as complement. When Stoller said "we talk about repetition as being something **which is unaesthetic**" or "that's something **one sees**," he employed embedded relative clauses, which function as adjectives.[5] Using as a rough-and-ready measure of the amount of embedding a count of finite nominal and relative clauses compared with total clauses, we find that Bryant's speech was quite similar to Stoller's in this respect. Twenty-seven percent of Bryant's total clauses and 31 percent of Stoller's total clauses were embedded. The difference is largely accounted for by the fact that Stoller framed more propositions than did Bryant as reports of speech, thought, and state of knowledge, so more clauses were structurally embedded complements of verbs such as *say*, *think*, and *know*. This structure results from his tendency, noted earlier, to speak for the group: "**We all know** that [nominal clause]"; "**We would all say** that [nominal clause]"; "**but perhaps we can generally say** that [nominal clause]."

Conjoining   When two clauses are conjoined, they are placed side by side. The relationship between them can be implicit, as when only a semicolon in writing or, in speaking, a slight pause separates them. This is referred to as asyndeton. Alternatively, the relationship between the two clauses can be explicitly marked by means of a conjunction. Explicit conjoining is traditionally subdivided into coordinate conjoining (relating two clauses, each of which could stand alone, with *and*, *but*, or *or*, and, in some treatments, *for* or *so that*) and subordinate conjoining (using a conjunction such as *because* or *after* when the clause being introduced is not a "complete thought" by itself). This is a vexed distinction, however. The concept of subordination is really pragmatic and semantic rather than structural, and no clause really "stands alone" in discourse, every clause always being in cohesive and semantic relationships with others.[6] I will not attempt here to differentiate coordination from subordination but instead look at conjoining in general in Bryant's and Stoller's speech, adding, in fact, a few items to the traditional lists of conjunctions.

Roughly the same percentage of clauses were asyndetic in Bryant's speech as in Stoller's: 40 percent for Bryant and 44 percent for Stoller. In each case, more than half the asyndeton occurred in a few special contexts. The first clause in a turn was often not explicitly related to anything preceding it. Thus Bryant began turns with unmarked "∅ I'll start" or "∅ It's *a* function." (I use the symbol ∅ for the absence of a conjunction.) Nor was a speaker's answer to his or her own quoted or rhetorical question, as in Stoller's "Isn't that what false starts are? ∅ They are, quote, language problems." Asyndeton is also common in syntactically parallel clauses. Clauses that are related by being structurally similar appeared not to need to have this redundantly marked with conjunctions. Thus, Stoller's

> And well in some places it's grammaticalized,
>> ∅in some languages it's grammaticalized,
>> ∅in others it's not.

Leaving aside these special cases, then, more than four-fifths of all the clauses that could have begun with conjunctions in both Bryant's and Stoller's speech did begin with conjunctions. Stoller used a larger variety of conjunctions than did Bryant, who used *and* more than Stoller did, often in combination with another conjunction: "and yet," "and so," "and when," "and again," "and so that." A signal of continuation, *and* is semantically the least marked conjunction in English. One of its uses is simply to indicate that a speaker is not yet finished talking (Schiffrin 1987, pp. 141–150). This was its primary use for Bryant, as is clear from her need to combine it with more specifically meaningful conjunctions. Bryant used *and* more than three times as often as any other conjunction.

While Bryant tended to mark semantic and pragmatic continuation with *and*, Stoller marked contrast as often as he marked continuity. Stoller employed *and* and *but* equally often. As Schiffrin points out (1987, pp. 152–177), *but* can signal contrast in several ways. Stoller used *but* to mark ideas that contrasted with other ideas as well as speech actions that contrasted with expectations for them. Here he uses *but* to return to his topic after a digression:

Well, I guess—people have spoken about this in different ways—
but I mean, what kind of pattern is there which doesn't involve
repetition?

Stoller also often used *but* at the beginning of a turn, to signal a point of
view that contrasted with another speaker's:

But you see that's the kind of thing we have to unpack for different cultures.

But some people get the floor this way, don't some people get
the floor this way, too?

Conversely, he used *but* to signal a concessive move in argument after
having disagreed with another. (Note how the disagreement is discretely
signaled with the ambiguously inclusive or exclusive *we all know*).

We all know that when you say the same thing that the referential meaning stays the same. So when we say the meaning has
changed we mean something other than the referential meaning has changed. Then we have to start to unpack the other kinds
of things besides referential meaning. **But** your example is
interesting because it forces us to have to tease our brains into
disagreeing with you until we can come up with an explanation.

The most frequent conjunctions, with the exception of *and* and, in
Stoller's case, *but* were *because* and *so* for both speakers. Bryant began
one nonembedded clause in eight with one of these conjunctions, Stoller
one in seven. The frequency of these conjunctions had to do, of course,
with the persuasive genre of the talk; one would expect more temporal
thens and *befores* in narrative, for example. *So* and *because* introduce what
Quirk and Greenbaum (1973, p. 327) refer to as "clauses of reason or
cause." As Schiffrin points out (1987, pp. 201–217), speakers give reasons and causes on several levels. *So* or *because* can be used to indicate
real causality, as when Bryant said, "You're going crazy **because** you're
getting your own talk back" or "Phatic community is still there [i.e., still
important], **so** you have to have that same damn conversation over and
over again." We can call these *causal* uses of *because* and *so*. Alternatively, *so* and *because* can mark logical inferences or warrants of the kind
that could be paraphrased in syllogisms. For example, Stoller used *so* to
introduce the inference in this argument: "When you say the same thing,
the referential meaning stays the same. **So** when we say the meaning has
changed, we mean something other than the referential meaning has
changed." *Because* introduces the warrant (that is, the supporting propo-

sition) in this argument by Bryant, discussing a Pinter play in which the expression "very nice" is repeated over and over: "The prior text is the course of the drama, **because** 'very nice' outside of that context just has a neutral, conversational [meaning]." These uses of *because* and *so* can be referred to as *inferential*.

On yet another level, *so* and *because* can give reasons for speakers' actions in the discourse, marking speakers' "motives," as Schiffrin puts it (1987, p. 202). Bryant used both conjunctions this way in making a point about the danger of imputing intention to speakers:

> Yeah. But intentions are always so dangerous. How can we know what someone's intentions are? And you sometimes end up imputing your intentions to other people. (*One* does, not *you*.) And I—to put it back on me—I can maybe say what effects are had upon me, but maybe there are other effects that I am feeling that I can't articulate. So it always seems like there is a little bit of danger in looking at intentions and effects, **because** how can anyone really know?

The best paraphrase for *so* as it was used here is not *therefore*, since what follows *so* is not a logical consequence of what preceded it. "X, **so** y" in this use means "x leads me to say y." "X **because** y," as Bryant used *because* here, means "my evidence for x is y." I refer to these uses of *so* and *because* as *evidential* uses; they mark relationships between assertions and reasons for uttering them.

In addition to these uses of *so* and *because*, all of which mark reasons on one level or another, *so* can also function to mark where a speaker is in his or her turn to talk. For both speakers, *so* sometimes introduced summaries or rephrasings at or toward the ends of the speakers' turns, as when Stoller said, "She was seeing [repetition] as a unitary phenomenon within a single culture and a single language, **so** she was finding the unity," or when Bryant ended turns with "**so** that's my little bit" or "I'm confused. **So** are you going to clear this up?" We can call these *boundary-marking* uses of *so*.[7] Table 3.1 displays the ways Bryant and Stoller used the conjunctions *because* and *so*.

For both Bryant and Stoller, causal uses of *so* and *because* were relatively infrequent, and neither used *so* as a boundary marker very often. The two differed, however, in the predominant function for which they used the conjunctions. More than half of Bryant's *so*s and *becauses* were evidential, introducing motives for saying what she said, whereas half of Stoller's were inferential, introducing steps in syllogistic argumentation.

Table 3.1   Uses of *because* and *so* by Bryant and Stoller
(Percentage of Total Uses)

	Bryant (N = 19)	Stoller (N = 30)
causal	16	16
inferential	16	50
evidential	52	23
boundary-marking	16	11

Parallelism   Conjoined clauses may or may not take the same syntactic form as their neighbors. When two or more clauses in succession have the same or similar structure, the pattern is referred to as syntactic parallelism. Parallelism is often used as a cohesive device in genres such as oral poetry (Lord 1960; Finnegan 1977); lines in a poem or song that carry the same weight have the same shape. Parallelism is also used to structure persuasive arguments in some contexts (Koch 1983a); successive pieces of evidence for a claim are couched in the same syntax. Parallelism has been identified with oral or unplanned sorts of discourse (Ochs 1979; Ong 1982), although it can of course also be the result of very careful planning, as in a poem, a sermon, or a political speech (Johnstone 1987b). Parallelism can take the place of explicit, lexically marked conjoining (with *and* or *furthermore*, for example) for showing that propositions are of equal significance to the same topic, though speakers can of course do both. Parallelism can be exact, as when Stoller repeated the same phrase,

> Oh that's repetition;
>   that's repetition

or nearly exact, as in Stoller's

> Now what will it   work for
> and what will it not work for?

There are also examples in both speakers' talk of looser parallelism, as when Bryant said

> . . . to direct a hearer back to something and say,
> "This is still salient;
> this is still   has potential meaning"

Note how Bryant seems pulled in the direction of parallelism, beginning the second clause with "this is still" and then having to shift syntactic gears to make the rest of the clause come out right: "has potential meaning."

As was pointed out earlier, Stoller and Bryant both tended not to mark parallel clauses redundantly with conjunctions. Stoller's parallelism was, however, more frequent and more consistent than Bryant's. There are only three examples of syntactic parallelism in Bryant's speech during the discussion. Two of the three (one of which has already been quoted) are in reports of speech. Bryant represents speakers, in other words, as repeating propositions in parallel clauses. Bryant's third use of parallelism was in presenting an example of parallelism:

> That's something I've thought about in terms of trying to classify or hierarchize different kinds of repetition or parallelism or cyclicity in [the language she studies], because the kinds of story cycles that you get in rabbit and coyote tales, for example,
> **there's something repetitive about that,**
> **there's something cyclical**
> **there's something parallel about that . . .**

Parallelism served specialized functions for Bryant, in other words. It did not appear to be a strategy she employed in the relatively unmarked presentation of propositions in disputation.

Stoller, on the other hand, made frequent use of parallelism to organize propositions as he verbalized them. As we will see, parallelism was a consistent structural element of his preferred way of organizing persuasive arguments. There are fourteen examples of parallelism in his talk. Some are short self-editings, when Stoller corrected or refined a term by repeating the old phrase with the new word:

> And well in some places   it's grammaticalized,
>   in some languages it's grammaticalized.

Other of Stoller's turns involved multiple parallelisms:

> . . . we could say it's identical:
> **its referential meaning's   the same;** we can
> record it and see that
> **its intonational pattern is the same,**
> but we would all say that—because we are committed to it—
> that it has a different meaning. Then it's our job to say what the
> different meaning is.

Well it's **the second refrain,**
    or the third refrain,
    or the fourth refrain,
or it's **creating cohesion**
or it's **giving poetic unity** to the song or poem or whatever.

Parallelism for Stoller, in other words, seemed to be a less marked, more normal strategy for connecting clauses than it was for Bryant.

To summarize, Bryant and Stoller displayed relationships among propositions expressed in different clauses in ways that were in some instances surprisingly similar and in others interestingly different. Both used exactly the same percentage of relative clauses to total clauses. Both favored explicit lexical conjunctions over asyndeton, employing conjunctions in 80 percent of the cases where they could employ them, and both conjoined clauses asyndetically in the same proportion and in the same contexts. Stoller used somewhat more nominal embeddings than did Bryant, phrasing more propositions as reports of speech, thought, and knowledge states. He used a larger variety of conjunctions than did Bryant. The conjunction Bryant used most was *and*, often to signal that her turn to talk was continuing and often supplemented with a more explicit conjunction such as *so*. Stoller, on the other hand, used *and* and *but* equally, signaling contrast on a variety of levels as often as he signaled continuity. Both used *so* and *because* often, no doubt because they were primarily engaged in making assertions and supporting them, but their uses of these conjunctions were different: Stoller overwhelmingly used *because* and *so* in inferential ways, to mark logical warrants and implications, whereas Bryant used *because* and *so* evidentially, to give reasons for her speech actions. Stoller used parallelism to display relations among clauses more often than did Bryant, and in a less restricted set of contexts.

Effectiveness

Being effective in persuasive speech—having one's claims accepted—requires, for Americans, that claims be supported. People have to give reasons for the propositions they want others to accept. Middle-class children begin learning this even before they start school, when adults challenge them to "tell why" they say what they say, and the teaching of strategies for "telling why" is a large part of what goes on in public speaking and basic writing classes in school and college. Articulate people support the claims they make. There are, however, many ways of doing this. To see how Stoller and Bryant provided support for their claims, let us look first at the content of their arguments—what persuasive strategies they chose—and then at aspects of how they deployed these strategies in clauses and turns.

The persuasive strategies that are most highly valued in Western cultures are the ones referred to as "logical." In everyday talk about persuasion, we use the term "logical" not only with reference to formal syllogistic logic of the "All men are mortal / Socrates is a man / Therefore Socrates is mortal" sort but also for arguments that sound like formal syllogisms but for one reason or another are not.[8] Logical or "quasilogical" (Perelman and Olbrechts-Tyteca 1969, pp. 193–260) syllogisms are rarely laid out in full in everyday rhetorical discourse; major premises ("All men are mortal"), minor premises ("Socrates is a man"), or even conclusions may be implicit. For this reason, Aristotle and the tradition he founded refer to these sorts of arguments as "enthymemes," a word having to do with the Greek root for "hidden." Somewhat less highly valued but also acceptable in the Aristotelian tradition is the strategy of supporting one's claims by giving examples. Other less-valued strategies exist as well. People persuade others by telling stories ("When I was your age"; "I remember once"), by making reference their own authority ("Because I said so"), by repeating and paraphrasing, or in some situations simply by making the claims in the first place (though we might not want to refer to this as "persuasion").

Bryant sometimes supported the claims she made in the conference conversation in "logical" ways. When another participant suggested that functions of repetition could be distinguished in terms of speakers' intentions or in terms of effects on hearers, she responded with an enthymematic argument:

> Yeah. But intentions are always so dangerous. How can we know what someone's intentions are? And you sometimes end up imputing your intentions to other people. (*One* does, not *you*.) And I, to put it back on me, I can maybe say what effects are had upon me, but maybe there are other effects that I am feeling that I can't articulate. So it always seems like there is a little bit of danger in looking at intentions and effects, because how can anyone really know?

Spelled out fully, the argument is this: if we cannot identify our explanatory concepts with phenomena we can observe, then these explanatory concepts are dangerous (a widely accepted premise among scientists). We cannot examine intentions or psychological effects objectively. ("How can we know what someone's intentions are?"; ". . . maybe there are other effects that I . . . can't articulate.") Therefore, "there is a little bit of danger in looking at intentions and effects."

One type of enthymematic argument particularly valued among academics is the argument from authority. Bryant used such arguments several times. Sometimes the authorities were other scholars ("I'm think-ing of Duranti's work"; "Elinor Ochs has done some really interesting stuff"), and sometimes the authority was her own scholarly self ("that's something that I've thought about . . . in [the language she studies]"). Bryant also sometimes argued by example. At one point, the discussion had to do with whether the recurrence of sounds and common words like *the* in discourse should be counted as repetition. Bryant responded with an example involving the effect of the phonological recurrence in "a little alliteration":

> But talking about the functions that repetition has and we look at the use of a little alliteration and, see, you think it's funny, right? And you laughed; it worked. There were a number of examples earlier today about repetitions being funny and so the function of my alliteration there was in effect the same as the multiple repetitions for creating a joke that worked, that were so funny, and the play and the conversations that we looked at earlier. So if we wanted to see a matchup of repetition, whether it's phonological, morphological or syntactic and a function, that—we've got it there [i.e., the function of repetition is the same on all levels]. There's got to be something going on; there's some kind of closeness there.

The example here—"a little alliteration" and its effect—is followed by an enthymematic argument that could be rephrased this way: If the func-tions of different phenomena are the same, then the phenomena can be classified together. One function of phonological repetition—humor—is, as has just been illustrated, the same as one function of repetition on other linguistic levels. Thus, "there's some kind of closeness there."

The contributions by Bryant that involved making and supporting claims were typically complex in this way: she tended to do more than one thing to support a claim. For one thing, Bryant frequently supported claims with reference to her personal feelings. In one of a series of turns devoted to persuading others of the validity of her objection to listing functions of repetition, she said that she "had a feeling" that the group was treating utterances as having only one function at a time and that "taxonomies like that make me nervous." She also sometimes simply reformulated claims without providing explicit support for them. In this extract she did so by posing questions suggesting but not asserting the claim that it might be useful to think about repetition from the perspective of repeaters:

> And what's the relationship between these cultural presuppositions and the saliency versus unconsciousness that we were talking about before? Does it, do we not want to call something as repetition if native speakers can't talk about it? Don't have the metalanguage or something like that?

On the whole, then, Bryant used a variety of strategies for persuasion, some highly valued by the culture and the academic subculture of the situation and others less so, often in combination.

Stoller relied on enthymematic, "logical" persuasion far more than did Bryant. In twenty-one turns that involved making and supporting claims, he provided twelve enthymematic arguments. A particularly explicit one is this:

> It was almost I think today stated as a theoretical principle of our workshop that when something is reproduced, its meaning changes. That is, it's got a new box around it because it happened a second time; and therefore, we're going to say that. We'll have to do something with your case. So what we'll do is say it's case number two and it tells us that the person has Alzheimer's disease and therefore it's different.

Only the minor premise is implicit here. The major premise is the "theoretical principle of our workshop": "when something is reproduced, its meaning changes." The case in point ("your case"), an Alzheimer's patient who initiates the same conversation over and over, was currently under discussion. The conclusion: "It's case number two . . . and therefore it's different." Note Stoller's use in this extract of conjunctions often used to link logical arguments to their conclusions: *therefore* twice and *so* once. Only one of Stoller's syllogistic arguments was an argument from authority, and the authority was that of the group: "We all probably know people who do that."

Stoller also argued occasionally by example (there are four such arguments in his talk). He supported his suggestion that the term "repetition" was perhaps being used too broadly with two drastically differing examples of situations to which the term could be applied: a conversation consisting of the greeting "hello" and the response "hello" and a poem structured by parallelism. Infrequently Stoller used traditionally less valued lines of argument. Several times he appeared to elicit support for claims by explaining what he meant by making them, as in this example:

> Why do we look at certain types of patterns and call them repetition and other types are not? Presumably because this is a cultural bias we have. We have come to think of certain things as being repetition and other things we call something else that we conceive of them or perceive them to be. Different societies and cultures do that.

What follows the claim here—that some patterns are called repetition and others are not on the basis of cultural bias—is an explanation of what this means: "We have come to think of certain things as being repetition." On the whole, though, Stoller's rhetoric was Aristotelian, involving enthymeme and example almost to the exclusion of non-"logical" modes of proof.

About half of Stoller's claim-making turns in the discussion had the same structure, revolving around a rhetorical question the answer to which was the claim he then supported. The structure, demonstrated here with one of Stoller's speaking turns, was this:

(a) a hedged, tentative-sounding claim to the floor, introducing his topic:
>> If you think of it in linguistic terms, reduplication as a grammatical process, like we heard about Creole and lots of languages have, and then parallelism in poetry . . .

(b) a question or suggestion:
>> okay, now do they have anything to do with one another?

(c) an answer or response:
>> I like to think they might, but we need a theory that shows how they work together.

(d) a longer sentence, sometimes rephrasing the answer and always providing support for it:
>> Some people have shown that the kinds of reduplications that one finds in everyday language are potentials for— and probably the grammars of languages—are potentials for artistic uses in the poetries of those same languages.

(e) a summation, sometimes introducing a corollary claim:
>> That's an argument for showing that there is a relationship.

A turn quoted earlier provides another example of the pattern:

(a) Introduction: Why are we—what you are calling a repetition pair of glasses,

(b) Question: why do we look at certain types of patterns and call them repetition and other types are not?

(c) Answer: Presumably because this is a cultural bias we have.

(d) Discussion: We have come to think of certain things as being repetition and other things we call something else that we conceive of them or perceive them to be.

(e) Summation: Different societies and cultures do that.

Stoller's use of *presumably* in stating this claim was characteristic. His claims were mitigated with *probably*, *presumably*, or *maybe* in most cases. Even at his most insistent (in his repeatedly arguing for the claim that repetitions by Alzheimer's sufferers had to be seen as inexact, because no repetition is ever exact, but failing to move the discussion off a sticking point), he mitigated arguments by attributing assertions to the group rather than presenting them as his own: "**We all know** that when you say the same thing the referential meaning stays the same. So **when we say** that the meaning has changed, **we mean** something other than the referential meaning has changed." The confident forcefulness Stoller displayed through the consistent strategy and structure of his arguments was thus always softened, made easier for others to hear, by forms of mitigation.

Bryant's arguments were, by contrast, hedged less frequently and mainly in her early turns (as when she began her first contribution with "I'm aware that I'm about to make all sorts of disclaimers"). More typically, she made bald assertions: "And **that's what's really happening** during the course of this play"; "But intentions **are always** so dangerous;" "... in different speech communities, different maxims **are** stressed." Her claim-making turns were not consistent in structure the way Stoller's were. Bryant tended to dramatize the points she made more often than Stoller did. One way Bryant provided drama was through constructed speech, as here, in giving an example:

> I've had the same conversation over and over with the same people. When I go to [her research site], one of the things that you, that we talk about is the crops. "How's the milpa doing?" "The milpa's fine." And that conversation you can have over and over with the same people, and it's satisfying.

In the extract discussed earlier in which she said "a little alliteration" and then commented on the group's laughter in response, she exemplified a claim by producing a spontaneous dramatization of it.

In sum, Bryant and Stoller both consistently supported the claims they made in the discussion. Not surprisingly, however, they did this in somewhat different ways. Stoller, on the whole, relied on the power of logic to persuade. His arguments were relatively consistent in structure and relatively careful and hedged. He presented claims impersonally, not as feelings of his own but rather as self-evident to all who could reason. (Although Stoller and Bryant used *you* equally often during the discussion, Stoller used *we* more than twice as often as did Bryant.) Bryant relied in the main on the persuasive power of presentation, presenting a more forceful, more dramatic, less tentative rhetorical *ethos*. The kinds of support she provided for her claims were more varied, less consistently drawn from the Aristotelian tradition of arguing by enthymeme and example and more often connected to her own feelings and observations.

Two Self-Portraits

Let us now review what we have said about Leo Stoller and Zia Bryant. Table 3.2 provides a sketch of the differences between the two styles of articulateness. Although he made a number of long contributions to the discussion, Stoller's turns at talk included fewer words on the average, because he tended more often than did Bryant to be a part of more competitive segments of the conversation in which many speakers were claiming the floor, all taking short turns. Bryant, on the other hand, tended to talk when there was less competition for the floor. After some "entrance talk" at the beginning of the discussion, Bryant took the first turn, immediately asserting her right to speak and to permit others to speak. In addition to asserting a dominant role at the beginning of the discussion, she claimed a voice in the discussion by deictically calling attention to herself with first-person pronouns. Stoller was quiet at the start of the conversation, achieving interactional fluency quite differently. Throughout the discussion, he praised others' contributions and made suggestions about what the group was thinking or how the group should proceed. Occasionally he became insistent about getting topics of his own taken up, but throughout the discussion he made far more frequent reference to *we* than to *I*.

There are more similarities than differences in the syntax of conjunction by which Stoller and Bryant show how propositions are related. Stoller used *but* more often than Bryant did, marking contrasts in ideas

Table 3.2 Summary of Features of Stoller's and
Bryant's Styles of Articulateness

Stoller	Bryant
A. Readiness: Personal and Interactional Fluency	
took shorter turns	took longer turns
made more short contributions	made fewer short contributions
joined in segments of conversations in which many people were involved	was less likely to join in when many people were involved
achieved interactional fluency by evaluating others' contributions, making suggestions about group's task, sometimes by being insistent about getting his topic taken up	achieved interactional fluency by asserting self and ratifying and speaking for others at the beginning of the conversation
made many references to group	made many references to self
remained quiet at beginning of discussion	took dominant role at beginning
B. Clarity: Relating Ideas	
used *but* more, to mark referential and pragmatic contrast	used *and* more, to mark continuation of her turn
used wider variety of conjunctions	used fewer different conjunctions
primarily inferential use of *so* and *because*	primarily evidential use of *so* and *because*
parallelism used more as unmarked strategy for creating cohesion	used parallelism only in marked situations
C. Effectiveness: Supporting Claims	
had less variety in persuasive strategies	had more variety in persuasive strategies; more complex arguments involving several strategies
used more "logical" enthymematic persuasion	used some "logical" persuasion, but also supported claims with reference to personal feeling, and by restating
referred only to the experience of the group for authority	used arguments from other scientists' authority
had consistent structure for presenting and supporting claims, revolving around question and answer	had no consistent structure for presenting and supporting claims
often mitigated claims with *presumably*, etc.	less frequently mitigated claims; made more bald assertions
dramatized infrequently	dramatized frequently

and expectations. Bryant used *and* more, a signal of continuity. On the whole, Stoller used more different conjunctions than did Bryant, and more parallelism. Both often employed *so* and *because*, but for different purposes: Bryant tended to display motives for speaking, while Stoller tended to display logical relations. Both consistently supported the claims they made, Bryant by means of a wider variety of strategies, some making recourse to syllogistic logic and others not. Stoller more consistently employed logical means of support. Unlike Stoller, Bryant made several references to outside authorities and to her own authority as a scholar; the only authority to which Stoller referred was that of the group. In about half the contributions in which he presented and supported claims, Stoller made use of a consistent structure involving a central question and its answer. He frequently hedged his claims with adverbials such as *presumably* or *probably*; Bryant did this less frequently, and mainly at the conversation's start, making more bald assertions throughout. Bryant's talk throughout included more dramatization—scenes recreated with constructed speech and spontaneous dramas involving the group's reactions to her—than did Stoller's.

What do we make of these contrasts? We could try to line up the features of Stoller's and Bryant's speech with social or cultural categories, seeking ways that Bryant sounds like a woman and Stoller like a man, for example, or examining their styles in terms of research findings about regional or ethnic "conversational style" (Tannen 1984). It turns out, however, that the categories and the features do not line up very well. Bryant displayed what might be thought to be the more masculine interpersonal style in the discussion, asserting herself more forcefully, referring less to the group, employing fewer hedges, claiming the right to the floor at the discussion's start. But her modes of persuasion—dramatizing and making reference to feelings—seem feminine.[9] The converse is true of Stoller. His interpersonal style was the more feminine of the two: he expressed more attunement to the group, was less eager at the beginning of the discussion to assert a role in it, and hedged more often. But his reliance on traditionally more valued logical modes of persuasion seems masculine. Likewise, both Bryant and Stoller displayed aspects of "involved," rapport-based conversational style as well as aspects of "considerate" or more detached independence-based style, to use Tannen's (1984) terms. Stoller's style was on the whole highly involved. He spoke for the group, he praised others, and he joined in when there was competition for the floor and sometimes insisted on winning the competition. But he made his points by means of rationality rather than by getting others emotionally involved or by expressing his own emotions. Bryant's style was more detached, on the whole—she spoke only for herself and talked less when there was competition—but she often employed drama, personal testimonial, and expressions of emotion in making her points, thus seeming more involvement-oriented than Stoller in this respect.

No student of variation in discourse structure and style would expect any individual to be a perfect match for the generalized descriptions of regions, classes, genders, and so on generated by research; no woman is the prototypical woman, any more than anyone is completely typical of his or her region or ethnicity or interactional role. Prototypes are, by definition, idealizations, rather than descriptions of particular cases. Aware as we may be of the fact that we are generalizing away from particular cases, and as well as we may understand what we gain and lose by doing this, there is still some danger in it. The danger is that idealized descriptions sometimes come to be used as explanatory devices. From discovering that, in some respects, an individual's style matches expectations generated in other studies of groups to which the individual belongs, it is a short and easy step to supposing that group identifications *account for* the individual's behavior. This step is often taken in casual interaction—a European says, "You do that because you're American," or a man says, "You just think that because you're a woman"—usually to the annoyance of the person whose behavior is thus spuriously explained. Scholars do not, if they are following the normal standards, make the unwarranted step from description to explanation overtly. As I have pointed out, however, the methodology of sociolinguistic studies of groups makes it all too easy to make the step covertly. Close analysis of talk by particular individuals, considered as individuals rather than as representatives of groups, reminds us that describing features of a person's talk and noting similarities between that person and others is not the same as explaining the mechanism whereby that person made those choices.

Bryant and Stoller made different choices because they were expressing and creating different individual selves in their discourse. Each identified with, and expressed identity with, various externally constituted groups. But this was only one aspect of the process in which they were centrally engaged: the expression of a multidimensional, unique self. Both expressed selves in such a way that they came across clearly to others; their identities were noticed, heard, taken seriously. This, I think, is what articulateness really is: successful self-expression. Successfully expressing a coherent, unique self in discourse requires the traditional elements of articulateness: readiness or fluency, clarity, and effectiveness. People who are not articulate are people who fail to "assert themselves" or, in everyday terms, to "make themselves felt."

The identity expressed by Bryant was direct, personal, and dramatic. Her motives for being articulate in this interaction seemed to be psychological ones, having directly to do with the importance and the pleasure of self-expression; she enjoyed the spontaneous process of successful self-assertion. She called attention to herself, talked about how she felt rather than referring to external standards of evidence. Primarily motivated by personal psychological needs, she was not managerial or interventionist. She allowed and sometimes encouraged others but did not try to shape their talk. Since she was not trying to demonstrate how things should be done, her approach to making herself heard was pragmatic (doing what would work rather than what should necessarily be done) and thus not always consistent. Bryant's pleasure in dramatizing herself was infectious; unlike people who seem driven to force others to notice their uniqueness, she was very well liked.

Stoller's self-presentation was more complex. On one level, he appeared to be presenting a role, that of the Socratic teacher. In this role, he was attuned primarily to the intellectual process of disputation rather than to the psychological process of expression. He oriented himself to the group, speaking for it, intervening to correct error, and managing others by evaluating their contributions and asking them questions to which he then gave the answers. He made consistent displays of culturally favored processes for disputation, such as logical argumentation, demonstrating also that insistence is sometimes called for. The role of teacher for Stoller was to some extent encouraged by the situation: he was, as we have noted, one of the senior scholars at the conference and had been in on its planning from the beginning. But this social position did not "speak him," to use some popular terminology. In the first place, he did not have to accept the role; another conferee in much the same position most pointedly did not act "teacherly." In the second place, being a good, fair teacher—enabling others to find out what they knew and to discover more—was personally important to him, part of his own image of his identity and thus part of the identity he expressed. So, on another level, Stoller was expressing an identity as personally as Bryant was.

Loci for the Expression of Self in Academic English

In some interesting ways, Stoller's and Bryant's ways of achieving articulateness were *not* different. Most generally, their behavior suggested that both were more attuned to the process of discussion—the exchange of ideas—than to the goal of the discussion—suggesting answers for the preset questions. In this way, both contrasted with some other speakers at the conference who appeared much more concerned with results, constantly nudging others back to the assigned topics, attempting to elicit conclusions from the group, sometimes rereading the questions aloud. Bryant's and Stoller's lack of concern about the specific assigned task was perhaps an aspect of their claim to articulateness; by not exactly following the rules, they asserted their right to a say in what would be talked about.

But both took the discussion seriously. Neither appeared to be primarily interested in just having a pleasant time talking; unlike some other participants, neither one initiated or colluded in the practice in some discussion groups of encouraging the group to dawdle (by standing in the hall, by joking, or simply by starting conversations about other topics) before getting to the work of the discussion. I suspect that this behavior had to do with two things. First, as part of the claim to articulateness, both displayed their acceptance of responsibility for monitoring and to some extent controlling the proceedings. Being cooperative is a way of ensuring that one will be liked, and being liked is, as we have noted, a key element of articulateness. People listen to others they like. Second, I think that Bryant and Stoller both enjoyed disputation of the kind they engaged in at the conference, a feeling no doubt connected with the fact that both were good at it.

Another interesting similarity between the two styles arises from the preceding observations about gender and conversational style. Both speakers managed both to be forceful and dominant (by being willing to compete, supporting claims with irrefutable evidence, taking charge of turn-allocation and topic) and to be gentle in manner (by hedging, mitigating, enabling others, cooperating). Strategies for asserting interactional force and dominance have been found to be reflected in the discourse of people with power in an interaction, and gentleness and mitigation have been found to be characteristic of those who are relatively powerless (O'Barr and Atkins 1980). By seeming to balance assertions of power with assertions of powerlessness, Bryant and Stoller suggest that, at least in relatively egalitarian situations, powerless speech and powerful speech are not in contrast. The real key to being articulate when people have more or less equal rights to be heard may be in effecting the right balance between relative power and relative powerlessness, between having control and being able to relinquish it.

Finally, it is interesting to speculate on why there was so little difference in syntax between the two speakers. Both, it will be remembered, employed equally complex syntax, and both combined clauses in the same ways, using almost the same amount of relative- and nominal-clause embedding and the same kinds of conjunction, in the same proportion, for the same purposes. There were much larger differences between Mattie Blair and Lon Bauer in the rhythm of their grammar. Though these two case studies by no means demonstrate it, they do suggest that there may be less flexibility in the relatively formal register of academic discourse than there is in the vernacular. This reminds us of Maurice Bloch's (1971) observation that formality in any aspect of culture is a matter of relative fixity of options. Since the syntactic register in Bryant's and Stoller's case is more or less fixed, resources for the expression of self must be found elsewhere, in choices of what to say and how to behave as a speaker rather than in choices of how to grammaticalize propositions. Standard English, often thought of as enabling people to express themselves, in fact may in some ways limit their resources for self-expression. (It should be noted, however, that creativity and limitations of options are often linked. Poets who write sonnets and musicians who play clarinets are constrained in different ways by their media, and completely unconstrained creativity, not responsive to any cultural limitations, would strike others as insanity.)

Social Identity, Rhetorical Adaptation, and Personal Style

In this chapter we have looked at a genre of talk—academic disputation—in which there is less of a cultural push towards self-expression than there is in the telling of personal anecdotes, and in which there are, one might suppose, fewer universal cognitive reasons for self-expression. Academic persuasive discourse is, we often think, more "canned," that is, less varied from speaker to speaker, than is narrative. This is, as we have found, true to some extent, but if speakers of standard academic English have fewer choices for clause-combining and the like, they find other ways to express their individuality. What emerges from a detailed analysis of how two professors manage to be heard and listened to and taken seriously by colleagues is not a description of professors acting like professors or a description of a woman acting like a woman and a man acting like a man but a description of two individuals, each using language to express a distinct self. What each does can be related in some ways to how each is externally defined in terms of the cultural categories we use in first attempts at understanding strangers—gender, social role, ethnicity, and so on—since their choices for speaking are, to some extent, "acts of identification" with such groups. But to correlate discourse choices directly with social categories is to abstract away from the real reason linguistic choices are made: in service of the expression and the creation of self.

Thinking about articulateness as the expression of an articulate individual self is not just a way of enabling ourselves to notice more of the fine detail that distinguishes one person's style from another's. If we fail to see articulateness as a matter of individual voice, we may mistake the answers to important questions about language. For one thing, we risk confusing correlation with causality, forgetting that demographic categories like gender, social positions like power and control, and cultural tendencies to relative involvement or detachment in interaction do not determine how an individual will talk. This is a point I have made before; I make it here again not because many linguists would be likely to disagree with it but because our deterministic ways of talking about language use make it so easy to lose sight of.

For another thing, we may miss seeing that rhetorical choices for how to persuade, like sociolinguistic choices for how to pronounce words and construct clauses, are mediated by individual choices about how to be. Rhetoric is often seen as a set of options or possibilities among which rhetors choose for strategic reasons having to do with topic, audience, and so on. What Aristotle called the "art of persuasion" is sometimes taught as if it involves no more than learning to assemble discourses from rhetorical Erector Sets of options for lines of argument, modes of organization, and methods of delivery. This sort of teaching has a long history, beginning with the Greek Sophists. The mechanical vision of rhetoric is descriptively adequate for most purposes, and it underlies methods for training people to write and speak that are as effective as any others, but it is not adequate as an explanation of what happens as people construct discourse. We have found that self-expression plays a crucial role in the process, mediating between the options and the outcome. Rhetorical *ethos* (or literary "voice") is more important than some have taken it to be. A model of rhetorical discourse that is adequate as an explanation must be a model in which the choices a speaker makes are understood as having to do with the adaptation to a situation not of a set of preexisting options but of a personal voice.

We have also uncovered something about what may be more likely to vary from speaker to speaker and what may be less likely to vary, and about the constraints on the expression of self imposed by formal, standardized varieties. The two speakers we examined made very similar grammatical choices. It would be interesting to learn whether it is more generally true that grammar is controlled by genre in formal situations in a way that other levels of choice are not. Quantitative research on generic styles like that of Biber (1988) is based on the assumption that this is the case; my study of these two speakers suggests that the assumption might be valid. But the two speakers made different interpersonal and rhetorical choices about how to interact with others and how to persuade, even though they were in many ways doing exactly the same thing, because they were expressing different selves. Even the relatively hegemonic standard variety of English they spoke could not keep them from sounding like the different individuals they were, because self-expression was the key to what they were doing with language.

— 4 —

Individual Variation
in Scripted Talk

In survey research or polling, the interviewer must be inflexible, bound to the predetermined wording schedule and sequence of options. . . . The interviewer . . . is trained to recite the questions as worded and in the pre-scribed order, without variation in inflection or emphasis.

> from a manual for survey-research interviewers
> (Harriet Nathan, *Critical Choices in Interviews*)

If your data is to have any meaning, it is essential that each respondent is put through the same experience.

> from a manual for interviewers (Marvin Gottlieb, *Interview*)

Canons of research demand that the interviewer operate somewhat like a computer with all the appearances of a fellow human being, but, so far as we know, persons in everyday life find it impossible either to present themselves as or to receive presentations of others (regardless of the form it takes) which conform to the strict canons of scientific inquiry.

> Aaron Cicourel, *Method and Measurement in Sociology*

Here is a transcription of a brief telephone conversation that took place one evening shortly after five o'clock:

[The telephone rang.]
   ME: Hello?
 VOICE: Hi, this is Fran with Olan Mills?
   ME: I'm not interested, thank you.
[I then hung up.]

Most Americans have interactions like this more often than they would like. Even if they are interested in the portrait sittings offered by the Olan Mills chain of photography studios or in newspaper subscriptions or tickets to police fund-raisers, Americans tend not to like calls of this sort. Their dislike has partly to do with the fact that such calls invade their privacy. But it also has partly to do with the fact that they know, as soon as they hear the first contribution by the caller, that his or her talk is canned, memorized or read from a script and hence in some sense not the talk of an individual.

And yet, even knowing that they are interacting with a business entity, people still hear an individual. Fran-with-Olan-Mills had a low physical voice for a woman, somewhat like my own. She drew out the vowel in "Hi," pronouncing it as a diphthong, and she spoke the word with a combination of speed and intonation that made her sound, to my ears, as if she weren't from my area. Overall, she sounded intelligent and likable. After hanging up on her, I felt a little bad about having done so, as I always do (though not bad enough to keep me from hanging up again the next time somebody from Olan Mills calls). Hanging up the phone when a real person is on the line is rude in a way that hanging up on a tape recording is not. Despite my knowing that she said exactly the same thing to whoever answered at each number she dialed, Fran still partly evoked the sense of etiquette that guides my interactions with people rather than the inconsiderateness with which I interact with machines. She had a physical voice and a way of using it that were her own, and if I had let her continue to talk I would have heard more that distinguished her style from others'.

In the preceding chapters we have looked at individual variation in two genres of talk: personal-experience narrative and academic disputation. In spontaneous recountings of personal experience, we found considerable variation from individual to individual at all levels of structure. Many models of language suggest that variation like this could, if we knew enough about the speakers and the situations, be fully accounted for on the basis of social and contextual facts. I argued that such explanations leave out a step, the step in which people select, from among the linguistic resources available to them, the ones that enable them to create and express individual selves in narrative. Given the genre, this is not a surprising finding; narrative is often seen as precisely the means by which people create themselves, their histories, their identities, in talk.

That the same thing appears to be true in academic disputation is somewhat more surprising, given the fact that persuasion is often seen as the strategic adaptation of rhetorical resources to situations, without reference to the people doing the adapting, and given the fact that the standard English employed by the academics whose talk we examined is often seen as a fairly fixed, inflexible register. Still, there are reasons for supposing that the expression of self is likely to enter into this kind of talk, too, much as it enters into narrative. Creating a self in talk has long been seen (under the designations *ethos* or "voice") as a key element of persuasion, and standard varieties are often seen as enabling people to express themselves fully and clearly.

We turn now to a genre in which, according to most people's understanding of how this speech event works, the existence of individual variation should be much more surprising. This is the anonymous telephone survey, in which a person who is paid to collect answers to scripted questions as quickly as possible interacts with a stranger whose name she or he never learns and about whom she or he is meant to know almost nothing until the last few minutes of the conversation. The other person in the interaction, the respondent, may or may not fully understand the interviewer's job, but if the respondent does not understand at the beginning that his or her own job is to make selections from choices presented by the interviewer or give succinct answers to open-ended questions, without elaboration and without time-consuming chat, he or she is to be instructed how to perform the task correctly.

For the purposes of the sociologists, political scientists, and media and marketing specialists who make use of such interviews, it is entirely possible that two respondents could behave identically. That is, it is possible for two respondents to produce exactly the same answers, as the answers end up being encoded by the interviewers. It is also possible—in fact, it is required by the theory that underlies the research methodology of survey interviewing—for two interviewers to behave identically. In theory, interviewers are required to conduct each survey exactly the same way, and exactly the same way as other interviewers do. Otherwise, the survey is flawed, respondents not all having been given precisely the same task.

One might suppose that such a situation would suppress individuality for interviewer and respondent alike. In many ways, of course, it does;

one has far fewer choices about what to talk about when following a script than when speaking spontaneously, fewer choices for how to phrase one's opinions when the choices are "excellent," "good," "fair," and "poor" then when options are open. It turns out, however, that what actually occurs in an anonymous telephone interview goes well beyond script reading and choosing from among fixed alternatives. We look in this chapter at talk by respondents and interviewers in a set of public opinion survey interviews conducted over the telephone. We find that there can be considerable variation from individual to individual in this genre, too, and we examine why this should be.

The Texas Poll

The Texas Poll, sponsored by Harte-Hanks Communication, is conducted four times a year.[1] Each quarter's survey includes questions asked by the Public Policy Resources Laboratory at Texas A&M University, which conducts the poll. The answers to these questions are syndicated to the press. In addition, the survey asks questions for nonprofit organizations, governmental agencies, and academic researchers, who pay to have their questions included and for statistical analyses of the answers. Respondents each quarter are approximately one thousand residents of Texas, selected by means of a "digit sampling frame," which generates random telephone numbers in different parts of the state in such a way as to ensure a demographically representative sample. Interviewers are trained and paid by the Public Policy Resources Laboratory. Most of the interviewers are college students, almost all are women, most are around twenty years old, and most are from middle- to upper-middle-class urban or suburban families from Texas.

Like other such surveys, the Texas Poll is a standardized, scheduled interview (all respondents are meant to answer the same questions, and the wording and order of the questions are specified), which includes both open-ended and "fixed-alternative" (multiple-choice) questions. Interviews are structured around a questionnaire that is part flow chart and part script. Once the telephone is answered (and if the number is not that of a business), the talk begins with an introduction by the interviewer. To avoid conducting a disproportionate number of interviews with women (since women are more likely than men to be at home and more likely to be the ones to answer the phone than are men when women and men are both at home), the interviewer then asks which adult in the household has had the most recent birthday and requests to speak to that person. If that person is the one who answered the phone and she or he agrees, the questions begin; if not, the appropriate person is summoned or arrangements are made for a callback.[2]

Questions are asked in topical sets. In the survey we examine here, questions include a set eliciting opinions about how various public officials were performing, a set about skin cancer, a set about the supercollider that was then under construction in Texas, a set about abortion, and several other sets. Whether or not some questions are asked depends on the answers to others (for example, people who said they had never heard of the supercollider were not asked any further questions about it), and questions in some sets are rotated to minimize effects of question order. The questionnaire prescribes exact wording for the introductory portion of the interview and for each question, as well as for topic shifts between sets of questions ("On a different topic"; "On another subject"; "Now we want to ask some questions about families"). If it started promptly and if nothing occurred except for question asking and answering, an interview for the January 1989 survey took about twenty minutes. Not all were that short, however. The tapes on which the interviews were recorded lasted forty-five minutes, and some interviews were longer than that.

We look here at thirty-six interviews from the January 1989 run of the poll. This set includes at least one interview conducted by each of the twenty-four people who did the interviewing for this survey. Three of these interviewers were men, twenty-one were women; one of the women was African-American, and one woman and one man were Hispanic. In order to be able to determine whether interviewers' styles were consistent from interview to interview, we examine seven additional interviews by one of the female interviewers (so that there are altogether eight by her) and five additional interviews by one of the male interviewers (altogether six). In addition, since some tapes begin with repeated attempts to locate an appropriate respondent, we can also look at multiple introductions by two other interviewers. Each respondent is of course different, so that there are thirty-six in all.

Individual Variation
Among the Respondents

Respondents did several sorts of things during the interviews. Sometimes they were asked to make a choice from a set of alternatives that were read to them and to state their choice in words that were the same as some of the words they heard, or at least similar enough that the interviewer was able to choose a single option to circle on the questionnaire she was filling out. For example, one item looked like this:

L1. Would you agree or disagree with a law that would require a one-week waiting period before a handgun could be purchased?

Agree	1
Disagree	2
Don't know	8
Refused/NA	9

The most efficient thing for a respondent to do in response to this question would have been to say just one word—"agree" or "disagree"—or one phrase—"I don't know." For the purposes of the survey, that was all anyone was interested in. Interviewers were trying to proceed quickly through the questions, and the people who processed the information that was collected in the survey, as well as the eventual consumers of the information, wanted and used only the numbers that encoded the choices. If respondents failed to produce, verbatim, one of the choices that had been read to them, interviewers almost always "probed" for an appropriate response, as in this case:

INTERVIEWER: Would you agree or disagree with passing a law in Texas requiring a person under eighteen to have parental consent or a court order before an abortion?
RESPONDENT: I'd say yes.
INTERVIEWER: **I'm sorry. Would you agree or disagree?**
RESPONDENT: Agree.

In the sense that respondents were almost always required to reproduce one of the words on the interview script, the answers to fixed-alternative questions could be called *scripted*. They were also *required*: except in very rare cases, the interview would not proceed until the question had been answered. One might thus suppose that there would be relatively little variation from respondent to respondent in the structure of answers to such questions.

Respondents were occasionally required to do things that were not scripted, such as answering open-ended questions. These were questions in which alternatives were not presented, such as "What do you think the most important issues are with respect to nuclear power?" or "I have a few questions about organizations that raise money for various health problems or mental or physical disabilities. Will you please tell me the names of all the organizations you can think of?" Interviewers recorded these responses verbatim, though they would later be encoded for statistical analysis. These questions could in all cases have been answered with a short noun phrase or two. "Radioactive waste" would, for example, have been the ideal sort of answer to the question about nuclear power from the perspective of the interviewer trying to write down exactly what the respondent said. Respondents who gave structurally elaborate answers were indirectly instructed to be more succinct; when answers were long and elaborate, interviewers often told respondents that they were trying to copy their exact words. As we will see, however, very few respondents answered open-ended questions with simple noun phrases. Most answers were somewhat more elaborate, and some were considerably so.

The ideal respondent, from the point of view of survey researchers, is one who does only the things he or she is required to do. Additional talk of any sort slows the interview down and does not add to the information encoded on the questionnaire. But respondents in fact did do things that they were not required to do, sometimes because the situation called for a departure from the question-and-answer sequence of the interview and sometimes for more puzzling reasons. Sometimes they were interrupted by other people in their households (or beeps from the other telephone line) and asked the interviewer to pause: "Would you wait again?;" "I'm sorry, hold on just a minute." They frequently asked the interviewers to repeat questions. These requests could sometimes be couched in very personal terms, as when one young man said to the young woman interviewing him, "I'm sorry, one more time. I- I know y- y- you've spoke all night and your voice is just going out but I didn't catch that one." Sometimes respondents commented on the survey—the format, the specific questions, the length—as did this irate woman:

RESPONDENT: You have to study these *damn* questions before you can answer.
INTERVIEWER: Okay, ma'am.
RESPONDENT: I don't (*two-second pause*) I think you should have told me to begin with how long this would
⎡take.⎤
INTERVIEWER: ⎣Okay⎦ ma'am. We'll be finished in two minutes, ma'am.
RESPONDENT: You better or I'm *hanging up.*

INTERVIEWER: Okay, okay, that's fine, ma'am.
RESPONDENT: I'm getting pissed off.
INTERVIEWER: I'm sorry, ma'am.

By far the most common way for respondents to deviate from their required tasks was to give reasons for the answers they gave.

Let us look now in more detail at three aspects of the respondents' performance in the survey interviews. First, we review ways respondents did something they did not have to do and for which they were not given preset options—justifications of their answers. These constituted an element of the interviews that was neither required of respondents nor scripted. We will expect there to be a relatively large number of ways of justifying one's answers, and we will not expect uniformity from respondent to respondent in the details of how it was done. We will want to know, however, why answer justification was so frequent in the interviews, why, in other words, people seemed compelled to explain why they answered as they did. Next, we will look at an element of the interviews that was required but not scripted: the answer to an open-ended question. We will see that the simplest way to answer the question, with a single noun phrase, was very rarely chosen. Respondents elaborated on the noun phrase, making it into a clause, and then adding hedges and other pragmatic markers to the clause. We will want to know why they seemed to have to do this and why they did it in so many different ways. Finally, we will examine the scripted, required answers to a fixed-alternative question, where we will expect to find little variation from individual respondent to individual respondent—but where we will find more than we might expect.

Justifications of Answers

Though respondents were not required to explain why they answered questions the way they did and were never asked to do so, they invariably did at one point or another. Every respondent justified at least one answer. Three provided elaborate, multiple justifications for every answer, so their interviews were incomplete when the tape ran out after forty-five minutes. Leaving out these three, which would raise the average considerably were they complete, the mean number of justifications per interview was 5.5.

Justifications of answers were of several types. Respondents sometimes explained their answers as they appeared to think aloud before answering. Examples of such prefatory justifications are these:

[question about gun control]

Ummm (*four-second pause*) **I'm not too fond of guns, but yet, I don't know about the waiting law,** [INTERVIEWER: Umhm, so] I'm not really sure.

[question about the economy in the next year]

(*two-second pause*) **Uhh gosh, that's a hard one to call. It really depends on,** I don't know on that.

[question about how good a job President George Bush was doing]

Well, he just got elected, so uh, I guess good?

[question about which form of skin cancer is most serious]

Uh, my mother has skin cancer, that's why I'm trying to remember now. I don't remember, she just, she had one that wasn't bad, I don't remember, say them again now.

More than 50 percent of the justifications that preceded answers were preambles to "don't know" responses. In syntax, they were varied, as the examples suggest.

Respondents sometimes included prefatory justification with answers on which they already appeared to be decided. These justifications sound like attempts to make the answer seem to be the only logical choice:

[question about whether it should be legal to carry a concealed gun, with a license]

Being a female, I agree with that.

[question about how well an elected official is doing]

Personally, he surprised me. I'm gonna say good.

[question about whether respondent thinks his financial situation will be better or worse next year]

Well, I can only live on Social Security. I can see no room for improvement for me at my age and as I say I live alone. [INTERVIEWER: Uh-huh] **So ah, I would say that** I ah, I hope to do as well a year from now as I am now.

[question about the strength of respondent's identification with the Republican Party]

Uh, I'm a member of the Young Republicans at school, so I guess strong.

[question about whether nuclear power plants cause health problems]

From the stories of it, I agree.

Alternatively, justifications of answers could follow the answers:

> [question about how respondent sees his financial situation in a year]
> Probably worse off **because I will have two kids in college. One of them next year.** (*laughs*)

> [question about whether motorcycle helmets should be required]
> Yes, **I never rode a motorcycle, but there's plenty of head injuries and you can get killed that way.**

> [question about whether judges should be elected]
> Not necessarily, **'cause the people don't know uh from uh Adam's off oxen, I mean, they wouldn't know how to vote. They d- they never do.**

> [question about whether respondent ever works on getting a suntan]
> Uh, no. **I'm black.**

Another way respondents sometimes justified their answers was to embed the answer logically in its justification. In some cases, the answer was easily inferable by the interviewer, and no probing was necessary:

> INTERVIEWER: President George Bush has said that the government will not raise federal taxes. Do you believe federal taxes will or will not be raised?
> RESPONDENT: I think he, he'll have to.

> INTERVIEWER: Do you use a sun block when in the sun?
> RESPONDENT: I don't get to lay out in the sun. (*laughs*)

In other cases, the interviewer probed for an answer with an acceptable format:

> INTERVIEWER: [Should state prisons be built] with bonds to be paid from taxes over several years?
> RESPONDENT: Not with current taxes. We can't do that. They're saying they're short a billion now. So how can they take from what they don't have?
> INTERVIEWER: Okay. So, you disagree or strongly disagr=
> RESPONDENT: =Yeah, I disagree.

> INTERVIEWER: Overall, how would you rate Texas as a place to live?
> RESPONDENT: Well, to me it's the only state.
> INTERVIEWER: Excuse me?

RESPONDENT: I said that ex- it's excellent 'cause it's, to me it's the only state.

Sometimes answers were not easily inferable from respondents' discussions of their opinions and motives. This could give rise to long negotiations between interviewers and respondents, like this one:

INTERVIEWER: Overall, how would you rate Texas as a place to live?

RESPONDENT: See I know, I was born and raised here, I know the state backwards and forwards, but you see, you've got about five basic s- areas or segments, honey. You can't just look at, I mean eh,

INTERVIEWER: How would you just rate it as a place to live?

RESPONDENT: The whole state?

INTERVIEWER: Well I mean you- what part uh, what parts have you lived in, I mean in
Tex⌈as? ⌉

RESPONDENT: ⌊I've⌋ lived in San Antonio, which is one of the finest inland cities in the world =

INTERVIEWER: = ⌈Okay   ⌉

RESPONDENT: ⌊(I've lived in)⌋
Florence, Italy, and Toledo, Spain, and maybe a couple of other places. And uh, you know, I've lived uh in Houston, which is an excellent uh has a beautiful climate, has high humidity and high heat, which I like and most people don't.

INTERVIEWER: ⌈Well⌉

RESPONDENT: ⌊I've ⌋lived in Wichita Falls, which is a, *hell*hole, cold as hell in the winter and hot in the summer.

INTERVIEWER: ⌈Okay⌉

RESPONDENT: ⌊( ) ⌋has nothing to offer, and I live in Waco now. I lived in Dallas at one time,

INTERVIEWER: Okay.

RESPONDENT: Uh, I'd say overall con- uh you want?

INTERVIEWER: Overall, uh-huh.

RESPONDENT: Compared to the rest of the United States?

INTERVIEWER: Uh-huh.

RESPONDENT: I think it ranks with the, with the rest of them, I think it ra- I would put it, now not right now, the economy is bad, but when the economy is normal,

INTERVIEWER:	⌈Uh-huh⌉
RESPONDENT:	⌊( )⌋I mean during the boom
	days =
INTERVIEWER:	=Right =
RESPONDENT:	=uh that uh Texas would, I rank it
	uh, except for climate, I rank it with California
	and Florida in places to live.
INTERVIEWER :	So would you rank it excellent or good?
RESPONDENT:	I rank it excellent!

Though this respondent was one of the three most talkative of the thirty-six, his insistence on explaining his responses to poll questions was not uncharacteristic. People appeared to feel a need to explain themselves, even when they were aware that their explanations were not being recorded and would not be used. They were often insistent about this, sometimes interrupting interviewers in order to finish their explanations and frequently continuing with justifications for several turns, even after their answers had been acknowledged by the interviewers.

Justifications of answers were not a required part of the interview. Nor were they encouraged by most interviewers; long-windedness of any sort on the respondent's part interfered with the interviewer's job of proceeding as quickly as possible through the survey in order to fill her or his quota of questionnaire forms, so interviewers tended not to provide much encouraging backchanneling and often tried to cut loquacious respondents off. And yet unsolicited justifications from the respondents were ubiquitous and took a large variety of forms.

More clearly than any other element of the interviews, justifications expressed the humanity and the individuality of respondents. In explaining themselves, respondents showed that they were people, not opinion-dispensing machines: people thinking about what they said, having reasons, being rational. They also showed that they were individuals. Structurally, the one thing almost all answer justifications had in common was reference to *I*: "I'm not too fond of guns"; "my mother has skin cancer"; "I never rode a motorcycle"; "I'm a member of the Young Republicans at school"; "I don't get to lay out in the sun"; "I was born and raised here, I know the state backwards and forwards." Respondents refused to behave like the clusters of demographic facts the poll required them to be, insisting instead on behaving as if they had unique motivations for their opinions—and expressing these motivations in individually varied ways.

Answers to an Open-Ended Question

The second question on the interview was this: "What do you think is the most serious problem facing the state of Texas?" A respondent's answer to this question was required—the interview would not continue without an answer—but the answer was not scripted. Not surprisingly, there was considerable variation in the structure of answers to this question, so much so that a syntactic rule generating all the possibilities would be difficult to imagine. The word or phrase that the interviewer would write in the appropriate blank on the questionnaire (the major problem) was usually spoken as a noun phrase ("drugs," "unemployment," "the economy"), but it could be an adjective ("economic") or the word *no*. The internal structure of the noun phrase was varied, and in only five cases did this phrase constitute the entire answer: "Taxes"; "Drugs"; "Your education"; "A lack of jobs"; "The oil company."

In addition to this key word or phrase, any of the following elements could occur, all describable only abstractly in pragmatic terms: requests for clarification, the framing discourse marker *well*, hesitation markers such as *uh* and *um*, descriptions of respondents' thought processes ("let me see," "I think," "I guess," "I don't know"), explanations and justifications of the answer, additional answer(s), hedges such as *probably*, *maybe*, or *right now*, and markers that the answer was complete ("but other than that, that's about it;" "yeah"). Hesitation markers and descriptions of thought processes usually preceded the key phrase; hedges could precede or follow; hesitation markers, descriptions of thought processes, and hedges could be repeated in any order. Requests for clarification typically came at the beginnings of answers, as did *well*, when it was used. Justifications could precede or follow answers; some were very short, while others were very long. Here are seven of the possibilities:

> Well, uh, the work economy, I mean the work. Lot of people out of work.

> Uh, economic.

> RESPONDENT: Um ummm Just think, I can't, do you have any examples?
> INTERVIEWER: Uhn-uhn. It could be anything, ⎡or if y-⎤
> RESPONDENT: ⎣I don't know⎦
> INTERVIEWER: Okay =
> RESPONDENT: =Uh the supercollider. You think that's, unh you know I've heard, about it, but I don't think it's going to affect anything here in Texas, if I think it's really good for it.

INTERVIEWER: Okay. So do you have, do, think that Texas has any serious problems facing it right now?
RESPONDENT: No.

Um, unemployment.

(*one-second pause*) Uh, probably unh, I don't know (*one-second pause*) inflation?

RESPONDENT: (*three-second pause*) The most serious problem?
INTERVIEWER: Um

RESPONDENT: (*two-second pause*) Uhh (*six-second pause*) I don't know. Uh (*laughs*) Uhh unemployment maybe.

Ooow. Politically, ah. I think that a, the a, employment is the ah most serious. That *and* the oil boom right now.

In one quarter of the cases interviewer and respondent formulated the answer together. Interviewers sometimes repeated answers, suggesting that more was required and giving the respondent time to expand:

RESPONDENT: Um, unemployment.
INTERVIEWER: Unemployment.
RESPONDENT: And there's taxes . . . (*laughs*)

Interviewers occasionally attempted to interpret answers that consisted mainly of justification, as highlighted in the following excerpt:

RESPONDENT: Well (*one-second pause*) one of the things that I, I feel like is that uh that sometimes it takes, uh went overboard when, when oil was um, got too high, and ah an- and we set up to budget things to, in order to, to go on the basis of that kind of income. And uh, then when it come down they had to reach for some other place. And ⌈uh, ⌉
INTERVIEWER: ⌊Okay⌋ **so you're saying the oil got too high, and** =
RESPONDENT: = Yeah, in other words they, they uh they took the money that they was normally getting, (let me) make it a little this way, what I'm saying.
INTERVIEWER: Okay.

RESPONDENT: Long about ten years ago, uh, w- we was still-
we's selling gasoline at the time somewhere
around 38, 39 cents ⌈and   ⌉ uh then
INTERVIEWER: ⌊Mm-hm⌋
RESPONDENT: when oil jumped on to where that uh, it got now
it's two dollars a gallon and oh, um uh we got the
state come in saying "Well, look how much
money we got coming in." This is one person's
opinion. That's my opinion ⌈of   ⌉
INTERVIEWER: ⌊Mm-hm⌋
RESPONDENT: what they've done. And then it- it caused us
to- to set up more things that we'd be um, uhh
(*one-second pause*) be uh, obligating for. And then
when uh, when it is no longer there, you have to
reach for somewhere else, get that income that
way. Uh, that's just one of the results, but uh, uh,
as far as the state is concerned, it has good
highways, it has uh, enough shoulders on the
highways that you can pull off to the side and
enjoy the, the state, where many of the states
don't, not even allowed to stop unless you have
an emergency. It's just, I could talk on all day on
how, how much I like Texas.
INTERVIEWER: **Okay. But the uh, problem you said is that the
oil, the oil prices are too high, got too high?**
RESPONDENT: Well, that's what I think, that it might maybe
bring um, our problem in at the state legislature
and places.

In one such case the interviewer disagreed with the respondent's re
formulation of his answer:

RESPONDENT: . . . Mexico is going to be another Cuba if we're
not careful. The, it's going to be totally commu-
nism and we treat them like *dogs*, we treat them,
we in*sult* them, we we we don't *help* them.
INTERVIEWER: Okay, I see.
RESPONDENT: I consider that our biggest problem.
INTERVIEWER: Okay, we=
RESPONDENT: = Drugs are no- is not our big
problem because eh, you know, they'll whip
the drugs or =

INTERVIEWER (formulates): =Texans or Americans don't
know how to deal with foreign people.
RESPONDENT (reformulates): **That's right, with the Mexicans.**
INTERVIEWER (disagrees): **Well uh I, not only the Mexicans,
unfortunately, just in Texas that they have
that, they're exposed to it . . .**

Interviewers sometimes helped formulate answers by commenting ("The
economy. Nice and general. Okay.") or by asking for more ("Anything
else?") and sometimes encouraged reluctant respondents:

RESPONDENT: Uh, gosh (*laughs*) um,
INTERVIEWER: Just, j-, just how do you ⌈feel?
RESPONDENT: ⌊I would say the homeless.

In almost all cases, the interviewer decided when the question had been
satisfactorily answered; we look later at how interviewers signaled this.

In this element of the interviews, as in the one discussed previously, no two respondents sounded exactly the same; even the short
snatches of talk I have used as examples hint at what these interviewers and respondents are like as individuals. Many of the respondents'
departures from what would have been the most succinct way of
answering the question had to do with their apparent need to fill processing time during which they were deciding on an answer. Discussions of the reasons for such "filled pauses" that are based on the analysis
of casual conversation often explain the *wells* and *uhs* and *let me sees*
with which speakers mark time by saying that if a person stops talking,
another person is licensed to start talking. If you don't want to lose
the conversational floor, in other words, you need to fill pauses while
you think of what to say next. But the survey interviews were not like
this. Interviewers had no motivation to take over the floor; they had
to wait for respondents to provide answers before they could get on
with the job. There were, accordingly, interviews in which there were
four- and even eight-second pauses, pauses that would seem agoniz-
ingly long and embarrassing in casual talk among people like these. Even
respondents who understood very little else about what the interview
was all about knew that interviewers were not going to cut them off if
it took them some time to formulate their answers; the centrality of
the interviewee's responses is the most basic feature of interviews, in
contrast to other kinds of conversations. Yet respondents seemed to
need to treat the interview as if it were casual conversation rather than
a mechanical answer-production task. They seemed to need, in other
words, to be people interacting with people, refusing to be confined to

the role of respondents interacting with interviewers. They needed to express their individuated humanity.

Answers to a Multiple-Choice Question

We look next at part of the respondents' performance in the interviews that was both required and scripted: their answers to a multiple-choice question. These responses were required in that the interviews did not go on until the question had been answered and scripted in that the answer was supposed to be, or at least include, one of the words on the list of possible answers read to the respondent by the interviewer. The question, as it appeared on the questionnaire, was this: "How would you rate the job Ronald Reagan did as President—excellent, good, only fair, or poor?" (Interviewers did not all ask the question this way. Some embedded the list in a clause: "Was it excellent, good, only fair, or poor?"; "Would you say he did an excellent, good, only fair, or poor job?")

The answers to the question almost invariably included one of the words from the list: "excellent," "good," "fair" or "poor." The one exception was "great," overlapping the question before the interviewer finished reading the list. (The interviewer failed to probe for one of the listed answers, apparently encoding "great" as either "excellent" or "good.") Fewer than half of the responses consisted only of an item from the list, however; most respondents added elements of structure. Of the responses that were elaborated, only two were structurally identical to each other: "I would say" followed by an item from the list. No two of the remaining thirteen responses were structurally the same. A number of respondents embedded their answers in clauses, as in these examples:

> I think, aw, Reagan did an excellent job.
>
> He did good.

Instead or in addition, other respondents added hesitation markers to their answers. One added a linking *also*, referring to a previous question about the governor of the state.[3]

> Uh, only fair.
>
> Ah, I'd say fair also.

One respondent expanded on her answer after the interviewer's acknowledgment:

> RESPONDENT: Poor.
> INTERVIEWER: Okay.
> RESPONDENT: Definitely poor.

In general, additions to the required single-item answer had the effect of adding syntactic explicitness and/or references to self, just as did justifications of answers. Some answers, however, were much longer and more radically different, involving elaborate justifications and requiring probes from the interviewers. In one case the question was never asked, and in some cases the question was never, strictly speaking, answered at all:

> RESPONDENT: Mmhmm, I think of sorry.
> INTERVIEWER: Excuse me?
> RESPONDENT: Uh, very sorry.
> INTERVIEWER: Okay.
> RESPONDENT: I have never known a man that could get up, use the illustration that uh, that he did about when it was Carter, I'm not upholding Carter, but I always felt like he got in there, just in with the plain man,
> INTERVIEWER: Mm-hmm
> RESPONDENT: but I think he was trying to do a good job and when I heard Ronald Reagan say if he couldn't balance the budget, he ought to get out and let somebody in there that could. Then when I see him bring the budget higher than two billion dollars—two trillion dollars, it didn't make me very happy. And he's also the one that helped t- to pass this bill over to where that uh, wealthier person didn't have to pay 45 percent of the income tax, but lower theirs to 28 percent, just the same as th- the people of us who had a little income and had to get out and get a little bit more work to substitute for it. And it's brought 'em back up into a bracket where they paid the same bracket amount wealthy ones did. I don't think Ronald Reagan did anything but create show.

This was not the only respondent whose answers were often much more elaborate than required; neither was this respondent the most long-winded.

In summary, there was considerable individual variation in the structure of responses to the multiple-choice question, a speech act in which one might expect variation from individual to individual to be maximally suppressed. Several respondents never did choose one of the alternatives read to them, and many others did something else in addition to making a choice. When they did so, they built a phrase or clause around the single-word choice or indicated that they were hesitating for thought. In their elaborations, they often made reference to themselves: "I think," "I'd say," "I always felt like." Here again, the interview's mechanical sequence of questions and prestructured choices among preanalyzed options was subverted or ignored by respondents expressing themselves as individuals, displaying personal motives for their opinions and acting as if they were engaged in normal conversations with other individuals.

What Were the Respondents Doing?

Why did the Texas Poll respondents behave this way? Why did they express themselves as individuals even though such self-expression was not required, not even encouraged, in fact officially ignored in the speech event they were engaged in? Perhaps they did not understand what the poll was intended to accomplish or did not know the rules for interaction in such a speech event. There were, certainly, respondents who did not understand what a public opinion poll was, even once it was explained to them, and who were mistrustful or even hostile throughout, perhaps suspecting that they would eventually hear a sales pitch or that the information they provided would be used against them by a loan-collection agency or the police.[4] Other respondents, however, knew exactly how a public opinion survey worked, even sometimes helpfully second-guessing what the interviewer was doing. This respondent, for example, displayed her understanding of the reason for the eliciting of personal information at the end of the interviews:

INTERVIEWER: Finally, I'd just like to ask you a few questions about yourself so that we can see how the different groups of people feel about these things.
RESPONDENT: Demographics? Huh?
INTERVIEWER: Excuse — yeah, demographics. (*laughs*)

In a study published in 1955, Strauss and Schatzman suggested that many Americans may not know how survey interviews are meant to proceed, lower-class respondents being more likely than middle-class respondents to be unfamiliar with the communicative expectations of this speech event.[5] It is likely that in the years since 1955 more and more Americans have come to know what a survey interview is and what the norms for its conduct are. Most adults have been approached at least once for a telephone survey interview of one kind or another, and even the most

cursory familiarity with the news means knowing specifically about public opinion polls. Still, some of the Texas Poll respondents may have had
only a vague idea of why they were being asked questions and what the
answers would be used for.

But although there were respondents who did not know what a
public opinion survey was, there were none who did not know what an
interview was. The interview is a familiar speech event for most Americans (Grimshaw 1969; Wolfson 1976). Television and radio talk shows,
in the interview format and sometimes including telephone interviews,
are extremely popular, and children conduct interviews for school
projects beginning in primary school. Though I cannot prove that each
of the thirty-six respondents had been exposed repeatedly to interviews,
I think it highly unlikely that any had not. In any event, it is clear from
the tapes that none failed to understand the basic mechanism: the
interviewer would ask questions and they would answer them, the collection of information rather than the development of an interpersonal
relationship being the goal. Male respondents occasionally teased female
interviewers, who sometimes teased back; women congratulated other
women on pregnancies and blessed them when they sneezed. But in the
end, respondents always remained anonymous. Whatever happened in
the interviews in addition to the proffering and collection of information was always subsidiary to the main purpose. Though every respondent departed from the bare minimum he or she would have had to say
to complete the task, in no case was this because, failing to understand
what it was, he or she had departed entirely from the task.

Respondents who did not know specifically how to answer the questions were instructed how. When one woman, for example, answered
the question "How would you rate Texas as a place to live?" with "I like
it just fine," and "fine" was not one of the options that had been given
to her, the interviewer said, "Okay. Most of our questions have a specific answer. You can just choose from the answers I read to you."
Another who said "Great" was told, "Okay, my — I've got four choices
down here, excellent, good. . . ." Respondents who hesitated in answering open-ended questions were instructed to give "just your opinion,"
and when they delivered their answers too quickly for the interviewer's
transcription (as they very often did) they were told that the answers
were being recorded verbatim:

INTERVIEWER: What do you think the most important issues are
with respect to nuclear power?
RESPONDENT: I think it's about uh the uh contamination of the
nuclear waste.

INTERVIEWER: Okay, let me write this down, the contamination, of nuclear waste. Okay.

Some respondents knew precisely how the questions were to be answered and made displays of this knowledge. This woman, for example, couched her answer to one of the demographic questions in terms of the code number she guessed the interviewer would be marking:

INTERVIEWER: Okay. Do you have adult children living away from home, young children at home, or no children?
RESPONDENT: Number one.

Other respondents checked on the appropriateness to the questionnaire format of things they said, asking questions like "Is that an answer?"

It appears, then, that respondents understood what they were doing in essentially the same way as interviewers did. Many knew specifically what a public opinion poll was, all knew what an interview was, and if they did not know how to answer the questions they were instructed. Their displays of humanity and individuality occurred in spite of the task they were engaged in, not because they were engaged in something else instead. Later in this chapter we engage in a more detailed discussion of the reasons for these displays. First, however, let us turn to the interviewers.

Individual Variation
Among the Interviewers

Much of the interviewers' task was scripted: they had questionnaires in front of them from which they were supposed to read. But interviewers did other things as well. Some of these other speech acts were required in order for the interviews to proceed. Interviewers needed, for example, to acknowledge the answers respondents gave them with some sort of verbal nod (they almost always used *okay*); they needed to signal when they were starting again after misreading a question (with a phrase like "I'm sorry, let me start over," for example); they needed to tell respondents who gave inappropriate answers what the proper format was ("I've got four choices here"). Interviewers also did things that were neither scripted nor required. They sometimes commented on the answers they heard. They sometimes asked the respondents extra questions. Sometimes, they got involved in conversations with respondents, about what interviewing was like in one case, about plans for law school in another.

Let us examine the interviewers' talk in the Texas Poll interviews in the same way we examined the respondents'. We begin with unsolicited comments on respondents' answers. Of all the speech acts in which interviewers engaged, this was the least scripted. We will not, accordingly, expect uniformity from individual to individual. We will, however, ask why interviewers seemed to need to depart from the script in this way, especially since they had been explicitly told during their training *not* to comment on people's answers except for a few reasons. Then we look at a task that was required and completely scripted: the introductory pitch in which the interviewer solicited the cooperation of the person who answered the telephone. This talk occurred before the interviewer knew anything whatever about the respondent except perhaps his or her sex, before any sort of rapport could have been established. There should, we might suppose, have been no reason whatsoever for interviewers to do anything except read from or recite the few sentences written on the script. But they did not all speak the introduction the same way, and we will want to know why.

Unsolicited Comments on Answers

We look first at an element of the interviewers' talk that was neither scripted nor required: interviewers' unsolicited comments during or about respondents' answers. To give a very elaborate example, one interviewer, during a respondent's anecdote about abortion, interjected:

> That's, ah-hah, that's, that's really neat. That happened with a friend of mine too. So, that happened with a friend of mine's family too. They adopted a baby, a little girl.

This sort of commentary is definitely not condoned by interviewer supervisors and directors of polling services; interviewers can lose their jobs for it. Most unsolicited commentary was not so extended: "I know what you mean," "goodness," "that's fine."

Unsolicited comments by interviewers appeared to serve a number of functions. Interviewers sometimes reassured subjects that a "don't know" answer was acceptable: "Okay, that's fine"; "That's okay." Sometimes they commented on respondents' justifications of their answers:

> RESPONDENT: (*laughs*) I guess [the president]'s done pretty
>   good. He had a good party the other day.
> INTERVIEWER: (*laughs*) That's a good start. 'Kay.

They sometimes apologized for asking difficult questions: "I know you're going 'Oh gosh'"; "I know it's kinda hard to think of 'em"; "Okay. (*giggles*) Poor thing, (*giggles*) confusing you." In these cases, comments always mentioned or alluded to "I" and "you," and such apologetic comments were always style-shifted toward the informal from the formal prose of the questionnaire.

In addition, interviewers sometimes commented on respondents' answers:

RESPONDENT: Uhh I'd just have to say fair since I'm not real wild about [the governor]. (*laughs*)
INTERVIEWER: Okay, that's fine, that's what we're looking for.

RESPONDENT: [justifies an answer about gun control]
INTERVIEWER: Right, I agree with you there.

RESPONDENT: [responds to question about whether she has ever gone to a doctor to be checked for skin cancer by saying "No, but I worked for a dermatologist part time."]
INTERVIEWER: Hey, hey there you go, you don't, hey, that's that's what you gotta do.

Interviewers' remarks sometimes involved commentary on the poll's procedures or questions,

RESPONDENT: Uh, well, that's kind of a loaded question. I'd say yeah, I'd say yes.
INTERVIEWER: Okay. Yeah, now they're real simplified questions, I guess they have to be more or less.

or allusion to other respondents,

RESPONDENT: [objects to the choices given in a fixed-alternative question]
INTERVIEWER: Okay. Well, talking to others I think we do need a, a middle category.

or evaluation of their own performance.

Ah, I wasn't trying to insult your intelligence . . .

Okay. Okay. I'm still trying to figure out how to spell Wichita Falls. (*laughs*) I'm stupid.

In one interview, the respondent sounded congested and sneezed, which provoked the interviewer to say, "Bless you. Did you sneeze?" and "Sounds like you're getting over a bad cold?"

Variation in interviewers' unsolicited comments, except in the case of reassurances, was enormous, both in structure and function. There were many ways to stray slightly from the task at hand, and many choices of words and syntax along each tangential path. What interviewers' unsolicited comments had in common, however, is that they tended to highlight the fact that interviewers were not machines, that real individuals were speaking with other real individuals. As we will see, there are pragmatic reasons for interviewers' having to depart from their scripts, and interviews would not have been successful if they had not. But interviewers had individual ways of doing this, ways that expressed their individuality and sometimes even encouraged respondents to express theirs.

Introductions

The introductory talk took place at the very beginning of the interaction, immediately after someone at the number being called picked up the phone and said "Hello." The script printed on the interviewer's questionnaire was this:

> Hello, this is _____ calling for the Texas Poll, a statewide, nonpartisan public opinion poll. This month we are conducting a confidential survey of public opinion in Texas, and we'd really appreciate your help and cooperation.

Twenty-one of the twenty-four interviewers gave the complete introduction. (Three others were calling back and did not need to.) Of these twenty-one occurrences of the complete introduction, only two were exactly the same as the script on the questionnaire, and only two others were identical to each other. (Both of these differed from the script in adding *I'm* before *calling*, adding two *ands*, and substituting *for* for *with*, and both the interviewers chose to use both their first and last names.)

Two introductions were very deviant, involving the reordering and deletion of information in the script and the addition of other information:

> Hello, uh my name is Lianne and I'm calling for the Texas Poll. We're doing a statewide, nonpartisan public opinion poll, and it's a confidential survey of public opinion in Texas, sir.

> Hello, my name is Elizabeth McMillan, and I'm calling for Texas A&M University? for a Texas Poll that we're conducting? [RESPONDENT: Uh-huh] And it's just a statewide, nonpartisan public opinion poll that we do three times a year. It's a confidential survey of public opinion in Texas? And we'd appreciate your help with it?

The remaining introductions differed from one another, and from the script, along two axes. The first has to do with how the five clauses in the script were connected. Any of its five clauses could be spoken as an independent clause. In the script, only three clauses were independent, but in the interviews all five could be. With the exception of the first, each clause could be connected to the preceding clause with *and*. Thus the partially hypotactic, mostly asyndetic script (there was only one *and* in the scripted introduction) could be spoken as a completely paratactic, polysyndetic passage:

> Hello. My name is Mary Porter **and** I am calling from the Texas Poll **and** this is a statewide, nonpartisan public opinion poll **and** in this month we are conducting a confidential survey of public opinions in Texas **and** we would really appreciate your help and cooperation but first of all ma'am. . . .

Five interviewers, on the other hand, connected clauses only once, in four cases between the third and fourth clauses ("**and** this month we are conducting . . .") and in one case between the second and third clauses ("**and** the Texas Poll is . . ."). In the middle of this range, two or three *and*s could be employed at the beginnings of any combination of clauses. The third clause, which appeared in the script as the reduced appositive noun phrase "a statewide, nonpartisan public opinion poll," was actually spoken that way by only six interviewers. More often, it occurred as a finite clause. Seven options were employed:

> It's a statewide . . .
> It's just a statewide . . .
> This is a statewide . . .
> This is merely a statewide . . .
> We're a statewide . . .
> We're doing the statewide . . .
> which is a statewide . . .

The other axis along which the introductions varied was in how often and in what way they made reference to the people involved in the interaction. On the script, reference was made twice to *we* ("we are conducting"; "we'd really appreciate"), and the interviewer was required to refer to him or herself by name ("this is_____"). In all except two of the non-callback introductions, the two required *we*'s were included, and in every case at least one extra reference to "I" or "we" was added. Elaine

Maldonado included the two required *we*'s, as well as three extra first-person pronouns:

> Hi, **my name** is Elaine, and **I'm** calling for the Texas Poll. **We're** a statewide, nonpartisan public opinion poll. And this month **we are** conducting a confidential survey of public opinions in Texas. **We'd** really appreciate your help and cooperation. Do you have a few moments?

There was in addition another marker of personality in Maldonado's introduction, the appended question addressed to and about the respondent: "Do you have a few moments?" Ten of the interviewers used only their first names, but the majority chose to state both their first and last names. This format suggested more clearly that they were real people than did the first-name-only format, which identifies roles in many service encounters. Thirteen interviewers added *sir* or *ma'am*. Four exchanged the script's *hello* for the more personable *hi*, though one made a shift in the other direction with *good afternoon*.

Let us now look at how the same interviewer presented the introduction in different interviews. The next three selections (the first repeated from a preceding example) were all spoken by Elaine Maldonado:

RESPONDENT: Hello. (man's voice)

MALDONADO: Hello, this is Elaine Maldonado and I'm calling for the Texas Poll, a statewide nonpartisan public opinion poll. And this month we're conducting a confidential survey of public opinion in Texas and we'd really appreciate your help and cooperation.

RESPONDENT: Hello. (man's voice)

MALDONADO: Hello, this is Elaine Maldonado and I'm calling for the Texas Poll, a statewide nonpartisan public opinion poll? And this month we're conducting a confidential survey of public opinion in Texas and we'd really appreciate your help and cooperation.

RESPONDENT: Hello? (child's voice)

MALDONADO: Hello, this is Elaine Maldonado and I'm calling for the Texas Poll, a statewide nonpartisan public opinion poll? And this month we're conducting a confidential survey of public opinion in Texas and we'd really appreciate your help and cooperation.

With the exception of rising intonation at the end of one clause in the latter two excerpts, the three introductions were identical: Maldonado always said the introduction the same way. This occurred not because she was reading it and the others were not: her version was not that of the script, either. Of six introductions by Timothy Kiefer, no two were alike, but each began with the same opening formula, "Hello, my name is Timothy Kiefer." Jose Santos's two introductions were different, but both included the idiosyncratic wording "this is **merely** a statewide, nonpartisan public opinion poll." Laurie Peters's six introductions were all different, though she always used her first name only, always added *and* before the third clause, and all but once expanded this clause to "**it's** a statewide, nonpartisan. . . ." All but once, she pluralized the script's singular *opinion* in "we are conducting a confidential survey of public opinions."

If any part of the poll interviews could be expected to display little individual variation, it would be the introductions. This segment of the interview occurred before interviewer and respondent knew anything about each other (except that the interviewer had heard the respondent's voice and may thereby have identified the subject's sex and ethnicity).[6] The introduction was completely scripted on the questionnaire. Yet the twenty-four interviewers presented the introduction in twenty-two different ways. The interviewers appeared in almost all cases to be responding to the same troubles with the script: it was too writerly—too hypotactic and asyndetic—to be easily understandable and too distancing to be effective in encouraging respondents to cooperate. But no two interviewers corrected these problems the same way. The result was twenty-four different individual voices.

What Were the Interviewers Doing?

Survey interviewers are trained to be invariant in their performance, and supervisors monitor them to enforce invariance. Manuals for interviewers and textbooks about interviewing reiterate that "differences among research interviewers must be minimized or eliminated" (Nathan 1986, p. 69). "Generally each vocalization should be planned word for word and used by each [interviewer] exactly as written. Only in very rare circumstances should an [interviewer] deviate from the planned wording" (Stano and Reinsch 1982, p. 65). Interviewers are to ask all questions in a "neutral, straightforward way" (Hoinville et al. 1978, p. 100), "without variation in inflection or emphasis" (Nathan 1986, p. 68). They are not supposed to rephrase or explain questions, provide any clues about their own attitudes, say anything about their own backgrounds, or provide any more than minimal acknowledgments of answers. They are never, for example, to respond to an answer with "Good" (Hoinville et al. 1978, pp. 99–100; Stano and Reinsch 1982, pp. 63–64), for "each communication segment you employ outside your planned approach will tend to contaminate your data since additional communication, unrehearsed and unplanned, provides an opportunity for questioner bias to enter the process" (Gottlieb 1986, p. 69). Interviewing manuals stress the importance of "playing a constructive role" in the interview by establishing "an easy, pleasant relationship with respondents" (Hoinville et al. 1978, pp. 99–100); interviewing involves the same skills as ordinary conversation, and interviewers "can and will add informality to the interview by adding link phrases and comments of their own" (p. 99). But the goal must be kept in mind: "If your data is to have any meaning, it is essential that each respondent is put through the same experience" (p. 59).

Scholarship about interviewing has demonstrated, of course, that language does not act as a neutral code for the exchange of facts in this speech event, any more than in any other. Research in the 1950s demonstrated that interviewers inevitably affect the results of interviews (Hyman et al. 1954) and that middle-class respondents adapt better to the communicative expectations of interviews than do lower-class respondents (Strauss and Schatzman 1955). In an examination of face-to-face interviews, Brenner (1981) found that interviewers "significantly altered" about one eighth of all the questions. Theorists such as Cicourel (1964, pp. 74–75) and Briggs (1986, pp. 23–24) point out that the two goals of survey research—validity and reliability—are incompatible: a completely reliable interview would be completely standardized so as to assure that the same results would occur another time, but a completely standardized interview is least likely to get at respondents' real feelings and opinions.

But scholarship such as this appears to have minimal practical impact. Directors of polls, interviewers, and consumers of survey information rely on deep-seated beliefs about language to justify the practice; the knowledge that completely standardized interviews are inherently invalid is glossed over. Practitioners like the director of the Texas Poll assume that variability, since it can lead to biased results, is error, and they train their staffs to stray from the written questionnaire as little as possible, and then only in order to keep respondents participating. The reputation of the polling agency, and hence its ability to attract clients, depends on assurance that interviews are always conducted the same way. Poll interviewers want mainly to get respondents through the scheduled questions as quickly as possible; they thus should have no reason to produce extra talk themselves or to encourage extraneous talk from respondents except when it is the only way to keep respondents from hanging up.

Why, then, did the interviewers keep departing from the script, and why did they fail to read exactly what it said when they were reading the script? Interviewers introduced their individual identities in these ways because talk would not continue unless they did. Seasoned poll interviewers are well aware of this. They acknowledge that even though they know they are not to deviate from the script, many successful interviewers do. Beginning interviewers who stick strictly to the script are less successful; potential respondents hang up the phone. There are several reasons for this.

Politeness in Scripted Talk

For Americans, unsolicited telephone calls from strangers are an infringement of privacy, a threat to a person's right to choose with whom to interact. Worse, the Texas Poll asked questions that could embarrass respondents, either by forcing them to admit ignorance or by making them divulge private information such as their income, age, and religion. Interviewers were thus required to violate strongly held beliefs about how people should treat one another. (For this reason, the job is very stressful, and many interviewers do not last long in it.) In Brown and Levinson's (1987) terms, the interviewers' calls were "face-threatening acts," and such acts are considered rude unless they are mitigated by means of various "politeness strategies".[7] The beginning of the call, before respondents had agreed to participate and hence before they had implicitly agreed to be imposed on, was especially crucial in this regard.

Some attempts to mitigate the rudeness the interviewers' task required were built into the script. The introductory pitch gave reasons for the imposition ("the Texas Poll, a statewide, nonpartisan public opinion survey . . . This month we're conducting . . .") and suggested that the interviewer and respondent could work together ("We'd really appreciate your . . . cooperation.") In these ways, the script incorporated "positive politeness," anticipating the respondent's desire to be informed and equal. "Negative" politeness strategies acknowledging the respondent's need to be left alone were also incorporated into the written script. The tone of the scripted introduction was deferentially formal and impersonalized the interviewer by employing *we* rather than *I*, and interviewers were put in debt to respondents, who would "help" them by participating.

The most personal questions were asked at the end of the interview. By the time respondents were asked to provide their age, income, ethnicity, and other demographic facts, interviewer and respondent had been conversing for at least fifteen minutes, and the original imposition had presumably been excused, at least implicitly. The new imposition of requesting items of information that Americans do not normally divulge to strangers, and about which it is normally rude to ask, required another scripted expression of politeness, in the form of a brief explanation: "Finally, I'd like to ask you a few questions about yourself so that we can see how different groups of people feel about the things we've been talking about."

Many of the interviewers' deviations from the script can also be seen as politeness strategies, of both the positive and the negative sort. Interviewers expressed positive politeness by sometimes allowing respondents to stray from the topic if it appeared that respondents wanted to do so. They expressed personal interest in respondents' answers. They created solidarity by identifying themselves with respondents and by asserting common ground. They explained what they were doing, and why. They reduced the imposition of requesting personal information by divulging information about themselves. And they consoled respondents who were forced to admit ignorance. Interviewers also employed negative politeness strategies. Their voices sometimes sounded tentative and hedged. They showed respect by using "sir" or "ma'am." They apologized for difficult questions. They thanked respondents and expressed indebtedness to them. In short, the scripted politeness markers did not appear to provide enough mitigation for the imposition of a "cold call," and interviewers appeared to be required to add more. It could in fact be argued that failing to add extra expressions of politeness would in itself be impolite, since reading from a script, no matter how polite the script is, is not polite.

But while all interviewers were bound by the special requirements of this speech event for politeness, not all fulfilled the obligation the same way. No two sounded alike. Some were successful using mainly deferential, businesslike, negative politeness; others were equally successful with friendly, sympathetic, positive strategies. Some used a mixture, the way the script did. The thirty-six interviews we have examined are too few and the interviewers too homogeneous a group to allow for comparisons among subgroups, but the data suggest that interviewers' choices of politeness strategies did not correlate in any simple way with social factors. Of the three male interviewers, one favored negative politeness (and sounds very cool and efficient), one favored positive politeness (eliciting, for example, long digressions from his respondent by acknowledging answers with "Oh, is that right?"), and the third employed both. Nor does audience design appear always to have been a factor. Of the two interviewers for whom there are multiple interviews, one sounded somewhat different depending on whom she was talking to, while the other sounded almost exactly the same in every interview.

In some cases, individual variation among respondents can also be related to requirements for politeness. Respondents were the ones being imposed upon, and in general they appeared to have the right to be rude, at least at the beginning of the interview. Some respondents made overt displays of mistrust and refusal to cooperate (as did the woman who announced that she was "pissed off" and threatened to hang up), and they could treat interviewers as inferiors. One respondent, for example, made a point of the fact that he had never heard of the Texas Poll, addressed the interviewer as "honey" throughout, and told her (albeit somewhat jokingly, in line with a traditional inter-university rivalry) that she had chosen the wrong school. On the whole, however, once respondents had agreed to cooperate, they appeared to have agreed, if not to be polite, at least not to be rude. Respondents' deviations from minimal requirements of the speech event seemed, however, to have more to do with their needing to present themselves as thoughtful, reasonable individuals listening carefully and critically.

Discourse Task Management

Not all the interviewers' deviations from the script had to do with politeness. In addition to ensuring that respondents continued to feel respected and liked so that they would continue to talk, interviewers, even those with cooperative respondents, had the more specific job of making sure the talk unfolded in a particular way. Survey interviews are unlike casual conversations in that speakers in an interview do not have equal rights to propose topics or allocate turns. The topics are predetermined, and interviewers ask the questions and respondents answer them, the interviewer deciding when an answer is satisfactory in form. As a result, interlocutors in an interview, unlike co-conversationalists, need special techniques to keep themselves on task and get their job accomplished smoothly. These techniques can be collectively referred to as "discourse task management" (Johnstone, Ferrara, and Bean 1992; Bean and Johnstone 1994). In the Texas Poll interviews, discourse task management involved seeing to it that the questions on the questionnaire were asked and answered, making sure that responses were in the appropriate format and were accurately heard, ensuring that answer formats were understood, coding or copying the answers, getting back to the task at hand after interruptions, and so on.

The need for discourse task management accounts for many of the deviations from the interview script. This is particularly true for the interviewers, who had the primary responsibility for managing the interview.[8] For example, interviewers sometimes guided respondents through the questionnaire, saying such things as "Okay. All right, that's the end of the cancer questions" or rephrasing responses to make them fit the required format: "Okay, so you would disagree with a law that would allow . . ." They requested respondents to repeat when they hadn't heard answers accurately, they clarified questions when respondents appeared not to understand them, and they notified respondents when they needed time to copy their open-ended answers exactly. Respondents were also involved in discourse task management. When they had to interrupt the interview, for example, they sometimes used "Excuse me" or "I'm sorry" to announce that this was happening and again when the interruption was over. They asked interviewers to repeat questions and indicated when they had made mistakes in answering or when they thought their answers were not clear enough. Not all respondents were equally cooperative in this way, but, as I have pointed out, all appeared to understand that the interview was not a casual chat but rather a job to be gotten through.

The need for discourse task management in the interviews accounts for many of the deviations from the script. But it does not account for the exact form of these deviations or for the variation among them. Just as all interviewers had to be polite, all interviewers had the responsibility of managing the interview. But just as not all were polite in the same way, not all employed the same strategies for discourse task management. Explanations based in pragmatic needs for politeness and discourse task management account for the fact that respondents and interviewers deviated from the script and from the idealized expectations of the pollsters who designed the survey, but such explanations do not account for the individually varied nature of the deviations. To understand the variation from individual to individual and the consistency of some individuals' talk from interaction to interaction in a speech task that is meant to be invariant and mechanical, we need to look for an explanation at a more specific level, an explanation based in what it means to be a person rather than a machine.

Cultural Individualism
and Linguistic Individuation

Being polite means acting like a person and treating other people as people. But what it means to be a person is not everywhere the same. For contemporary Americans like the Texas Poll interviewers and respondents, being a person means expressing one's uniqueness. Americans' individualism has been remarked on for as long as Americans have been a nation. Writing in the 1830s, Alexis de Tocqueville (1966) used the then new term "individualism" to describe Americans' "calm and considered feeling which disposes each citizen to isolate himself from the mass of his fellows and withdraw into the circle of family and friends," leaving the larger society to "look after itself" (p. 477). According to de Tocqueville, democracy fosters individualism: when people do not have hereditary duties to others and are more mobile and less likely to remain with extended family throughout their lives, and when government is less intrusive, individuals are concerned mainly with their own interests (1966, pp. 477–480; 1960, p. 51). This self-interest is counterbalanced by the interpersonal bonds created by free political institutions. Citizens have to depend on each other if they are collectively responsible for government, especially on the local level (1966, pp. 481–484).

The American individualism described by de Tocqueville is, on the whole, individualism in the "utilitarian" sense (Bellah et al. 1985), that is, political and economic individualism that makes people seek power for themselves and look out for their own financial interests. But de Tocqueville also spoke of the interactional consequences of this ideology, pointing out that Americans are less bound by social convention than are other nations: "Everyone behaves more or less after [his or her] own fashion, and a certain incoherence of manners always prevails, because they conform to the feelings and ideas of each individual rather than to an ideal example provided for everyone to imitate" (1966, p. 582). This second important strain of individualism, usually said to have arisen during the nineteenth century, has been referred to as "expressive individualism" (Bellah et al. 1985). Expressive individualism, associated with writers of the "American Renaissance" and the culture their work reflected, is the idea that freedom and authenticity result from looking inward to the self and expressing the truths one finds there.[9] One of the best-known expositions of the idea is Ralph Waldo Emerson's in "Self-Reliance" (1990, pp. 27–52).[10] "Nothing is at last sacred but the integrity of your own mind," Emerson wrote; a person should "go upright and vital, and speak the rude truth in all ways" (pp. 31–32). (Emerson spoke of "men" rather than "people," and it is not clear whether or to what extent nineteenth-century expressive individualism was meant, by men, to apply to women. Bean [1992] points out that nineteenth-century women were not viewed as individuals, being treated instead as types, while Brown [1990] argues that nineteenth-century individualism was intertwined with nineteenth-century domesticity, with its feminine values.)

Expressive individualism means relying on conscientious introspection as the source of judgments about truth and morality. Crucially, it also means finding ways to express these judgments. Freedom is the freedom to use language in new, idiosyncratic ways, to express oneself "against all constraints and conventions" (Bellah et al. 1985, p. 34). For Emerson, "The maker of a sentence . . . launches out into the infinite and builds a road into Chaos and old Night, and is followed by those who hear him with something of wild, creative delight" (*Journals*, October 18, 1834; quoted and discussed in Becker 1981). Walt Whitman expressed a similar conviction in his *American Primer*, a paean to the creative potential of American English: "The Real Grammar will be that which declares itself a nucleus of the spirit of the laws, with liberty to all to carry out the spirit of the laws, even by violating them, if necessary" (1987, p. 6). As the critic James Perrin Warren (1990) has shown, Whitman was influenced by the transcendentalist aesthetic linguistic theory of von Humboldt as it was somewhat inaccurately popularized at the time. Whitman wrote unpublished notes and published articles about language in which he discussed the idea of language as a "spiritual organism," evolving through a series of morphological strategies towards perfection, that expressed the spirit of a nation. English, he said (with no worse misunderstanding of the linguistics he read than most people's), allows more freedom for individual expression than do Greek or Latin, because ideas in English are connected not by inflection but rather with unbound lexical markers such as prepositions and conjunctions. Unlike writers in Greek or Latin, writers in English can connect ideas "any way we please" (Warren 1990, p. 46). In his poetry Whitman illustrated the creativity of the "Real Grammar" by using new foreign borrowings and by shifting existing English words into new morphological categories. "The general effect of all his verbal turnings," writes Warren, "is to dislodge words from any fixed grammatical categories in order to emphasize the 'floating and movable' possibilities of American English" (p. 47).

Americans continue to be individualists. Arieli (1964) traces the history of individualism in American political ideology, pointing out that although de Tocqueville disapproved of individualism, Americans commenting on de Tocqueville have consistently reinterpreted the term in a positive light (pp. 195–204). Reisman (1950) described the "autonomous character" as one of four American types; Varenne (1977) studied the interaction of expressive and utilitarian individualism in a town in Wisconsin. Bellah et al. (1985) interviewed representative Americans, finding them torn between individualism and commitment to community; the authors are critical of American individualism on moral grounds, believing that it is eating at the fabric of interdependence necessary for the health of a society. Recent literary and cultural critics condemn individualism as an epistemological illusion, historicizing literature and other cultural artifacts in order to show how defined and constrained people are by external forces. As two such critics put it, "from the latter half of the nineteenth century to the present, the individualist order of the modern Western world has met with challenges that have rendered its beliefs and doctrines problematic" (Heller and Wellbery, 1986, p. 1). The authors go on, however, to note that "especially in America, the poststructuralist critique of individuality has had only a feeble impact on the persistently individualist imagery of our institutions and popular culture" (p. 12).

Moral self-reliance and creative self-expression are seen by mainstream contemporary Americans as crucial for mental health and social acceptance. Sincerity is valued more than conformity, in speaking as in thinking, and even the most traditional forms of speech (such as wedding vows), which must elsewhere be repeated verbatim, are often seen as meaningless unless done differently by different people. "Playing a role" or speaking "lines" is dishonest, and not true to the self. What it means to be a "character" is not to play an ordained part, but rather the opposite; if someone is a "character," it is because she behaves differently from others and thus sets herself apart for special notice. It is insincere, rude, and, increasingly, illegal to treat a person as the filler of a role rather than as a distinct individual.[11] People persist in treating others as idiosyncratically motivated individuals even when they are not, as for example in the Jerzy Kosinski novel *Being There* (1972), in which the infantile protagonist mindlessly repeats whatever he hears and is taken for a creative genius.[12]

The required expression of individuality occurs in many modalities, among them language.[13] To use language completely idiosyncratically would be to be incomprehensible, but the existence in humans of strategies for figuring out what someone might mean even if one has not heard it said that way before means that it is possible to do idiosyncratic things with language. And, crucially for our purposes here, it is more polite to be idiosyncratic, to do things differently, than it is to be completely conventional, because being different means being engaged, paying attention to what one is doing, not "being a machine." This, then, is why politeness and discourse management strategies in the survey interviews take the varied form they do, rather than a more consistent, conventional form. Variation from individual to individual, in short, is polite, because Americans are culturally required to act as individuals and treat others as individuals. Self-expression is thus not only necessary for the psychological and rhetorical reasons uncovered in previous chapters; it is, for some, required for social reasons as well.

Consistency and
Individual Style

No institution plays a greater role than language in holding together the fabric of human society. At the same time, nothing is more intensely personal than the language habits of individuals, a tight-fitting yet flexible garment around the ego of each.

C. F. Hockett, *Refurbishing Our Foundations*

My discussion so far has been mainly about the various ways different people perform linguistic tasks we might in one way or another think of as the same. I have tried to show that different people do things differently with language even when they might be expected to do things similarly because doing things differently from others is how we express selfhood, and expressing selfhood is both an important function of talk and a prerequisite for successful talk. In this chapter I explore linguistic individuality from another perspective. Rather than asking, as I have up to now, how different people do the same thing, I ask here how the same people do different things. This is in order to suggest answers to some important and usually unasked questions about linguistic consistency. I am interested here in how individuals' styles are consistent across situations and how they are not, and I am interested in how people use consistency and inconsistency as strategic resources in the expression of moral personae.

The way a person comes across to others, the way he or she is known for being, is partly a result of using language in consistent ways. I mean by this not just that a person's physical voice is recognizable or that character and interests may lead one to bring up the same topics or express the same opinions repeatedly but that a person's linguistic choices are in some ways consistent no matter what the purpose of the talk is, who the audience is, or how planned and edited the speech or writing is. In other words, individuals have characteristic styles of talk, just as they have characteristic gaits, facial expressions, and ways of dressing. But some people seem to be more consistent than others. Some of us dress more or less the same no matter what the situation, whereas others change their appearances from occasion to occasion; similarly, some people are always relatively formal with language, or always casual, whereas others shift styles more markedly.

Inconsistency across language tasks figures in traditional thought about language use in a complicated way. On one hand, inconsistency is seen as bad. Inconsistency is part of what is meant when a person's writing is called stilted. Stilted writing and speech are pinched, too limited in their use of the resources of the author's idiosyncratic style. Talented writers, it is traditionally thought, are consistent; they let their own voices come across no matter what they are writing. Conversely, however, inconsistency is traditionally thought necessary for rhetorical flexibility. College writing courses encourage students to take on different styles for different tasks; self-effacing adaptation to audience is treated in many syllabi as much more important than the projection of a consistent personal voice. There are, in other words, strategic reasons for inconsistency.

I deal in what follows with speech and writing by two women, one of whom would strike even an untrained listener as remarkably—perhaps impressively, perhaps intimidatingly—consistent in speech as in other aspects of self-presentation, the other of whom would not, to the casual listener, seem markedly consistent. Using as a measure of consistency the amount of variability in the frequency of a number of features across a variety of genres, I show what accounts linguistically for the differences between the two. I then explore reasons for the differences, suggesting that ethical choices about how to be and act are expressed in linguistic choices, including the choice between relative consistency and relative inconsistency. The texts I scrutinize most closely are transcripts of the speech of Barbara Jordan, a former Texas state senator and U.S. congresswoman and now a professor of public policy. I also examine speech and writing by Sunny Nash, a novelist, writer of screenplays, historian, photographer and former jazz singer from Bryan, Texas. I came to collect data from Nash and Jordan because they are two of twelve public-language users who are part of a study I am engaged in with Judith Mattson Bean and Delma McLeod-Porter about resources for the expression of personal and regional identity in Texas. I singled out Barbara Jordan's talk for my present purposes because Jordan struck me, as she seems to strike everyone, as a person with a remarkably consistent style. I picked Sunny Nash's talk and writing because, as an African-American woman, she draws on some of the same linguistic and cultural resources as Jordan, but to very different effect; in the course of the analysis I discovered that the different effect is in large part due to Nash's quite deliberate flexibility of style.

The Barbara Jordan Style

Barbara Jordan came to prominence through astute politics partly conducted through public oratory that seems to her audiences both inspired and inspiring. Jordan was raised in a historically black neighborhood in Houston, to which she returned to practice law after graduating from college in Houston and law school in Boston. Most of her career has been in politics, however: Jordan was the first African-American woman elected to the Texas Senate and the first African-American woman from the South to serve in the U.S. House of Representatives. She first gained wide national attention as a result of the televised speech she gave in 1972 as a member of the House Judiciary Committee deliberating whether to impeach President Richard Nixon. While other committee members made political pitches, Jordan analyzed the Constitution. In 1976 Jordan gave the keynote address at the Democratic National Convention, and in 1992 she did so again. She is frequently interviewed for magazine and newspaper articles and on radio and TV, and her courses in the School of Public Policy at the University of Texas are immensely popular. She is seen as a model for African-Americans, for women, and for politicians and as an expert on governmental ethics.

The way Barbara Jordan talks is known as "the Barbara Jordan style." African-Americans who teach or have studied public speaking know what the term refers to, though the Barbara Jordan style has never to my knowledge been systematically analyzed. Both in public oratory and in face-to-face interviews, Jordan speaks slowly, in a low, intense voice, articulating clearly and making it apparent that she is choosing words carefully. But her fame as a public speaker is not just a result of her delivery. She projects tremendous personal authority in her speaking. She seems believable because of the strong, upstanding, powerful character she displays. This, I think, is what most contributes to her effectiveness. To use

MOST EDITED ....LEAST EDITED

prepared	edited	unedited
speeches	interviews	interview
(3,219 words)	(6,411 words)	(2,237 words)

Figure 5.1   Texts by Barbara Jordan

the terminology of Aristotelian rhetoric, Jordan's appeal is primarily ethical, primarily a result of the compellingly believable persona she presents.[1]

The Texts: Two Case Studies

Because I wanted to see what elements of Jordan's style were consistent across speech tasks, I examined six transcripts that range from her most public, formal speeches to a relatively relaxed, unedited oral interview. In all, I worked with 11,867 words of Jordan's speech. To offer a sense of how she sounds, I will provide excerpts from each text genre before describing my analysis of them. Figure 5.1 summarizes the text types I used.

My coworkers and I conducted the unedited interview in Jordan's University of Texas office in February 1992. One of our goals was to elicit, in this interview as in others we conducted for our Texas speech project, a variety of speech styles, but with Jordan we despaired for a time of doing so. Jordan sounded as careful and formal in her talk with us as in the speeches we had seen on videotape. At the end of the hour, however, she told a story about a recent visit with elementary-school children, during which her speech speeded up considerably and she pronounced several words in characteristically African-American ways. Jordan does, as will become clear, display a much smaller range of stylistic variation than do many other speakers, but we were in the end able to elicit the variety she had available for an interview. For this analysis, I use three excerpts from the interview, totaling 2,237 words in all. One is from the beginning of the interview, one is from the middle (pages 9 and 10 of the twenty-one-page transcript), and one is from the end. The excerpt that follows, from the middle of the interview, is about how politicians with Southern accents are perceived.

> BEAN: Do you think either he or you or any other Texas uh or southern speakers for that matter encounter some degree of prejudice as speakers? . . .

JORDAN: No one ever, no one has ever uh said anything in a negative sense about the uh the way the way I speak and I think that for some, a southern accent sounds uneducated.

BEAN: That's the impression.

JORDAN: And that is the impression that the listener gets and y- Jimmy Carter you know you're president of the United States and you have a heavy southern accent and people still do not excuse it. In my opinion they they do not and uh uh and you know Jimmy Carter was just a very bright person, mm some people would say brilliant, not Republicans would say brilliant but some people would say that.

(Interviewers laugh.)

BEAN: This is true.

JOHNSTONE: So should he have learned not to speak that way, or?

JORDAN: N- No, I think you talk the way you talk I and if if people are going to relate to you on the basis of how you talk that kind of a relationship is nonsubstantive to me and too much surface and I don't want to be friends with them anyway.

JOHNSTONE: Um-hm

JORDAN: Um that should have nothing in my opinion to do with the way you regard people.

JOHNSTONE: But it does, it did have to do with how people regarded Carter.

JORDAN: Yes it did, and that was unfortunate.

JOHNSTONE: Just his, his misfortune, there's nothing he should have done about it.

JORDAN: No.

JOHNSTONE: Hmm. *(Waits.)*

JORDAN: There probably wasn't anything he could do about it.

JOHNSTONE: I think you're right. There probably wasn't.

JORDAN: Yeah.

On the other end of the spectrum, I analyzed published transcripts of two samples of Jordan's formal public oratory: excerpts from her House Judiciary Committee speech about the Nixon impeachment (1,415 words) and her Democratic Convention keynote speech of 1976 (1,804 words). These represent speech having a different purpose than our interview and with a different audience (viewers of national TV in both cases). The settings were also less intimate, and Jordan had time in both cases to plan, edit, and revise what she was going to say. Jordan claims not to write out her speeches in advance but rather to work from note cards, and material in her archives at Texas Southern University bears her out; notes for her many speeches typically consist of brief phrases and quotations. But though the speeches cannot be said to be written, they represent Jordan's speech at its most planned. To check that the printed transcripts I used corresponded to what Jordan actually said, I audited both speeches on videotape as well. The following excerpt is from the beginning of the House Judiciary Committee speech:

> "We the people"—it is a very eloquent beginning. But when the Constitution of the United States was completed on the seventeenth of September in 1787, I was not included in that "We, the people." I felt for many years that somehow George Washington and Alexander Hamilton just left me out by mistake. But through the process of amendments, interpretation, and court decision, I have finally been included in "We, the people."
>
> Today I am an inquisitor. I believe hyperbole would not be fictional and would not overstate the solemnness that I feel right now. My faith in the Constitution is whole, it is complete, it is total. I am not going to sit here and be an idle spectator to the diminution, the subversion, the destruction of the Constitution.
>
> "Who can so properly be the inquisitors for the nation as the representatives of the nation themselves?" [The Federalist Papers, No. 65] The subject of its jurisdiction are those offenses which proceed from the misconduct of public men. . . . In other words, the jurisdiction comes from the abuse or violation of some public trust. It is wrong, I suggest, it is a misreading of the Constitution for any member here to assert that for a member to vote for an Article of Impeachment means that the member must be convinced that the President should be removed from office. The Constitution doesn't say that. The powers relating to impeachment are an essential check in the hands of this body, the legislature, against and upon the encroachment of the Executive. In establishing the division between the two branches of the legislature, the House and the Senate, assigning to the one the right to accuse and the other the right to judge—the framers of this Constitution were very astute. They did not make the accusers and the judges the same persons.

In the middle of the spontaneous-to-planned continuum, I examined three published interviews with Jordan, two conducted by journalists and one by a professor. Linguists will object that such interviews are edited and thus do not represent exactly the words Jordan (or the interviewer) said. But this was precisely the point of choosing to analyze them. I wanted to see whether elements of Jordan's style would carry over even into texts edited by others, for a variety of general audiences. If characteristics of syntax, word choice, and discourse marking repeatedly survive cutting and recasting by different editors for different readers, then we can be sure they sound distinctive to others as well as to us. One of these short interviews appeared in a collection of conversations with prominent people published at the time of the U.S. Bicentennial (Murchland 1987, pp. 39–49; Jordan's speech totals 2,818 words), one was an interview in the weekly news magazine *Time* (Angelo 1991; 1,725 words), and one was an interview conducted by Liz Carpenter, an old Texas friend, in the general-circulation feminist magazine *Ms* (Carpenter 1985; 1,868 words). In this excerpt from the Murchland interview, Jordan discusses amendments to the U.S. Constitution.

INTERVIEWER: So I take it you would not be opposed to amendments.

JORDAN: I would not be *per se* opposed to amendments. But the next question is: Well, what amendments would you like to see added to the Constitution. I don't have any of my own, and I don't see any proposed that I would like to have added.

INTERVIEWER: What about the Equal Rights Amendment? I read somewhere that you favored that amendment.

JORDAN: When I was in Congress I supported ERA because I was in favor of what it stood for. But as an amendment it would be redundant. All of our basic rights are covered in the Constitution or in existing amendments.

INTERVIEWER: Many people suggest something should be done about the length of terms of office for elected politicians.

JORDAN: I don't agree with that either. I know there are those who think representatives ought to be elected for a four-year term. I don't. If I hadn't been running for reelection every two years when I was in Congress, I wouldn't have been getting on an airplane and returning to my district every other week. I think that was the original idea. This is the people's house, and the representatives who serve them have got to make themselves present to the people and hear their concerns, and represent them at the federal level. I say *re-present* because that is what a representative is. And it works the other way, too. The issues that are debated in Washington have to be represented to the people to get their views on them. I think the Founders were very wise in establishing this avenue of exchange between the people and the government and I wouldn't want to see it changed.

In order to be able to make some suggestions about the role of consistency in the speech of a person who presents a self quite different from Jordan's, I also examined texts by Sunny Nash. Nash is an African-American in her forties. She grew up in Bryan, a small city in east-central Texas, and graduated from Texas A&M University as one of its first African-American female students. Her bachelor's was in journalism, and she has worked as a reporter, editor, and TV and radio producer. She has also been a musician, performing advertising jingles in San Antonio and singing jazz in clubs in Houston and New York. Most recently she has worked in photography and as a free-lance writer, writing short memoirs and articles on African-American history for the Bryan newspaper and the *Houston Post* and occasional longer pieces based on personal history for the *Houston Chronicle*, one of which she turned into a short story published in an anthology of stories by Texas women. She also briefly published and edited a desk-top-produced magazine for the local African-American community. She now lives in the Los Angeles area, where she is collaborating on a screenplay based on African-American history and writing for a Western history magazine.

I used part or all of six samples of Nash's language for this analysis. As with Jordan, I took excerpts from the beginning, middle, and end of the unedited transcript of the interview my colleagues and I conducted with Nash for the Texas speech project. My research design would have been neater if I had been able to use the same two other genres of Nash's discourse as of Jordan's: published interviews by others and prepared speeches. But to do this would have muted precisely the facts I am interested in about the two voices. Nash and Jordan do not do the same things with language, and their choices of media are self-expressive choices. (Jordan is not primarily a writer, for example; though she does of course write, she prefers the immediacy of oral expression.) Even the two conversational interviews, though conducted by the same people with the same purposes, were in fact quite different. The Nash interview was full of talk by all, laughter, and the sharing of personal experience. Its tone was that of acquaintances talking over coffee. This excerpt from the transcript, in which we talk about one of Nash's screenplays, is from the middle of the interview.

> NASH: Day before yesterday (*laughs*), I got a letter, (*laughs*) from a Hollywood producer, her name was Romelle Foster-Owens, and she's an independent producer, and she was, she studied at the American Film Institute in Hollywood, and she's won lots of awards, and she's very legitimate—she got hold of this script from somebody who had had it and they got it from somebody else—it's registered so it can float around for years—she got it, and read it, and really liked it, and so, based on the fact that we had gone through the pro- through the trouble of registering it, and having several drafts done, she went through it, and critiqued it, and sent me thirty pages of notes.
>
> BEAN: Wow. (*laughs*)
>
> NASH: Saying "If you can, if you can turn this around in two weeks we'll we'll we'll uh sign an option on it." (*laughs*)
>
> JOHNSTONE: Thirty pages of notes!
>
> NASH: I'm saying there, I was in Dallas the last couple of days, and I took my laptop with me, and I, "Oh I'm gonna work on it," right? And I just sat there, I was so stunned by these notes I couldn't believe, all the stuff that I might have to *do*. Now I'll have to call her and tell her if she'll give me three weeks I'll do it.

I also looked at excerpts from two newspaper pieces based on Nash's or her family's history, one about her former father-in-law (Nash 1986) and one about a fiddler who was her grandmother's cousin (Nash 1993b). These are written in an informal narrative style that seems on casual inspection to emulate conversation in some ways. This excerpt from the 1986 article describes tent meetings organized by traveling faith healers:

Curious listeners, serious worshipers and restless children crammed hot, musty meeting places. Raspy voices yelled to the heavens and sang off key. Oil lamps flickering dimly against tired faces, the slight discomfort of body heat and the humble odor of overworked muscles created an atmosphere full of mystery. Desperate and despairing souls clung to the edge of their hard benches waiting to see a miracle.

From the congregation, a planted spectator who professed blindness or other affliction was led forward by the healing preacher's helper.

The healing preacher laid a sweaty palm on the "afflicted" and with a lion's voice made the rafters rumble. Through the quake, tiny flakes of plaster fell from the ceiling upon the crying worshipers. Amen! A woman overcome with emotion slumped aisleward in a spastic heap. Shrieking until his voice vanished, the healing preacher sprinkled the pretender with water from a small bottle. Worshipers whispered praise until the room fell dead in silence when the lame pretender ascended to human perfection.

Nash's most formal style is that of her historical pieces, of which I selected three: an article about photographs of turn-of-the-century slave descendants in the area (Nash 1992a), one about the lives of former slaves at the end of the nineteenth century (Nash 1992b), and a short piece in her magazine *Legacy* about the history of the African-American holiday Kwanzaa (Nash 1992c). Here she describes Kwanzaa:

Kwanzaa emerged during an era when African people in the United States and other parts of the world were in turbulent change. It was the 1960s when people were struggling for civil rights, yelling *black power*, protesting wholesale drafting of Black males into Vietnam and searching for racial identity.

In response, sociologist, **Dr. Maulana Karenga** fathered **Kwanzaa** some 25 years ago. Significant during the traditional Christmas season because it begins on December 26, **Kwanzaa** is Swahili for *first fruits*. The celebration, which lasts until January 1, is neither religious nor political. Based on seven principles, *Nguzo Saba*, the cultural holiday celebrates the heritage of Americans of African descent. Thought by many to have been borrowed from African custom, **Kwanzaa** is celebrated only in the United States of America.

According to an *Our Texas* article by **Angela Ransome**, University of North Texas, each day of **Kwanzaa** a different principle is celebrated. *Karamu* or *the feast* on December 31 is the most important day of the **Kwanzaa** celebration because all of the **Kwanzaa** principles are demonstrated.

In all, I looked at 3,972 words of text from Nash. Figure 5.2 summarizes them.

Linguistic Correlates of Personal Authority

It would of course be impossible to describe every element of the style of these texts, or even every element of their syntax, the level on which I will concentrate. So I take the approach taken in many studies of literary style: I describe a salient effect and test hypotheses about its probable linguistic causes. Thus I begin by looking for possible linguistic causes of the most consistent rhetorical effect Barbara Jordan produces: her compelling claim to be believed because of who she is. Having identified twenty-five features of word choice and syntax that I thought might characterize an authoritative style such as Jordan's, I counted their occurrence in all the Jordan texts and in the texts by Nash to see if these were in fact relevant factors. Nash's rhetorical appeal is not primarily based on *ethos*—she tends to support claims by telling stories—so features that she and Jordan used about equally often are probably not the ones that make Jordan sound authoritative. I then compared the various texts by Jordan with one another to see whether the impression Jordan gives of consistency of style was reflected in consistency in the use of these features. I did the same with the Nash texts to examine patterns of consistency there.

What might Jordan be doing with language, other than speaking deliberately and clearly, to create and reflect the powerful aura of personal authority I have described? In the first place, a speaker whose appeal rests on being perceived as a moral and intellectual authority probably encourages less overt negotiation of meaning with the audience than would a speaker whose appeal was more egalitarian. (Though the meaning of an utterance is always a matter of negotiation, the audience's con-

MOST EDITED ....LEAST EDITED

| historical articles (1,805 words) | personal memoirs (1,130 words) | unedited interview (1,037 words) |

Figure 5.2   Texts by Sunny Nash

tribution to the determination of what a speaker means is sometimes not highly valued and hence not very overt. To give just one example, midwesterners apparently value overt audience suggestions about the points of others' spontaneous stories less than do New Yorkers, as evidenced by relative paucity of commentary and evaluative backchanneling when a story is being told [Johnstone 1990b]). A speaker claiming personal authority might be expected to be fairly detached from her audience, relatively likely to be making assertions of fact and relatively unlikely to be engaging in phatic attempts to create rapport. She might also sound—as Barbara Jordan unquestionably does—formal, precise, and careful rather than informal or relaxed the way a more audience-centered, rapport-building speaker might.

To develop hypotheses about what these characteristics might amount to syntactically, I turned to the work of Douglas Biber (1988), who analyzed hundreds of English texts to determine the dimensions along which they differ. One dimension uncovered through Biber's analysis is the one he labels "Involved versus Informational Production." Texts at one end of this dimension—samples of academic prose, press reports, sports broadcasts—had relatively many nouns, prepositional phrases, and attributive adjectives, relatively long words, and a relatively high proportion of word types to word tokens, indicating a varied vocabulary. These features can all be correlated with the density of information in a text and the carefulness of its encoding. Texts at the other end—casual chats, business conversations—were verbal rather than nominal in style and represented more overt attempts to involve speaker and audience with each other. They were characterized by relatively high frequencies of the present tense, by relatively many verbs like *think* and *feel*, which express private states of knowledge and emotion, by relatively many *wh-* questions and emphatics and amplifiers, and by relatively many first- and second-person pronouns, all of which reflect the face-to-face phatic exchange of conversation.

"Involved" texts were also characterized by relative fragmentation, syntactic reduction, and "generalized or uncertain presentation of information" (Biber 1988, p. 106): they contained contractions and stranded final prepositions (*the person I talked to* rather than *the person to whom I talked*) and hedges. *Well* and *anyway* got these texts back on track when coherence began to derail. They used *do* rather than more explicit verbs, and *it* and demonstrative (e.g., *this, these*) and indefinite pronouns (e.g., *some, anything*) rather than more explicit noun phrases. Clauses were loosely connected with coordinators such as *and*, *but*, and *or*, rather than being more tightly connected through subordination; *be* appeared as a main verb relatively frequently (*the car was red*), substituting for tighter ways of expressing attribution (*the red car*). Certain kinds of subordination were used to convey speakers' feelings and attitudes.

Bearing in mind characteristics of my data (for example, one interviewer's asking Jordan to reminisce about her past would skew her verb tenses strongly away from the present, so I did not count present-tense verbs), I selected from among these features a set of seventeen, most of which I suspected might put all the Jordan texts on the informational, noninvolved end of the scale. Table 5.1 lists these features.

The second set of features that I suspected might contribute to the impression of personal authority in Jordan's speech are features correlated with speaking with confidence and with showing that one's confidence is based on faith in one's own thoughts and feelings. The stance an authoritative speaker like Jordan takes vis-à-vis the claims she makes is likely, I hypothesized, to display certainty about their truth. Such a speaker argues from personal principle and experience, rather than from external authority. To do this, she probably needs to refer to herself and to private cognitive and emotional states, saying things like *I believe* or *we felt*. I thus looked at Jordan's uses of first-person pronouns and what Biber (1988, p. 105) calls "private verbs": *think*, *feel*, and so on. In the case of first-person plural pronouns, I was interested not only in their number but in whether they were inclusive (*we* meaning you and I and perhaps others) or exclusive (*we* meaning others and I but not you).

An additional way of expressing confidence is to choose verbs, adjectives, and adverbs that convey certainty. To identify these, I used lists of "certainty verbs," "certainty adverbs," "certainty adjectives," emphatics, and predictive modals developed by Biber and Finegan (1989) in a study of "styles of stance" in English. (For complete lists of these, see Biber and Finegan 1989, pp. 119–122.) Table 5.2 lists all eight stance features I looked for.

Barbara Jordan: Speaking Consistently from Moral Authority

Barbara Jordan's speech turned out to differ from Sunny Nash's in some but not all of the ways I expected it to. Jordan's talk is, as I hypothesized, similar in several respects to the kinds of texts Biber labels "informational." The highlighted lines in table 5.3 display the relevant figures. Jordan used more long words than did Nash (3.76 per 100 words overall to Nash's 2.48), especially in the relatively unedited, spontaneous speech of our face-to-face interview, where there were more than twice as many words of four or more syllables than in the Nash interview (2.59 per 100

Table 5.1   Features of Informational,
Noninvolved Discourse

Feature	Hypothesis
Information is integrated, dense, carefully encoded	
1. nouns	many
2. words of 4 or more syllables	many
3. type-to-token ratio of long words*	high (great variety)
4. prepositions	many
5. attributive adjectives	many
Audience is not overtly interacted with	
6. second-person pronouns	few
7. *wh-* questions	few
8. sentence relatives	few
Text is explicit, nonreduced	
9. *that* deletion in relative clauses, as complementizer	infrequent
10. contractions	infrequent
11. *do* used as pro-verb	infrequently
12. stranded final prepositions	infrequent
13. indefinite pronouns	infrequent
14. demonstrative pronouns	infrequent
Text is coherent, not fragmented	
15. *be* used as main verb	infrequently
16. clauses coordinated	infrequently
17. *well; anyway*	infrequent

*Biber's finding was that integrated, dense texts were characterized by high type-to-token ratios of all words, not just words of four or more syllables. But the potential for lexical variety increases, roughly speaking, as words get longer: there are more ways to express the abstract concepts encoded in "big words" than there are to express the meanings of articles, pronouns, and such. Since calculating type-to-token ratios of all words would have been too cumbersome for the equipment I had available, I did the calculation only for the long words, on the theory that this would result in roughly the same information.

Table 5.2   Certain Personal Stance Features

Feature	Hypothesis
Makes reference to self	
1. first-pers. sing. pronouns	many
2. first-pers. pl. pronouns	many
inclusive/exclusive?	exclusive
Refers to own thoughts, feelings	
3. "private verbs" such as *think, believe, feel*	many
Expresses certainty	
4. certainty verbs such as *ascertain, know, prove*	many
5. certainty adverbs such as *actually, of course, unquestionably*	many
6. certainty adjectives such as *evident, true, unmistakable*	many
7. emphatics such as *a lot, for sure, so* + ADV. or ADJ.	many
8. predictive modals *will, would, shall*	many

words versus 1.11).[2] In the interview, Jordan used more than twice as many attributive adjectives as did Nash (2.82 per 100 words versus 1.27), though in the edited samples Nash used far more. Overall, Jordan used slightly fewer contractions (though, of course, in transcribing speech the choice between a contraction and a noncontracted form is often difficult). Excerpts from the interviews give a sense of these differences. Long words are in boldface; attributive adjectives, italicized. In the first of these Jordan was responding to a question about regional differences in political campaigning.

Table 5.3   Noninvolved, Informational Features in Jordan and Nash Texts (feature/100 words unless otherwise indicated; raw numbers in parentheses)

	JORDAN *unedited interview*	NASH *unedited interview*	JORDAN *edited speech*	NASH *edited writing*	JORDAN *all texts*	NASH *all texts*
nouns	13.05 (292)	12.59 (229)	19.62 (1893)	32.39 (702)	18.41 (2185)	23.99 (929)
long words	2.59 (58)	1.11 (20)	4.03 (388)	3.51 (76)	3.76 (446)	2.48 (96)
prepositions	7.86 (176)	7.31 (132)	10.13 (976)	11.21 (241)	9.71 (1152)	9.63 (373)
attrib. adj.	2.82 (63)	1.27 (23)	3.73 (359)	8.54 (185)	3.56 (422)	5.37 (208)
2nd-pers. pron.	2.01 (45)	1.61 (29)	0.91 (88)	0.04 (1)	1.12 (133)	0.77 (30)
wh- questions	0.04 (1)	0.05 (1)	0.20 (19)	0	0.15 (20)	0.02 (1)
sentence relatives (#)	0	0	1	0	1	0
that deletion (%)	47 (15/32)	18 (2/11)	37 (60/160)	9 (1/11)	39 (75/192)	14 (3/22)
contractions	3.22 (72)	5.26 (95)	1.02 (98)	0.78 (17)	1.43 (170)	2.89 (112)
do as pro-verb	0.80 (18)	1.72 (31)	0.56 (54)	0	0.61 (72)	0.80 (31)
stranded final preps.	0.22 (5)	0.16 (3)	0.05 (5)	0	0.08 (10)	0.08 (3)
indef. pron.	0.98 (22)	0.72 (31)	0.35 (34)	0.50 (11)	0.47 (56)	0.61 (24)
demonstr. pron.	1.56 (35)	1.00 (18)	1.14 (110)	0.14 (3)	1.22 (145)	0.54 (21)
be as main verb	2.86 (64)	1.99 (36)	3.19 (308)	1.71 (37)	3.13 (372)	1.88 (73)
clauses coordinated	4.69 (105)	4.10 (74)	1.43 (138)	0.37 (8)	2.05 (243)	2.12 (82)
well/anyway (#)	7/1	4/1	5/0	0/0	12/1	4/1

Oh, I think uh it's not so much the style of campaigning, the issues are different. The issues of **womanizing**, to take one *current* one, are responded to differently, **regionally**, in my opinion. That you will find in the South more people, and this may be too much of a **generalization** but I am not sure, more people who place a *greater* store in *marital* **fidelity** than some other regions, now that may or may not be true but I get that sense, and the polls will indicate something like this if you will look at some *national* Gallup or Harris and how people have responded to the uh **machinations** of the Clinton uh you may find some difference in how that is regarded. So the issues, the *political* issues I think may play out differently **regionally**, rather than campaign styles.

This fairly typical contribution by Jordan in spontaneous interview talk displays how her use of long words and adjectives results in denser, more compact presentation of information than other choices might. For example, in *one current one* an attributive adjective helps make the phrase shorter than *one that is current* or *one that people are talking about now* would be. The expression *marital fidelity*, a long legalistic term modified by an adjective, is more compact than the possible alternatives *being faithful to one's spouse* or *not fooling around*.

An excerpt, also about regional differences, from our interview with Nash gives some impression of how her speech contrasts in these respects with Jordan's, offering new information at a slower rate and in less compact fashion. She had been asked whether she noticed anything different about New Yorkers' style of talk when she was living there. (Aware that she was dealing in stereotypes, Nash was being somewhat facetious here.)

It's, has to do with phrasing, like, uh the way people cluster words together. The speed with which they speak. I found that people in New York do speak a lot faster than people in Texas. And they speak while they're moving. They *(laughter)* they're s- they're moving along and "Da da da da da" and and I I've heard the tail end of many sentences in New York *(laughing)* because pe- We stop and we make ourselves perfectly understood and we speak at a, at a speed that we can understand so therefore, we hope that other people can too. But it doesn't seem to be as important to, as far as I can see in New York it doesn't seem to be as important that people understand what other people are telling them. There's a lot of hand gesturing and just a lot of movement. . . .

There are examples in this extract of relatively self-conscious, planned syntax ("the speed with which they speak," for example, or the elaborate conjunction "so therefore"); the difference between Jordan's and Nash's styles in the interviews is not just that Nash was more casual and Jordan more formal. Information emerges clause by clause here, rather than being packed into brief phrases. Neither Jordan or Nash had previously been asked the questions to which these excerpts are responses; both were speaking spontaneously. But here as elsewhere in the interview, Jordan seemed always to plan her answers before uttering them. Nash, on the other hand, planned as she went along, speaking faster and adapting phrase by phrase to the audience's responses. The result is that Nash's response is less dense, less tightly "informational," and, as suggested by our laughter during it, somewhat more entertaining.

Turning to the features I suspected might mark certainty of stance (table 5.4), we find, as I expected, that Jordan employed more of almost all of them. In spontaneous speech, edited speech, and overall, there is consistently more expression of certainty by means of verbs and adverbials such as *know* and *of course* (neither Jordan nor Nash used many certainty adjectives), more predictive modals such as *will* and *would*, and many more "private verbs" such as *believe* and *feel* in the first person. In the edited excerpts (the transcripts of speeches and the edited interviews), Jordan used more first-person pronouns, singular and plural, than did Nash, though in spontaneous talk Nash used first-person singular forms more. (This reflects the fact that her responses to almost all our questions were autobiographical, her primary line of argument being from personal experience.) The only certainty features Nash used slightly more than Jordan were the ones that make the least overt claim to personal authority: emphatics like *just* and *so* or *such* in *so important* or *such a good idea*.

The Jordan excerpt includes several markers of certain stance: *I think* (twice), *I get that sense*, three uses of *will*. She was making a distinct display of hedged uncertainty here ("this may be too much of a generalization"; "that may or may not be true"), but the fact that the authority for her claims comes from her own knowledge and moral belief is still apparent.

But there are a number of features of informational texts that the Jordan material does not share, and in some ways Jordan's talk seems rather more audience-centered than, as I hypothesized, the converse. These characteristics of Jordan's style can, however, also be seen to contribute to her particular authoritativeness.

For one thing, while Jordan's spontaneous interview talk sounds in

Table 5.4   Authoritative Stance Features in Jordan and Nash
Texts (feature/100 words unless otherwise indicated; raw
numbers in parentheses)

	JORDAN *unedited interview*	NASH *unedited interview*	JORDAN *edited speech*	NASH *edited writing*	JORDAN *all texts*	NASH *all texts*
1st-person singular pronouns	8.09 (181)	10.25 (185)	2.62 (252)	1.01 (22)	3.64 (433)	5.21 (207)
1st-person plural pronouns	0.49 (11)	0.44 (8)	2.60 (250)	0.23 (5)	2.19 (261)	0.33 (13)
% incl.	9	37	81	0	78	23
% excl.	82	63	16	0	18	38
% other	9	0	3	100	4	38
private verbs	1.87 (42)	0.77 (14)	2.46 (237)	0.01 (2)	2.35 (279)	0.40 (16)
certainty verbs	0.49 (11)	0.33 (6)	0.35 (43)	0.23 (5)	0.37 (45)	0.27 (11)
certainty adverbs	0.40 (9)	0.17 (3)	0.10 (10)	0 (0)	0.16 (19)	0.07 (3)
certainty adjectives	0.18 (4)	0.11 (2)	0.02 (2)	0.05 (1)	0.05 (6)	0.07 (3)
emphatics	1.21 (27)	1.38 (25)	0.66 (64)	0.46 (10)	0.76 (91)	0.88 (35)
predictive modals	1.03 (23)	0.89 (16)	1.11 (107)	0.23 (5)	1.09 (130)	0.53 (21)

some ways *more* planned and edited than Nash's, her planned, nonspontaneous discourse sounds in many ways *less* edited than that of Nash. Although Jordan uses more nouns and attributive adjectives in relatively unedited talk than does Nash, thus compressing information more than Nash does, she uses fewer nouns and attributive adjectives in the planned, edited samples. In unedited speech, Jordan uses the relatively noninformational *do* as a main verb half as much as Nash does (Nash says "You got to *do* some more," for example, rather than "write some more" or "prepare some more"); in the edited samples Nash always chooses more informational verbs while Jordan uses *do* at an only slightly lower rate than she does in spontaneous talk. In both edited and unedited modes, Jordan uses demonstrative pronouns (*this*, *those*, and so on) more than Nash does; these are often said to characterize talk whose interpretation requires immediate context, like face-to-face conversation, rather than more context-free, noninvolved talk. Particularly striking are the demonstrative pronouns in short style-shifted codas that Jordan appends again and again to long, carefully worded sentences. Here are two examples from her 1976 Democratic convention speech and one from our interview:

> We believe that the people are the source of all governmental power; that the authority of the people is to be extended, not restricted. This can be accomplished only by providing each citizen with every opportunity to participate in the management of the government. They must have **that**.

> We have a positive vision of the future founded on the belief that the gap between the promise and reality of America can one day be finally closed. We believe **that**.

> I did not learn to speak differently, I learned to think, in law school, that was the, the difference. I cou- I, I stopped, I stopped writing from the surface of my mind and decided to go inside and see if there was really something there because it was important, to get to the bottom of an idea and be able to uh uh make it hold up in uh legalese, in legal argument. **That** was important.

Jordan connects clauses with the relatively nonexplicit coordinators *and*, *but*, and *or* somewhat more frequently than does Nash in spontaneous talk, and almost three times as often in edited talk. She uses the transition marker *well* more often than Nash does in unedited speech and is the only one to use it in edited talk. In sum, Jordan's edited samples are much more like her spontaneous speech than are Nash's, much less edited-sounding.

This has something to do with the fact that Jordan does not, in fact, write out even her most formal speeches. Jordan's decision not to prepare her speeches completely in advance is evidence of the value she places on extemporaneous oral articulateness, an attitude that comes from the preaching tradition of the Baptist church (her father was a minister), from her high school and college debate training, and from her training as a lawyer. Her presence and that of her audience are, for her, the source of the power of her words: "after [a speech] is given," she told us, "it's dead." It should be clear from the samples of Jordan's speech reproduced earlier that what she values is not just the ability to think of something to say in any situation but the ability to think of the one *right* thing to say and to phrase it accurately, precisely, and with meticulous care. By choosing to speak extemporaneously rather than read from a script and by choosing to speak on preplanned occasions the same way she does on unplanned ones, Jordan makes displays of easy thought-fulness and mastery of language. This contributes to her aura of personal authority.

Jordan also uses *you* and its variants more than does Nash, especially in the edited samples, and *you* refers to a person in the speaker's presence, not an indefinite "one," more often for Jordan than for Nash. Jordan also uses *we* and its variants more often, and many more of Jordan's *wes* are inclusive, meaning "you and I" rather than "others and I." The effect of Jordan's inclusive *wes* can be sensed in this extract about freedom, taken from one of the edited interviews:

> You have to start with the basic freedoms of speech, the press, assembly and so forth. All else flows from that. Freedom is the linchpin of **our** federal system. When **we** get to the Fourteenth Amendment **we** get the incorporation of equality into the basic ethos of this country. But **we** can't be equal unless **we** are free.

While I expected that Jordan's style would involve less overt interaction with her audience than Nash's less authoritative style, it in fact seems to involve more. I think the explanation for this is in the particularly situated nature of her appeal and in her conception of her ultimate audience. The truth, for Jordan, is not to be discerned in abstractions; it is here and now, in this interaction. Her authority is a result of her effect on *you*, her audience, in *our* shared experience of her talk. But Jordan's audience is never limited to the people sitting in the room with her. Always a public speaker, she always appears to be speaking for the record, to her "fellow Americans."

Jordan also uses more *wh-* questions than does Nash. Asking questions could be seen as a way of involving one's audience, making hearers responsible for meaning and thus relinquishing a degree of personal authority. But the involvement of the audience here is symbolic, an artifact of Jordan's being much more overt about attempting to persuade than Nash is. Jordan's questions are all rhetorical, not questions to which she expects the audience's answers. "How many times do you read of a defection by Americans to some other form of government?" she asks in the Murchland interview. "Who can so properly be the inquisitors for the nation as the representatives of the nation themselves?" she quotes Madison in the Judiciary Committee speech. In contrast, Nash consciously attempts not to persuade but rather to lay out facts and let them speak for themselves. This is because, she told us, "I have found that we as African-Americans have been accused of being emotional about *everything*. And therefore, you start to lose the material, you lose the event, you lose the point in the emotion."

A final feature of Jordan's talk that seemed surprising at first, in light of my expectations that her style would be denser and more integrated than Nash's, was her frequent use of *be* as main verb. *Be* conveys a great deal less information than do other verbs, and it is often used in situations in which there is a more concise alternative. To say "the car *is* red" and then to say something about it conveys less information per word than to say something about "the red car." But Jordan's main-verb use of *be* has to do with another fact about this verb: copular *be* is useful in stating universal, eternal truths. The statement of such truths, with the implicit claim to the authority to do so, is very much a part of Jordan's style.[3]

To summarize, with the aid of hypotheses based on Biber and Finegan's work on styles and speech stance, we have uncovered a number of features of Jordan's style that differentiate her talk quite clearly from that of Sunny Nash. We have noted in passing that some of these differences are more marked in less edited speech, some in more edited speech; some of the differences have in fact to do with the amount of difference between the two modes. Let us now turn to a closer examination of similarity and difference between the two individuals' texts and genres.

To make it possible to compare degrees of similarity across speech samples, we first need a way of calculating stylistic consistency. The texts by Jordan and by Nash can be divided into three categories. One category consists of the spontaneous interview. Another consists of each speaker's most edited, formal discourse. For Jordan, this is her public speeches; for Nash, her historical essays. In between is an intermediate category: Jordan's written, edited interviews and Nash's personal memoirs. Figures 5.1 and 5.2, cited earlier, display the texts ranged from most to least edited. I selected eighteen of the twenty-five speech features analyzed earlier to count. These were features that occurred in at least two of the three text types by Jordan (for example, sentence relatives, of which she used only one, were excluded) and for which frequencies per hundred words of text could be calculated. (Deletions of the complementizer *that*, for which the appropriate calculation is the proportion of deleted *thats* to possible *thats* rather than deletions per hundred words, were excluded, for example.) For these eighteen features, frequencies were noted for each speaker and each text type. If the lowest figure for each feature is subtracted from the highest, we arrive at a number that represents the degree of difference between text types. Having this number we can compare the degree of difference between text types for Nash and Jordan.[4] For example, Jordan used 13.05 nouns per hundred words in the spontaneous interview, 18.28 in the edited interviews, and 22.39 in the planned speeches. Subtracting 13.05 (the lowest figure) from 22.39 (the highest) yields 9.34. Nash's use of nouns ranges from 12.59 in the spontaneous interview to 34.00 in the most formal texts, giving a difference of 21.41. Thus, Nash's texts differ from one another in their use of nouns more than twice as much as do Jordan's. In other words, Jordan is twice as consistent as Nash in the proportion of her words that are nouns.

The figures that result from this procedure are displayed in table 5.5. On the whole, the three text types differ from each other, for both speakers, in the ways one would expect. Both Jordan and Nash use more nouns, long words, prepositions, and adjectives in more formal styles than in the unedited interviews. Both use the most contractions, coordinate the most clauses, use *do* as a pro-verb the most, and use first-person pronouns the most in the interviews. In fact, for Nash, the linguistic progression from least to intermediate to most edited discourse corresponds in almost every respect with what Biber and many other students of the linguistic effects of spontaneity versus planning would lead us to expect. For Jordan there are three anomalies: contrary to what one might expect, she uses *wh-* questions, private verbs, and first-person plural pronouns more in the most planned texts than in the less planned ones.

Differences in the speakers' degrees of consistency are striking. Jordan's style is more consistent across text types than is Nash's for twelve of the eighteen features I tabulated and less consistent for only six. Table 5.6 lists these features. In most of the ways I have looked at, Jordan's style varies less depending on audience and situation than does Nash's. This finding confirms my own and many others' casual impression of Jordan's speech. Her consistency is perhaps the principal reason she strikes people the way she does, as a strong, authoritative person whose word can be believed. That she makes relatively little concession to circumstance in her linguistic style, as indeed in her dress and carriage and in the content of her talk, is taken as a sign of moral constancy.

Jordan's speech is consistent with itself within texts, too: once she chooses the mot juste for a concept, she uses the same word again and again. I calculated type-to-token ratios (comparing how many *different* words of a given type there were with how many words altogether of that type) for the two sets of individual lexical items I had examined in the texts: words of four or more syllables and private verbs. For both sets,

Table 5.5   Range of Frequencies of Features Across Text Types (lowest number/100 words subtracted from highest; figure indicating greater consistency italicized)

Feature	Jordan	Nash
nouns	9.34	21.41
long words	*2.53*	5.35
prepositions	*2.34*	5.03
attributive adjectives	*1.45*	7.60
second-person pronouns	1.86	*1.61*
wh- questions	0.21	*0.05*
contractions	*2.94*	4.76
do as pro-verb	*0.34*	1.72
indefinite pronouns	0.70	*0.34*
demonstrative pronouns	*0.63*	0.92
be as main verb	0.89	*0.49*
coordinate clauses	*3.64*	3.84
first-person singular pronouns	6.79	10.25
first-person plural pronouns	2.80	*0.34*
private verbs	2.97	*0.77*
certainty verbs	*0.18*	0.29
emphatics	*0.75*	1.19
predictive modals	*0.10*	0.89

Jordan's type-to-token ratios were considerably smaller than Nash's, as table 5.7 shows. While Nash's word choice is relatively varied, Jordan tends to reuse words once she has chosen them. This reflects the concern she expressed in our interview with finding the right word:

> [T]he beauty of, of expression is finding the, the right word [where] really no other word would suffice for communicating that idea. That's what appeals to me about language.

Jordan's repeated use of carefully selected and precisely articulated multisyllabic words is one way she displays this concern.

Sunny Nash: Inconsistency and Pragmatic Flexibility

Nash's spontaneous interview speech shares some features with Jordan's. Both use roughly the same proportions of personal pronouns to total words, for example, and both employ emphatic markers of certainty (e.g.,

Table 5.6   Consistency Across Text Types for Jordan and Nash

Features on Which Jordan Is More Consistent Than Nash	Features on Which Jordan is Less Consistent Than Nash
nouns	*wh-* questions
long words	indefinite pronouns
prepositions	*be* used as main verb
attributive adjectives	first-person plural pronouns
contractions	private verbs
do used as pro-verb	second-person pronouns
demonstrative pronouns	
coordinated clauses	
first-person singular pronouns	
certainty verbs	
emphatics	
predictive modals	

really, such) in the same proportion. But as the texts become more edited, the difference between the two women's styles grows. This reflects the most salient fact about Nash's style: it is not of a piece, as the figures presented earlier show. Her edited text differs much more from her unedited text than is the case for Jordan.

This is particularly the case for the features most associated with integration, density, and care in encoding. In edited text, Nash adheres to established canons of prose style. Her style is characterized by carefully chosen adjectives modifying most nouns, by syntactic complexity, by lexical variety, and by little use of potentially vague, prior-knowledge-requiring elements such as the verbs *do* or *be* or indefinite or demonstrative pronouns. This is evident in the following excerpt from one of her newspaper columns on the topic of local history (Nash 1992a):

> Turn-of-the-century slave descendants in Brazos County were as socially and economically diverse as their counterparts of other racial backgrounds.
>
> To date, records pertinent to the study of African-American culture and contributions have consisted of sketchy biographies, diaries and an incomplete reporting of American history. These records are being supplemented today by ordinary photograph collections, casual letters and simple birth documents, revealing the real history of an extraordinary people.

Table 5.7   Type-to-Token Ratios for Long Words
and Private Verbs

	Jordan	Nash
long words	66	78
private verbs	27	56

Words like *counterparts* and *pertinent* are more elevated than is typical of this newspaper's style, *to date* more compact than *up to now* would be. Almost every noun is modified, as in the final sentence with its *ordinary* photograph collections, *casual* letters, *simple* birth documents, *real* history, and *extraordinary* people.

Nash's memoir writing, though somewhat closer to her speaking style, is still relatively compact, rarely conversational in tone. In this excerpt from an article about her elementary-school gym teacher (Nash 1993a), the only casual elements are one use of *well* and the nonuse of the complementizer *that* with *afraid:*

> We were afraid the tumbling and gymnastics team would be picked based on who had the longest ponytail or the lightest skin or whose parents were school teachers. Well, those things may have counted with some teachers, but not with Mr. Pruitt.
>
> "You have to put that hair up," he said to me one day. "I don't want you getting tangled up in it and strangling yourself."

Even the gym teacher's speech is represented in a relatively writerly style. This is generally true of reports of speech in Nash's memoir writing.

Nash's interview speech is full of reported dialogue, and the dialogue she tells is far more realistically conversational than the dialogue she writes. Here, for example, she responds to my question about how she got the idea of writing a novel as a series of prayers:

> [W]hat happened was I had tried so many other things, telling this story and people'd say, "Well you can't use that, everybody's already *done* that, you can't use letters, you can't use-." I said "Okay, well *what* is *left?*" (*laughter*) So, the only thing that I could think of that was left and interesting enough for me to pursue, 'cause I don't want to just sit down and just start writing, that isn't, I want to entertain myself, that's the whole reason I write, so I started thinking about prayers and I remembered my grandmother praying all the time she would be walking around the house dusting and "Oh Lord, please, let such and such happen."

All the characters even alluded to here—other people, Nash herself, her grandmother—are given words to speak. In between, information emerges clause by clause in an additive style that sounds almost completely unplanned. For example, we learn in the middle of a sentence about thinking about prayers that Nash writes exclusively to entertain herself.

It would be possible to explain Nash's linguistic inconsistency in evaluative terms. It could be argued that she is not as persuasive in planned, edited modes as she is in face-to-face speech and that this is partly because her voice does not come across in her writing. To put it in the traditional terminology of writing pedagogy, perhaps she does not express herself in writing as well as she might. A somewhat less elevated tone in her newspaper columns might make them sound—at least to the middle-class Anglos who constitute most of the readership of the papers they appear in—more as if she were speaking with her own voice rather than with an adopted one. But this is only one way of thinking about reasons for the inconsistency.

If Jordan's primary appeal is her relatively detached, formal projection of own moral authority, Nash's is her immediacy and enthusiasm. She is a compelling conversationalist who draws interlocutors into her many schemes and dreams—from local art education projects for youthful criminals to photography projects in New York to Hollywood screen plays and back to a local magazine for African-Americans, all pursued at once—through her profession of faith that she can do anything. Being able to do anything is in fact at the core of Nash's presentation of self. She values flexibility more than consistency, and this shows in every mode of self-presentation. Sunny Nash, for example, is an adopted name, taken on because her original name was not suitable for the person she wanted to be. She has followed one career after another, as journalist, musician, photographer, educator, and free-lance writer, and taken up one project after another. Even her appearance is flexible: she does not appear to be the same person in different photographs. Thus it is not surprising that her language is so varied.

Inconsistency is, for Nash, an ability, a resource to be used in the presentation of different personas for different situations. (For a time after college, she sang advertising jingles for a San Antonio radio station, sometimes in a Hispanic voice and sometimes trying to sound Anglo but bound by contract not to sound black; she concurrently performed Aretha Franklin shows in nightclubs, sounding as much like the African-

American singer as she could.) It has been noted (e.g., Abrahams 1976; Balester 1993) that African-American traditions of speech performance value versatility, ranging from witty spontaneous comebacks in the most vernacular style to the highly elevated, fancy style of formal oratory. Nash partakes of this tradition in her construction of her own image for herself and for others, an image based on pragmatic flexibility of style, linguistic and otherwise. As there have always been, there are practical reasons for this. As Nash puts it (personal communication, September 7, 1993), "My flexibility—a much wider range than I thought you could imagine—gets me into all kinds of doors that other people could never budge. That's why I know intimate things about people and subtle things about society that other people don't know."

Strategies for Personal Style

Linguists and rhetoricians have repeatedly and convincingly shown that speech styles vary across contexts. People adjust their speech to suit their perception of their audience, to suit the topic, to express temporary or permanent identification with one socially defined group or another, and for other reasons. However, this chapter has suggested that speakers are also in some ways stylistically consistent, sometimes on the linguistic surface and perhaps most of the time in their underlying representations of themselves as actors and speakers. For Barbara Jordan, linguistic consistency is a sign of moral constancy. It is itself consistent with the other ways Jordan makes this point about herself, including her disregard for appearances and her lifelong refusal to adapt to social expectations about how a southern black woman should live and behave. For Sunny Nash, consistency of self-image expresses itself as flexibility of style, and linguistic inconsistency displays pragmatic flexibility. For both women, consistency and its opposite are resources used in the display of self in discourse.

As an individual decides, sometimes consciously and sometimes not, how to be, act, and sound, he or she selects from among the available linguistic resources. There are many ways to choose among and utilize the resources that are at hand. Ways of acting and talking provided by regional, ethnic, vocational, and gender models (among others) can be adopted or resisted, used predictably or creatively, as can ways of acting and talking provided by certain audiences, situations, or topics. An individual's style at any moment is the result of a complex set of calculations and choices. In previous chapters I have suggested that the expression of an autonomous, unique self is always a factor in this equation. This chapter has highlighted another variable in the equation—how a person expresses a self that is morally consistent from one encounter to another. This, too, turns out to be complex: underlying consistency of self-image can express itself in surface consistency of style, but it can also express itself as strategic inconsistency.

– 6 –

Idiosyncracy and
Its Interpretation

*Language, too, can be seen as a hierarchy of constraints, from the
species-wide constraints on all humans (and perhaps birds and whales,
too), to the particular constraints that make me sound like me—and
work out of my memory, shape as I shape, relate to others as I do, and
live in my world with some kind of coherence. One can study this
continuum at any level, but language is not reducible to just one
level. . . . If we are interested in language in full context—real language—we must take care not to exclude the individual voice, which is
the only place where self-correction, i.e. change, happens—where the
living organism interacts with the environment.*

A. L. Becker, *"Beyond Translation"*

In Chapter 1 I described a word, my father's *aaahh*, that I have heard
only two people use. *Aaahh* has a meaning for my father, for me, and by
now for readers of this book. But *aaahh* is idiosyncratic—so much the
property of one particular speaker that when my sister used it I was
startled, amazed to hear the word uttered in another voice. If *aaahh* is
idiosyncratic, how does anybody understand what it means? That question is the subject of this chapter. I will suggest that people understand
new uses of language by noticing and interpreting repetition. I understand what *aaahh* means because I have heard it before; my father's current uses of the form are repetitions of prior uses. Diachronic repetition
like this is useful in interpreting almost new forms, forms used for the

second and subsequent times. But what of the first time? I will suggest that the telephone information-givers to whom it is addressed understand what *aaahh* means because my father paraphrases it, in one way or another, as he uses it. *Aaahh* is always accompanied by a translation—a synchronic repetition, in a more conventional form, that conveys enough of its meaning to make it interpretable.

If people used neologisms like *aaahh* in every utterance or made nonce choices about how to structure phrases or pronounce morphemes, communication would be slow and awkward. Understanding one's neighbor or colleague or friend is not, typically, like understanding James Joyce; choices for how to mean and how to interpret most often involve the use of grammatical rules and conventional strategies. Chafe (1986), Coulmas (1981), Tannen (1989, ch. 3), and others are right in pointing out how much of our speech is phrased in prepatterned formulas, and linguists are right to devote most of their energy to describing the conventions of phonology, morphology, syntax, semantics, and pragmatics. A series of completely conventional utterances, generated by a closed set of rules that allows no individual creativity, can, at least under certain circumstances, be mistaken for language. (A well-known computer program called Eliza utilizes a relatively simple set of rules to emulate a psychotherapist's echoing questions and prompts—"Why do you mention your mother?"—and people are sometimes taken in.)

On the other hand, we are also often exposed to utterance forms and functions that are entirely new. Especially obvious examples are language learning situations, in which children and foreign-language learners have to figure out how to interpret words and structures they cannot have heard before. But idiosyncrasy is a part of all talk. Subphonemic variation routinely results in individual idiosyncrasy: different speakers have different articulatory targets for sounds, and speakers do not always hit the bull's-eyes they are aiming for, so precisely identical pronunciations (even assuming that identical articulations in different mouths would result in the same sounds) are very rare. Because there are far fewer distinctive sounds in a language than there are words or syntactic possibilities, one might expect less idiosyncrasy on this level than elsewhere in the system. It should, for example, be far more difficult for an individual speaker to create a new phoneme than to create a new word or sentence pattern. Phonemic idiosyncrasy has, however, been documented by Labov (1979) in his description of Nathan B., the speaker I described earlier who failed to recognize a contrast that was meaningful for other members of his speech community. And one's phonemic representations of individual lexical items can be inconsistent with those of one's community.

Every middle-class American family can cite examples of lexical idiosyncracy. "Family words" often arise from children's overgeneralizations or misgeneralizations or from adults' baby talk. To my Arizona nephews, for example, *ouchie* for a time meant cactus. The baby-talk form entered the adult lexicon when I used it in describing a southwestern landscaping style in which "ouchies make major statements." Morphological and syntactic idiosyncracy appears in slips of the tongue and in misprocessed "performance errors," and also in poetry and other creative speech acts. *Anyone*, for e.e. cummings and his readers, can be a proper noun, and *how* an adjective. The ironic postposed negation pattern ("You're home alone—not") that was common for a while in American English was the invention of a television scriptwriter. There is a series of creative morphological neologisms in this flirtatious telephone conversation between a college-aged couple:

RICK: Have you had dinner yet?
         (0.4-second pause)
CAROLE: No I haven't. ⌈Have you.   ⌉
RICK: ⌊I- I'm   ⌋ so hungry,
         (*laughing*)
CAROLE: Are you starving?
RICK: Yes.
         (0.3)
CAROLE: Have you **ate** today?
         (0.4)
         Eaten.
RICK: (*laughs*)
CAROLE: (*laughing*) I said **eated**. (*laughs*) =
RICK: = No I-
         I- I already **eated**. (*laughs*)
CAROLE: You already **eated**?
RICK: Yes.
CAROLE: What did you eat at? (*laughs*)
RICK: But I'm going to go- I'm gonna go, **ran**
         now. (*laughs*)
CAROLE: You gonna go **ran**.
RICK: I'm gonna go **ran**.
CAROLE: (*laughs*)
RICK: (*laughs*)
CAROLE: Fuck you. (*laughs*) (He's) gonna go **ran**
         now. (*laughs*) ⌈Leave me alone.   ⌉
RICK: ⌊And the- and then-   ⌋ and

then I'm gonna- and then I'm gonna
[**go:n**] to a movie. (*laughs*)

CAROLE: Gonna **gone** to a movie?

RICK: Gonna **gone** to a movie.

CAROLE: *Are* you gonna **gone** to a movie?

RICK: Yeah.

(0.2)

You wanna **comed?**

CAROLE: (unintelligible)

RICK: (*laughs*)

CAROLE: I wanna **came.**

RICK: (*laughing*) Wanna **come.**

CAROLE: (*laughs*) You wanna **came.** (*laughs*)

(0.4)

(*laughing*) Leave me alone.

RICK: (*laughs*)

Rick and Carole use what was presumably originally a slip of the tongue (Carole's "Have you ate") as the basis for a series of playful uses of preterit and participle forms in inappropriate contexts. Robert Hopper (1990; Hopper and Glenn 1994), to whom I owe this example, shows how the idiosyncratic-morphology game serves as a framework for a series of suggestions by Rick and Carole about potentially romantic activities. Courting couples relish shared idiosyncratic experience like this, as it gives them an element of history that is exclusively theirs.

One might wonder how an analyst could ever be sure that a use of language was really new, that the audience of an utterance had in fact never before been exposed to the linguistic strategy in question. If it were, in fact, crucial to prove that in a given case a given addressee had never before heard the particular linguistic item he or she was being exposed to, then this objection would be very difficult to deal with; people are not always aware of what they have heard before and what they are hearing for the first time. But this is in fact not crucial. To establish the necessity for a model of interpretation that can explain how people understand the idiosyncratic, it is enough to show that it is *possible* for a person to interpret complete newness, not that this is actually what has happened in a given case.

Just as there is idiosyncracy in the sounds and structures of language, there is also idiosyncracy beyond the sentence, in how discourse is structured and in how discourse structure is marked. An example of idiosyncracy on this level will be the main text for this chapter.

Discourse Markers
and Conventional Interpretations

It is widely recognized that speakers use various linguistic and para-
linguistic resources as they talk to indicate how their talk is to be inter-
preted. Pause and final intonation can signal the end of a turn at talk
(Sacks, Schegloff, and Jefferson 1974); *well* often marks the introduction of something unexpected into a conversation (Schiffrin 1987,
pp. 102–127); a codeswitch may indicate a shift from background to foreground information (Gumperz 1982, p. 79). Linguistic elements that
serve functions like these like these have been referred to as "contextualization cues" (Gumperz 1982, pp. 130–152); a lexical subset including *and, so, well,* and the like have been called "discourse markers" (Schiffrin 1987); cues to a shift into a performance mode of discourse have
been described as "keys" (Bauman 1977, pp. 15–24); other terms have
been used as well.

Metacommunicative strategies such as these are typically thought
of as belonging to shared sets of conventional options among which
speakers choose and to which hearers turn as they interpret speakers'
utterances. In other words, discourse markers are seen as having meanings in much the same way as other linguistic items have meanings,
though the meaning of a discourse marker may not be referential: *well,*
for example, signals unexpected conversational action because, and only
if, the speaker and the hearers share the prior knowledge that *well* is one
of the strategies that can be used for this purpose. According to Gumperz,

> this channelling of interpretation is effected by conversational
> implicatures based on conventionalized co-occurrence between
> content and surface style. That is, constellations of surface features of
> message form are the means by which speakers signal and listeners
> interpret what the activity is, how semantic content is to be under-
> stood and *how* each sentence relates to what precedes or follows. (1982,
> p. 131)

But not all discourse markers are conventional. Nonconventional ways
of showing what one is doing as one talks are one aspect of a person's
individual voice; they are among the things that enable us to recognize
a specific person's style as distinct from those of other people. As I discuss three linguistic items used as discourse markers—one a lexical item,
one various permutations of a phrase, and one a set of nonlexical
sounds—I will suggest how hearers manage to interpret each in its discourse marking function. For conventionalized discourse markers and
for discourse markers whose function is inferable from their semantic

content, my discussion of the strategies by which the markers are inter-preted will be based on familiar models of semantics and pragmatics. For completely idiosyncratic, nonsemantic discourse markers, I will suggest a model of interpretation involving two processes: (1) hypothesis for-mation based on synchronic paraphrastic repetition in the linguistic and extralinguistic context, and (2) hypothesis confirmation based on dia-chronic formal repetition of the item in question.

My examples of discourse marking strategies are from spontaneous, fairly monologic narratives that arose in conversations. As I have pointed out (ch. 2), one of the things narrators do as they tell stories is to indi-cate what the parts of their stories are and where each part begins. Labov (1972c), for example, describes some of the ways narrators mark the divisions of their stories into functional parts—abstract, orientation, ris-ing tension, resolution, coda. Hymes (1981) and others speak of sub-units similar to poetic and dramatic verses, stanzas, scenes, and acts. Van Dijk (1981) speaks of "episodes," Longacre (1976, p. 262 et passim) and Grimes (1975, pp. 101–111) of "paragraphs," Chafe (1980) of "centers of interest."

It is clear that, for purposes of intelligibility if nothing else, spoken narrative must be produced in chunks, which narrators need to mark off from one another, and that there are a variety of ways in which this marking can be done. Some narrative discourse marking strategies are so conventional as to be clichés: "meanwhile, back at the ranch," as a marker of a return to the main sequence of events at the end of a digres-sion, is one such. Other choices, however, are considerably less conven-tional. In fact, discourse marking strategies may be completely uncon-ventional, completely idiosyncratic.

Strategies for Discourse Marking

In what follows, we look at three discourse markers used as signals of discourse chunks in oral narrative, beginning with the most conventional and ending with the most idiosyncratic.

So: *Conventional Marking and Interpretation*

We begin with a conventional way of signaling the beginning of narra-tive chunks—through the use of *so*. What follows is a conversational narrative about a car wreck that was mistakenly attributed to alcohol when the real cause, the audience is encouraged to believe, was the driver's suffering a collapsed lung.[1] The word *so* consistently signals shifts to increasingly crucial and suspenseful episodes in the story. (Not all uses of *so* serve this function, of course. Those that do are highlighted.)

Did I ever tell you about when I wrecked my '73 Mercury, er a Comet GT actually? Well I was bowling and uh, there was—it was the day after Valentine's Day, and we had the day off from work.

So I went bowling with a couple guys from work and uh, I had about a beer when I went over there and I had about a beer per game while we were bowling and uh — Well, we bowled about four games, and it was in the middle of the afternoon.

So I was driving home, and it was on Washington, nnuh, it was on Jefferson, and I was going eastbound, and I got about a quarter of a mile, and my lung collapsed, and I blacked out and folded the car in a tree. And, I was still unconscious, and when I woke up and I saw all these sirens around me and everything, and I looked over to my left, and you know, about eight inches away was the tree, you know. And I opened my mouth and I pulled out a piece of glass about this big out of my mouth, and I have no windshield at all, and the car was half smashed, and there's just this cop in the passenger's side window reaching in to see if I was okay. And he dragged me out of there, then he stood me up, asked me a couple questions, and looked in the back seat and saw all those beer cans in the back seat you know. And uh, I, standing out there with the guy, and I just woke up from being unconscious, and he goes, "You been drinking?" And I said, "*Well*, yeah, I had a few beers this afternoon," which was a mistake saying that right there.

So he puts me in this car and drives me downtown. And meanwhile, I was supposed to go to Bloomington at four o'clock, so I was supposed to go home, and John and Jon were gonna pick me up.

So there's—while I was taken downtown, they're standing outside my door, wondering if I'm home, 'cause they're all set and all packed for Bloomington. And they turned around on the porch, and they see this tow truck driving my car all bashed up down the road, and they're wondering where the hell I am. Well, down to the police station, they took me downstairs, and they gave me the breathalyzer test, and they told me to breathe in this thing. I got a .14. And then they made me walk this straight line while they videotaped me. And I had only been conscious for about fifteen minutes you know, after this wreck.

So they took me downtown, down to the, they booked me and took me down to the basement, opened the cell door, took all my possessions, put them on the table, and opened the cell door, and I was just about to walk in there, and I sat down on the chair, and the nurse—there was this lady—goes, "You sure you don't want to be checked out?" And I go "*Hell yes* I want to be checked out!"

So she goes "Okay," and I get up and the cop, get back in the cop car, go back downtown. He drives me up to Saint Joe hospital, checked me into the emergency room. I ended up lay-ing on the bed, they cut me open, put a chest tube in. And so here I am sitting with this big tube coming out and oxygen going up my nose and a big intravenous thing. And I end up being in the hospital for a whole week you know, and I still got arrested for drunk driving.

So is conventionally enough chosen as a discourse marker that Webster's Collegiate Dictionary (9th ed., 1983) lists "used as an introductory par-ticle" as one of the definitions of *so*. Far more thoroughly, Schiffrin (1987, pp. 191–227) devotes a chapter to *so* and *because*, in which she shows that *so* marks superordinate material on structural and semantic levels as well as on the level of speech act and action. (I have discussed Schiffrin's analysis in chapter 2.)

The first two *so*'s in the car wreck story introduce story sections that gradually narrow the orientational focus from Valentine's Day to the afternoon of Valentine's day, drinking beer and bowling to the car, going eastbound on Jefferson.

It was the day after Valentine's Day,
and we had the day off from work,
So I went bowling with a couple guys from work and uh,
I had about a beer when I went over there,
and I had about a beer per game while we were bowling
    and uh —
Well, we bowled about four games,
and it was in the middle of the afternoon.
So I was driving home,
and it was on Washington, nnuh,
it was on Jefferson . . .

Subsequent *so*'s introduce new stages in the action. There are two attempts to start a section about being taken downtown to the police station, the first one aborted when the teller digresses to an evaluative side story about his friends' reaction to seeing his wrecked car towed by.

> **So** he puts me in this car,
> and drives me downtown,
> and meanwhile—I was supposed to go to
>   Bloomington at four o'clock . . .
> **So** they took me downtown, down to the,
> they booked me,
> and took me down to the basement. . . .

The final *so* begins the denouement of the story—the section Labov (1972c) calls the resolution. The teller is on the verge of being thrown in jail when a nurse finally notices him and asks, "Are you sure you don't want to be checked out?"; he says, "Hell yes!," and the nurse's "okay" means that instead of going to jail he is taken to the hospital.

> **So** she goes "Okay,"
> and I get up
> and the cop, get back in the cop car,
> go back downtown,
> He drives me up to Saint Joe hospital. . . .

So fills a not unusual set of functions in this story, a story that has been told many times and probably conventionalized in the process. What gives this story its individual flavor is not the use of *so* or the use of *so* for this set of purposes. A model of understanding that sees the speaker and the audience as sharing a set of possibilities for discourse marking, a set from which the teller chooses *so* and to which the hearers go to find the interpretation of *so*, could explain this example well. The next example could probably also be explained with such a model, though its interpretation involves somewhat more inferencing.

One Time in Particular:
Semiconventional Marking, Semantic Inference

The narrative that follows was part of a conversation in which a girl was encouraging her father, who was somewhat reluctant, to reminisce about his past. He searched his mind for anything interesting he might have done and began to talk about his experience in Naval Aviation, where in order to draw extra flight pay he and others were required to spend a certain amount of time in the air. As he incrementally moved from general images of "just fly[ing] around on pilot-training hops, and sleep[ing] in the back of the plane" toward a specifically oriented and dramatically evaluated story about a trainee pilot who, flying only by instrument, very nearly crashed into a cliff, the teller used permutations of "one x I remember in particular" in exactly the same way as the teller of the car wreck story used *so*.

JILL: What are you thinking of? (*laughing*)

DAD: Oh, I was thinking about uh when I was in the Navy, in Naval Aviation. Used to have to, put in our time basically, to draw flight pay which was kind of nice. It was like a bonus.

JILL: Right, you told me about that.

DAD: That uh, sometimes we'd just go up and fly around on pilot-training hops and sleep in the back of the plane or read books and just put in the necessary amount of time.
One time in particular I remember uh we used to also fly observer, which was standing on a stool with your head sticking up in a plastic dome on the top of the airplane.

JILL: Well where were you though?

DAD: Uh Patuxent River Maryland, Naval Air Test Center.

JILL: No I mean in the plane were you, like right behind the pilot?

DAD: Yes in the area behind the pilot and the flight engineer.

JILL: And you had to look out through the top?

DAD: Umm. They, there was, some plastic dome that the navigator would use if he was shooting stars or something for position.

JILL: Oh wow.

DAD: What I was supposed to be doing is looking for surrounding aircraft. They'd usually do this when they were practicing takeoffs and landings. They'd just be looking for anybody else that might be in the way, or any hazards or problems.
But uh one time I remember in particular, when we were doing this uh, was a pilot-training hop, they were checking ah qualified pilots but they were checking them out on four-engine aircraft, teaching them to fly with larger airplanes. And they used to fly them *blind* when they became somewhat just proficient, which consisted of uh covering up the windshields and the side windows and the

trainee's side of the airplane, and they would fly GCA or Ground Controlled Approach, takeoffs and landings, primarily landings. And it used to make me a little nervous sometimes, since he couldn't see I hoped the, instructor was pretty good, be able to take over the controls if anything really bad happened.

But I remember one pilot in particular, I don't know if he ever got checked out or not (*chuckles*) or passed, but he scared me to death about three times. One one time at Naval Air Station Patuxent River uh, where the Patuxent meets the Potomac and meets the Chesapeake Bay, and one of the main runways we always came in over the water. The runway was about ohh probably thirty feet, built up, from the level of the water and—

JILL: You mean like a cliff?

DAD: Well yeah cliff or drop-off if you were on the runway right.

JILL: To the water.

DAD: But you used to come in over the water and land on the runway.

Um **the first approach this one particular trainee made**, when he was flying blind or couldn't see, mm came in very high and, basically *chopped* the throttles. I don't- I think we must have gone down about fifty feet immediately and *bounced* on the runway and *bounced* back up and bounced back down. Really a lousy landing you know. (*chuckles*)

JILL: But you were above the runway at least.

DAD: Yeah we were above the runway. Next time he came in, fairly decent level-wise but he didn't get lined up with the runway, and he ran *off* the runway. Fortunately uh there was a taxi strip there rather than grass, which might have spun the airplane, tipped it over or something like that. But the last one was the one that *really* got me. He was coming in low, and they kept telling him to correct and correct, and he kept trying and he wasn't doing very well. And I was, my head poked up through the plastic dome looking at a *dirt bank* the drop-off at the end of the runway.

JILL: Ooohh.

DAD: Aand it was a toss-up as far as I could see whether we were gonna hit the water, plow straight into the dirt, or whether he was gonna get it on the runway but uh— The other pilot uh did have to take over this time it, it felt like—

JILL: You mean this was the same guy?

DAD: Yes. Felt like what we really did was, aimed into the dirt and at the last minute the, the instructor grabbed the controls and hit the throttle. Looked like we just, jumped up onto the end of the runway, without plowing into the bank.

JILL: Hmm.

DAD: At this point in time I wasn't too sure the extra money was worth it.

JILL: I bet—

DAD: I think there might have been a lot a lot of people that might have had to change their shorts when they got down too. But that was, well the money was *good* and so- most of the time you didn't have to do a whole lot. But there were a few times like that that I didn't really care for it too much.

The first "one time in particular I remember" moves the story from general reminiscences about possible ways to draw flight pay to one specific way to draw flight pay: by flying observer, "looking for anybody else that might be in the way or any hazards or problems."

> Sometimes we'd just go up and fly around on pilot-training hops
> and sleep in the back of the plane or
> read books and just put in the necessary amount of time.
> (*two-second pause*)
> **One time in particular I remember** uh we used to also fly
>   observer. . . .

The next "one time I remember in particular" introduces the more specific theme of flying observer on pilot training flights.

> They'd just be looking for anybody else that might be in the way,
> or any hazards or problems.
> But uh **one time I remember in particular,**
> when we were doing this uh,
> was a pilot-training hop,
> they were checking ah qualified pilots but they
>   were checking them out on four-engine aircraft. . . .

Part of this checking out involved the pilots' "flying blind," or blindfolded, relying only on the plane's instruments for landing. Even more specifically, "I remember one pilot in particular" begins the actual story.

[S]ince he couldn't see I hoped the, instructor was pretty good,
be able to take over the controls if anything really bad happened.
But **I remember one pilot in particular,**
I don't know if he ever got checked out or not . . .

Finally, "the first approach this one particular trainee made" gets the story
back on track after Jill's request for extra detail about the setting.

DAD: The runway was about ohh probably thirty feet,
   built up, from the level of the water
   (*gestures to illustrate*)
   and—
JILL: You mean like a cliff?
DAD: Well yeah cliff or drop-off if you were on the runway right.
JILL: To the water.
DAD: But you used to come in over the water and land on the
   runway.
   Um **the first approach this one particular trainee made,**
   when he was flying blind or couldn't see,
   mm came in very high and, (*audible breath*) basically
   chopped the throttles. . . .

This storyteller was clearly not using *one time in particular* simply to signal that what followed referred to a single punctual event. This can be
seen from his first use of *one time in particular*, which precedes a reference to a nonpunctual series of events—"we used to also fly observer."
Although *one time I remember in particular* is not a member of any list of
conventional narrative-chunk-introducing particles or phrases, it is easy
to see how the meaning of the phrase might suggest its use in this capacity. Both *one* and *in particular* have meanings that have to do with speci-
ficity, and the phrase is reminiscent of the highly conventional story-
beginner *once upon a time*. A speaker's extending the lexical meaning
"specific" to the discourse-marking function of indicating the beginning
of a unit with a narrower orientational and evaluative focus than the
preceding one is not difficult to imagine.

Nor is it difficult to imagine the process of inferencing by which a
hearer might understand *one time I remember in particular* in its function
as a discourse marker. It is in fact possible that, for many speakers, *I
remember one time in particular* may actually be part of a conventionalized set of possible discourse markers. Its use in this capacity, or at least
the use of something similar, such as *one time* or *once in particular*, is
familiar.

We turn now to a case in which the discourse marker is neither a member of any conventionalized set of possible discourse markers nor semantically interpretable as a possible member of such a set.

And uh, uh:
Nonconventional, Uninferable Marking

What follows is the whole of a story told under much the same conditions as was the story about flying. A son was encouraging his father to reminisce. The teller was at one time the press agent for a semiprofessional softball team. (His reference to amateur softball is inaccurate.) His narrative style is hesitant, with lots of *uh*s and pauses. A combination of hesitation noises, *and uh, uh* serves in his story as the marker of the beginnings of episodes.

> Ehn any newcomer whether it's a player or part of management, maybe particularly part of management uh, you have to be proven, uh, they uh give you an initiation, just like they do in a fraternity or sorority.
> **And uh, uh,** in 1947, we're at the Hollandin Hotel in Cleveland Ohio, and we just won the our third straight world championship. And that was my first year with the club and, one of my first road trips with them, and uh we were uh then amateur softball we didn't drink champagne, we drank beer, hah—
> **And uh, uh,** so Bobby Jones, who was usually the ringleader of, all the off-field activities, like uh dropping water bags on people walking out in the street out of the hotel rooms and so forth, uh, came over, as I was sitting there and, reasonably well dressed uh, after I'd called the story in to the paper about the, winning, and he, turned a whole bucket of, water and ice on me, and, I started singing "Stormy Weather" and, it almost gave me immediate acceptance uh, from the, from the ballplayers.

The first part of the story is its abstract, in which the teller introduces the expectation that the story will be about an initiation ritual, "just like they do in a fraternity or sorority." The first *and uh, uh* separates this section from the next, in which temporal and spatial orientation is provided: the event, we learn, took place in 1947, in Cleveland, after the team had won its third straight world championship. Another *and uh, uh* begins the narrative proper. (More orientational material, to the character of Bobby Jones, is introduced in an embedded clause here.)

And uh, uh is clearly not a member of any conventionalized set of possible discourse markers. Nor is its discourse-marking function inferable from the semantics of the phrase, since *uh* has no semantic content and since, as we have seen, *and* is most often a marker of a continuation, not a marker of a shift. Yet *and uh, uh* just as clearly serves as a discourse marker in this story, and in others told by the same teller. If there is nothing outside of the story to indicate that *and uh, uh* should be taken as a discourse marker—no shared set of conventions to which we can turn to find out what it means, and no sentence-level meaning on which to base inferences about discourse-level meaning—how are we able to interpret *and uh, uh* this way?

Repetition and
the Interpretation of Idiosyncracy

The interpretive process necessary for figuring out what *and uh, uh* does in the "Stormy Weather" story can be seen as involving two steps. In the first, the hearer forms a hypothesis based on redundancies in the linguistic context: co-occurring markers of the same thing. Each *and uh, uh* occurs immediately before another element that also signals the new chunk's beginning. The first precedes "in 1947," a fairly clear signal that what follows will be orientational as opposed to summary; the second precedes "so," which, as we have seen, is a conventional chunk marker. In addition, each *and uh, uh* comes between the end of one sentence-like unit—with final intonation and syntactic closure—and the beginning of another. The beginning of each chunk is signaled more redundantly in this story than in either of the other two. Paraphrase—repetition of meaning—is one key, then, to the interpretation of idiosyncratic discourse markers.

The other key to the interpretation of idiosyncracy is repetition of form. While it is possible to *guess* about what an unfamiliar linguistic item means upon hearing it once, it is possible to *know* what it means only on repeated hearings. The meaning of an unfamiliar form emerges as the form is used and reused in varying contexts. *And uh, uh* is clearly not a discourse marker at the outset of the story in which it is used; it becomes a discourse marker in the course of the story's telling. The repeated item—*and uh, uh*—comes to signal new chunks of the story. The fact that it is repeated signals that the item serves a discourse-marking function. This signaling of potential meaning and the establishment of actual meaning are thus emergent as the talk proceeds; understanding is to this extent retrospective.

The same applies to *one time in particular* and its variants in the trainee flyer story. The use of expressions like this as discourse markers is relatively conventional, as has been noted; it is possible to imagine speaker and auditors looking the expression up in a mental lexicon and deciding on that basis what it might mean in this context. But coming to a conclusion what the expression *actually* means as used in the flyer story involves the use of situated cues. It requires noting what co-occurs with the expression and that the expression is repeated. The first *one time in particular* in the story is, as we have noted, in an odd context, followed as it is by the nonpunctual "we used to also fly observer." This anomaly provides a basis for hypothesizing that *one time in particular* is not here simply orienting specific events in time but that it may instead be working cohesively, pointing to particular parts of the story rather than particular events in the narrated sequence. This hypothesis is verified by subsequent repetitions of *one time in particular*, which occurs before each inward focusing of the storyteller's lens.

It appears, then, that it is only in the case of *so* that the interpretation of the marker can be modeled as a looking-up process in which auditors figure out the meanings of forms by referring to preestablished conventions. Native-speaker interpreters of the car wreck story presumably already know (though of course without being aware of it) that *so* can mean "beginning of new discourse unit" and should be able to bring this knowledge to bear the first time they encounter the conjunction in the story. Even here, though, the dictionary model fails to explain the process completely. For one thing, "beginning of new discourse unit" is not the only meaning of *so*, which also functions, among other things, as a semantic marker of result. Even hearers who are familiar with the conventional meaning of *so* do not know, when they first encounter it, which meaning is intended. Furthermore, as Schiffrin points out in her discussion of *so*, the word can work more than one way at a time. Many words are less polysemic and polyfunctional than *so*, but many words are more so. In order to produce an interpretation of the function of *so* in this story, the pattern of its occurrence in this story must be referred to. Just as they do in the less conventional cases, interpreters must listen for repetition. Repetition thus augments grammar—what interpreters already know about what words mean and what their order and morphological markings signify—and convention—what interpreters expect stories to be like because of what they expect social interactions to be like.

Grammar, Convention, and Repetition

Audiences bring several kinds of knowledge to the task of interpreting what they hear. For one thing, they bring *linguistic knowledge*, in the form of one or more grammars. Evidence from comparative studies of syntax suggests that human beings have an innate tendency to approach language differently than we approach other potentially meaningful phenomena (Chomsky 1986; Bickerton 1990). We are apparently born with the ability to figure out the grammars of one or more languages, based on innate knowledge about the general principles on which all grammars work and the parameters along which languages can vary. This means that we are likely to make certain kinds of generalizations about what we hear and not others. In this very general sense, all speakers of all languages share a universal Grammar, a Grammar that encourages us, for example, to pay attention to differences in word order and word form and to interpret syntactic structures not only on the basis of what they are like but also in relation to other structures.

Partly because of the shared tendencies of universal Grammar, people who have the same linguistic experiences are likely to make similar grammatical generalizations about them. To the extent that two speakers do share linguistic experiences, they can be said to "speak the same language," or to "share a grammar" in the more specific sense used when we refer to "the grammar of Arabic," for example. Linguists and nonlinguists alike tend to think about things this way, in terms of languages shared by large groups (such as "English" or "Greek") and the grammars that generate those languages. This way of thinking captures the fact that speakers do not have to create language de novo every time they converse, since they can draw on preexisting knowledge of meaning and structure. But labels like "the English language" also encourage a way of imagining language in which language grammars are too easily confused with universal Grammar. In this way of conceptualizing what linguistics is about, languages are treated as if they were superorganic, existing outside the individual and available for logging into, like mainframe linguistic computers. Paul Hopper (1988) calls this way of conceiving of language the "A Priori Grammar attitude." From the A Priori Grammar perspective, people are seen as acquiring one or more languages, shared with other members of their speech community, which they then use when they talk. As Hopper puts it, the A Priori Grammar perspective assumes that "grammar is complete and predetermined and is a prerequisite for generating discourses" (p. 118). But no two people do in fact have exactly the same history of linguistic experience, so no two grammars can be exactly alike. Since each individual's grammar is distinct, speakers have to negotiate, as they speak, what their words should be taken to mean.

Speakers also bring *social knowledge* to the job of interpretation. Perhaps the most basic of the social conventions is the assumption hearers make that utterances have purposes, that what is said has some bearing on the situation at hand. Sperber and Wilson (1986) argue that the assumption that utterances are relevant gives rise to all the other kinds of inferencing that are required in figuring out what people mean by what they say. Others propose more specific strategies. Grice (1975), for example, suggests that people can interpret what others say only if they assume not only that speakers are saying relevant things but that they are being honest, clear, orderly, as concise as necessary, and as complete as necessary.

Whichever formulation best reflects what happens in speakers' minds, it is clear that assumptions like these have to be made if language is to be communicative at all. In addition, there are cultural and subcultural conventions about what utterances should be taken to mean, conventions of the sort studied by ethnographers of communication (Hymes 1972). What counts as relevant, orderly, or polite in a given situation can vary from group to group (Saville-Troike 1982; Bauman and Sherzer 1974). Like grammar and for the same reasons, however, social knowledge is never completely shared and must be renegotiated as people interact.

The conventional ways of structuring words and sentences that we call grammar and the conventions of language use that are part of culture provide a convenient shortcut to meaning when these conventions are mutually shared. But grammars and cultures are never completely shared, and sometimes, as often in the language contact situations that give rise to pidgin varieties, they are barely shared at all. To the extent that grammar is not available, people make do with basic *cognitive strategies* for creating utterances and understanding them. Perhaps the most basic of these is the sensitivity to pattern without which intelligence of any sort is hard to imagine. The tendency to notice pattern and take it to be significant is at the root of people's linguistic and social knowledge about language, since if we did not attend to repeated forms and repeated contexts we would never learn the shortcuts to interpretation that linguistic and social knowledge represent. Since patterns are the result of repetition, one formulation of language-users' most basic task might be "Notice repetition and figure out what it could signal."

Repetition can create many different specific effects (Johnstone 1987c, 1994). For example, lexical paraphrase can function as a modificational strategy, as when the words in couplets like *clear and concise* take on elements of each other's meaning (Koch 1983b, 1984). Repetition of others' talk can create interpersonal rapport, as people display their identification with others by repeating parts of what others say (Tannen

1987a, 1987b, 1989). Repetition can be a strategy for keeping people talking, as when psychotherapists echo clients' utterances to encourage them to say more (Ferrara 1994) or when nonfluent speakers repeat themselves to force their interlocutors to keep guessing what they mean (Knox 1994) or when teachers repeat and reformulate to guide students toward correct responses (Merritt 1994). Patterns of parallelism may serve to indicate that a speaker is engaged in verbal artistry (Bauman 1977; Sherzer 1982); repetition in literary discourse can act as a magnifying glass for characters' conversational quirks (Schnebly 1994) or mark overlays of various worlds or points of view (Ehrlich 1994). There are few functions repetition *cannot* serve, in fact. As one group of analysts put it,

> Repetition functions didactically, playfully, emotionally, expressively, ritualistically; repetition can be used for emphasis or iteration, clarification, confirmation; it can incorporate foreign words into a language, in couplets, serving as a resource for enriching the language. People repeat to produce trance, as in mantras or the Lamaze method for overcoming pain. Actors repeat to learn their lines; academics copy out quotes when they read in a new area. Repetition can be a bridging device in conversation, a way of dealing with an interruption, or a way of validating what another speaker has said. Repetition is a persuasive device. It is one of the primary forms of play. (Johnstone et al. 1994, p. 6)

Repetition is available to serve these and other semantic, interactional, and aesthetic functions because repetition is crucially present in all discourse, as a higher-order cue to structure and meaning. In an important sense, all understanding is the result of repetition: new experiences can be made sense of only in terms of old experiences, or "prior texts." As Becker puts it,

> Everything anyone says, to the extent it is understandable, has a history. Everything said evokes prior texts, lingual memories. Appropriating prior text is a necessary, nonfaultable plagiarism . . . that we all practice every time we speak or write. It's an ordinary thing. (1994, p. 164)

Greg Urban points to the necessity of repetition in the replication of culture in ritual:

> Internal repetition is, of course, linked to linguistic intelligibility. Individuals must be exposed to the sound inventory over and over again, and similarly to the lexical items, idioms, and other nonrecursive aspects of language. These are facets of the discourse that they cannot generate spontaneously. Correspondingly, their repeated

exposure to forms is a sine qua non of mutual interpretability. They must be able to pick out the sameness—repetition indicating the significance of the facet—across the stream of discourse whose meaningful segmentation would otherwise be impossible. Repetition is, in this sense, the ground of intelligibility. (1994, p. 157)

When a linguistic item is repeated, we attend to it for the same reason we attend to pattern in all our sensory media. If we did not, the world would be chaotic.

There are cases in which people rely in the main on linguistic and social knowledge in interpreting what they hear. At least for adult speakers in relatively homogeneous speech communities, it is possible to understand most utterances with reference to grammatical and sociolinguistic generalizations made long ago. This is, after all, convenient and efficient. If all linguistic communication were like reading *Finnegan's Wake* or being a monolingual Japanese speaker in the United States, understanding would be slow and difficult. But though most talking does not in practice take place across large gulfs in prior linguistic experience, the sort of attention to pattern that it takes to understand poetic license or a foreign language is always required. We never stop making grammatical and sociolinguistic generalizations, and it is repetition that makes these generalizations possible.

This becomes most obvious when there is no grammar. Russell Tomlin (1994) has studied the very beginning of foreign-language learning, the stage at which everything one hears is new and (from the hearer's perspective) completely idiosyncratic. Tomlin videotaped Indonesian-speaking tutors and nonIndonesian-speaking students mutually engaged in the attempt to enable the students to follow simple commands in Indonesian. Students and tutors relied on the social expectation that what the tutors said would be as relevant as possible to the task at hand, and tutors relied on the expectation that students' thought processes would be like their own. But the students had no linguistic knowledge to bring to bear except for the abstract principles of universal Grammar. Only the tutors spoke; students responded by moving objects on computer screens. The tutors' discourse, as they guided the students along their cognitive way, was richly repetitive. Referential redundancy was necessarily the first step; tutors pointed to objects and simultaneously uttered their labels to get students to associate objects and words. Once the student saw in this way that *kotak*, for example, meant "square," the tutor's next repetition of *kotak* could be taken as a request that the student point to a square on the screen. Later, the tutor's repetition of part of an utterance could signal material that was new to the student and needed to be focused on. For example, once students knew words for some shapes and colors, tutors could begin talking about spatial relations, repeating new ways of referring to places: "Put the small black square between the white squares. Between the white squares," or "Put the small black square to the right of the large white circle. To the right."

Tomlin's ingenious interactions are miniaturized, refined versions of what all interactions are like, since people never completely share grammars or ways to use them. Grammar emerges gradually in these interactions, shaped by repetition and paraphrase. There is no other way things could work. Repetition underlies grammatical and sociolinguistic knowledge because the strategy of understanding by noticing and interpreting repetition is at the basis of cognition. This is by no means a new idea, nor am I suggesting that pragmatics—the use of general, not specifically linguistic strategies—is all there is to language. When people can make use of grammar and semantics, they do. What I have tried to highlight through the discussion in this chapter is what I have been suggesting throughout this book, namely that newness, idiosyncracy, personal choice, and creativity are more pervasive in language than traditional ways of conceiving of language lead us to think. How speakers and discourses differ is as meaningful as how they are alike; appeals to conventionality and descriptions of conventions go a long way toward enabling us to understand what people do when they talk and listen to talk, but they do not go all the way.

— 7 —

Toward a Linguistics
of the Individual Speaker

Every man's language varies according to the extent of his knowledge, the activity of his faculties, and the depth or quickness of his feelings. Every man's language has, first, its individualities; *secondly, the common properties of the class to which he belongs; and thirdly, words and phrases of universal use.*

Samuel Taylor Coleridge, *"Biographia Literaria"*

The most difficult task for the philologist is to hear the individual voice.

A. L. Becker, *"On Emerson on Language"*

This book results from the intersection of three lines of thought: thought about language, thought about artistry, and thought about individuality. In my work with language, I have needed increasingly to consider social reasons for conventionality and variation. Studying the uses of narrative in a midwestern American city (Johnstone 1990a), for example, meant thinking about how region, community, and social roles and relationships influenced the shape and functions of people's stories about themselves. In work I am doing now in Texas (Johnstone, Bean, and McLeod-Porter, forthcoming) I am trying to model how these factors and others—ethnicity, gender, vocational identification, urbanity—constrain and facilitate speakers' choices. But as my work has moved toward the sociolinguistic I have more and more been bothered by the implicit determinism of much sociolinguistic theory, by the idea, espoused or suggested in some work, that we are linguistic creatures of our social environments, not the agents of our speech at all but rather "spoken by" our positions in society. The questions, or perhaps the question, to which I have kept returning have to do with how the social and the individual influence each other. I find myself wanting always to talk about particular speakers rather than about groups of speakers, even though that seems to defeat the generalizing purposes of sociolinguistics. I have tried to grapple with that concern here.

My interest in artistry has its methodological roots in my training in a kind of philological linguistics I have described earlier and will return to later. It also arises from reflection about the artistic media in which I work: writing and music. As a writer, I am—as all writers are—continually struck by how many ways there are to balance conventionality and originality and by how important it is constantly to maintain that balance. I am also struck by how self-expressive even the most formulaic genres can be—academic book reviews, for example, or thank-you notes to friends—in the hands of good writers. As a student of music, I struggle with precisely the same set of competing demands for conventionality (as I try to play the standard repertoire the way my teacher and his teacher do, and as I learn the complicated rules that must be followed in writing even the simplest few measures of music in the classical tradition) and originality (as I try to develop a style of my own as a clarinetist or figure out what makes a Mozart sonata distinctive). That struggle has entered in here, too.

My interest in individuality has to do with my inevitable interest in myself and my sense that other people must have senses of self either like mine or comparable along some common axis. I have always been motivated by the sense of being different from others, consistent in most traits from day to day and year to year, and unique. I have always found it annoying to have choices I made ascribed to my membership in one group or another, to be told "You think that because you're an American" or "You act that way because you're a woman." I have brought that into this work as well. More generally, my concern with individuality springs from an analytical predisposition to notice small differences, sometimes more readily than I notice big ones.

In this chapter, I first return to a methodological concern that has been a theme throughout: how can linguistic work be done in such a way as not to lose sight of people speaking? Paying attention to small differences, the way people do when they talk about works of art or pieces of music, is part of the analytical mind set that is required. I discuss how linguistics can benefit from ideas and techniques borrowed from the study of verbal art. In the final section, I reiterate what I have learned in the process of thinking simultaneously about language, artistry, and individuality.

Language as Art

It was only fairly recently, well into the twentieth century, that branches of linguistics developed that had more in common with formal logic (in the case of generative syntax and semantics) or sociology (in the case of variationist sociolinguistics) or anthropology (in the case of interactional sociolinguistics) than with literary studies. But these subfields have come to dominate the discipline, with the result that it has become fashionable to look to analytical philosophy or sociology or cultural geography for ideas to borrow and unfashionable to look to literary theory. ("Critical discourse analysts" like those represented in the pages of the journal *Discourse and Society* do make use of literary theory, but this is mostly a European trend and the Americans who work in this vein are still for the most part communications scholars rather than linguists.) We talk about logical operations and their scope, about social status and social networks, about the nature of community and gendered divisions of linguistic labor, relentlessly trying to position ourselves as pure or social scientists in the face of university administrations and granting agencies that keep classifying us as humanists. It is in part because of this that we have neglected the linguistic individual. But linguistics has its roots in philology, the close reading of texts considered to have historical or literary value. A linguistics once again willing to borrow ideas and techniques from literary studies would be equipped to supplement the results of linguistic inquiry about languages and dialects with a deeper understanding of speakers.

There are, in fact, some linguists who do call themselves humanists and who look to literature for ideas about how to understand language in general. This is not so much an identifiable school or camp as a loose group of scholars who tend to share ideas and cite each other. Their work harks back, explicitly or not, to that of earlier humanists with linguistic goals: von Humboldt, Sapir, Roman Jakobson. The most visible exponent of what she and others have called "humanistic linguistics" is Deborah Tannen, who organized a National Endowment for the Humanities summer seminar with that title in 1985 (see Tannen 1988). Many humanistic linguists identify themselves, or are identified by others, primarily with something else: ethnopoetics in the case of Dell Hymes, grammaticalization in the case of Paul Hopper, generative semantics in the case of

J. R. Ross, Southeast Asian linguistics in the case of A. L. Becker, Central American languages and cultures in Paul Friedrich's case. What these humanistic linguists share is nothing much more specific than the idea that literary ideas and literary-critical techniques are relevant to the goal of linguistics, namely, understanding what language is and how it works. In what follows, I describe some of these ideas and techniques.

Literary studies provide two kinds of insights for linguists: insights of theory and insights of method. Among the insights of literary theory is the reminder that language users are creative, that people can say things in new ways, break the rules, make new rules, be unique. This idea is as old as artful language is. Despite the professed determinism of some schools of literary theory, according to which people's choices are completely constrained by class, gender, and ethnicity, readers of literature cannot help thinking about creativity, because artful language, at least in the West, is precisely creative language. Artists are supposed to innovate, so in order to understand them one has to note and understand their innovations. The literary theorists who paid perhaps the most overt attention to creativity were the Romantics, for whom literature was the spontaneous outpouring of emotion. The idea that authors have idiosyncratic voices, idiosyncratic ways of meaning, is so much a part of our most basic understanding of literature that it largely escapes comment. *Of course* only Hemingway could have written Hemingway's fiction: that is why the results of Hemingway write-alike contests are so funny. And while another poet could be Whitmanesque, only Whitman could use language exactly the way Whitman did.

When linguists think about the role of creativity in linguistic theory, we bring Chomsky to mind. But what creativity means in Chomskyan linguistics is simply people's ability to produce sentences they have not heard before. This notion of creativity does not, most emphatically, cover people's regular departures from the grammar of their language. Not many other linguists talk about the subject; we prefer, on the whole, to pin down the forces that limit creativity in language. But in focusing their attention on the margins of languages and speech communities, LePage and Tabouret-Keller find it crucial to acknowledge and describe linguistic creativity:

> In the contact situations in which pidgin languages develop[,] any ploy is tried which may make for communication under difficult circumstances—language is, as Roger Brown (1958) once called it, a game, in which the players invent the rules and, we would add, also act as umpires. . . . In our data from the West Indies we can see that, even though there may be several fairly highly focussed broad creole ver-

naculars with fairly regular rules, Creole speakers coming into contact with speakers of more standard varieties of English will nevertheless try a variety of code-switching or code-mixing or modifying devices, adjusting their Creole to meet the needs of the situation. . . . In fact, in any community we find that language use ranges from the highly inventive and idiosyncratic to the highly conventional and regular. (1985, pp. 11–12)

LePage and Tabouret-Keller see discourse as a series of "acts of identity" performed as speakers use whatever resources they have to express shifting personal identities and group identifications.

If LePage and Tabouret-Keller are right, then grammar is not a homogeneous, shared, preexisting set of tools for discourse. This is the point Paul Hopper makes in his discussion (1988) of "emergent grammar." "The Emergent Grammar view" of the object of linguistics, says Hopper, "entails the investigation of the way in which strategies for constructing texts *produce* the fixing of the forms which are understood to constitute grammar" (p. 121). As speakers and writers invent and reuse effective ways of structuring texts, they mutually create conventions which will continue to be reused. As Hopper and Thompson put it (1993, p. 357), "grammatical regularities arise because of certain strategies people habitually use in negotiating what they have to say with their hearers, in terms of what the hearer is likely to know or be able to identify, what needs to be highlighted or presented as newsworthy, what makes a good story, and so forth." The Emergent Grammar view enables us to ask about linguistic creation, about the first time a word or a structure is ever used, as well as about words and structures that are fully grammaticalized.

Another insight from literary theory is that language is expressive of self and moral character. Like the idea that speakers are creative, this idea is fundamental to Americans' everyday understanding of language use. Learning to write and speak well enables people, we say, to "express themselves" clearly. Particularly clear exponents of the self-expressive aspect of literature were the nineteenth-century American expressive individualists I discussed in chapter 4. For Melville, Emerson, Thoreau, Hawthorne, and others, democratic freedom meant the liberty to express oneself. Among the most overt statements of the linguistic ramifications of expressive individualism are those of the poet Walt Whitman, who famously wrote a "Song of Myself" as part of *Leaves of Grass* that begins "I celebrate myself, and sing myself . . ." (1966, p. 23).

Sociolinguistics has shown us a great deal about how linguistic choices reflect social status, class, gender, ethnicity, and group identity but little about how language differentiates individuals from other individuals. Formal syntax abstracts away from the self altogether. But linguists who work in depth with particular extended instances of language use sometimes come to connect them with their producers in ways that those who work with constructed data or with many small excerpts from speech do not. Dell Hymes (1981), for example, identifies the Northwest Coast myths he analyzes by the names of their tellers, talking, for example, about "Louis Simpson's 'The Deserted Boy,'" although he does not (and could not, not knowing much about Sapir's informant) talk about what in the story is particularly expressive of Simpson's individuality. Deborah Tannen, much of whose work is based on detailed analyses of taped conversations, calls for more investigation of individual styles. "Cultural patterns do not prescribe the form that a speaker's discourse will take," Tannen says (1989, p. 80), "but provide a range from which individuals choose strategies that they habitually use in expressing their individual styles." I have suggested in this book that the need for self-expression helps explain aspects of language use that are puzzling from the point of view of the social determinism that characterizes much work in sociolinguistics and discourse studies.

Literary studies can also provide methodological insights for linguistics. One of these has to do with the possibility and the value of close-reading techniques of analysis. Close reading, or *explication de texte*, has long been at the core of the literary curriculum and remains so despite over a decade of increased attention to literary history and to sociological theories of literary production and reception. Literary scholars more and more stress the importance of context in the interpretation of literary works and the possibility of varying interpretations, but they still require their students to be able to describe exactly what is in the words of a text and how it means what it does. Radically relativist objections to the possibility of doing this are, in the words of one overview of the field, "more often stated than believed" (Preminger 1974, p. 160).

The critic George Steiner (1989) describes literary explication as involving "opportunities and obligations" (p. 155) like those involved in hosting a guest. The process crucially requires *cortesias*, "courtesy," the willingness and ability to encounter people and events with full attention and an open mind. Critical courtesy requires "an ethic of common sense": "What we must focus, with uncompromising clarity, on the text, on the work of art, on the music before us, is an ethic of common sense, a courtesy of the most robust and refined sort" (p. 149). The process of interpretation is provisional for Steiner, tentative, a gradual approximation, like translation. Its rigor comes not from replicability but from conscientious fidelity to the text.

The linguist A. L. Becker (1979, 1982a) describes what he calls "modern philology" in very similar terms. The goal of traditional philologists was typically critical: the understanding of specific texts. What differentiates modern philology is that it is linguistic in aim. Becker uses the analogy, and usually the actual technique, of translation in the process of coming to understand how specific texts mean and, through that, how discourse works in general. Part of the courtesy Becker extends to the texts he studies is the systematic consideration of contexts of various kinds: contexts created by relationships of texts to generically or historically related texts; immediate context, or the interrelationships of units within texts; the contexts of relationships between the text's creator and the audience and of relationships between texts and the world (i.e., how worlds are reflected in and created in texts); the context of the text's medium; the context of what was or could not be said or written. This systematicity adds rigor to the interpretive process described by Steiner and others but does not alter it in the most fundamental ways. Like translation, interpretation is approximate. What makes it useful for linguistics is this: finding out where translation is most and least approximate (most "deficient" and most "exuberant") is, for Becker, how one finds out what languages and discourses in them can be like and what language in general can be like.

A second insight for linguistics from literary critical method is that there is always an aesthetic facet to interpretation. I dare say that we all know this, but few of us ever admit it. We come to love our data and the people who produce it, no matter what sort of linguistic work we do. Language appeals to many of us the way music does. (In fact, linguists are often people who treat their mouths and ears to other pleasures in addition to language: many of us are gourmet cooks or food connoisseurs, musicians or music lovers.) What we can learn from literary criticism is that our aesthetic responses to language are methodologically useful because they help us to see that linguistic structure and language use are constrained by societies' and individuals' senses of symmetry, harmony, and beauty. Paul Friedrich (1986, pp. 54–64), for example, describes linguistic fieldwork in Mexico in which his informants included unusual, poetically virtuosic people. These informants enabled Friedrich to see, in relief, the ways in which speakers' choices are influenced by cultural and individual aesthetics. In *Talking Voices* (1989), Deborah Tannen combines analyses of spontaneous casual conversation with analyses of novels and plays. Very much aware of the aesthetic side of linguistic analysis, Tannen explicitly looks for "literary" schemes and tropes in her conversational data. She explores repetition, imagery, and fictional dialogue, all long thought of as especially literary things to do with language, showing that a crucial element of all talk and the main purpose of some is that it has to appeal to people's senses of harmony, rhythm, and completeness. Tannen refers to this aesthetic as "involvement" and claims that understanding is impossible without it:

> It is the central theme of my analysis that involvement strategies are the basic force in both conversational and literary discourse by means of their sound and sense patterns. The former involve the audience with the speaker or writer by sweeping them up in what Scollon (1982) calls rhythmic ensemble, much as one is swept up by music and finds oneself moving in its rhythm. . . . Sense patterns create involvement through audience participation in sense making: By doing some of the work of making meaning, hearers or readers become participants in the discourse. (p. 17)

Clearly, the methodological willingness of linguists like Friedrich and Tannen to accept the aesthetic facet of interpretation has theoretical consequences. Both see language as reflecting and creating ideas of beauty in the most basic ways. In Friedrich's words,

> language, whether at the individual, sociocultural, or some universal level, is inherently, pervasively, and powerfully poetic. . . . It is in poetry, properly speaking, that the poetic potential is most fully realized, through various kinds of intensification that call attention to the form of the message. This calling of attention must be consonant with the aesthetics, implicit and explicit, of the language and culture. Certain musical potentials of language, in particular, must work together with certain kinds of meaning. (1986, p. 17)

In other words, the underlying structure of a language is most obviously on display in its poetry (Sherzer 1975 also makes this point vividly), and people's uses of language are variations on themes made possible by structure.

Major Themes Reiterated

Linguists of all persuasions acknowledge, on the basis of their everyday experience of language, that no two individuals talk alike. But few study individual variation and voice; the linguistic individual is thought to be outside the purview of linguistic theory. Saussurean *langue* is essentially social, not the property of any particular individual; Chomskyan competence is that of an idealized representative speaker-hearer; for variationist sociolinguists and historians, an individual's innovation is not a change until it is adopted by a community of speakers. We have learned a great deal about language by abstracting away from the relatively chaotic individual to the relatively tractable social fact; we have been able to focus our attention on things we are good at—phonology, morphology, syntax, discourse structure—and set aside things we are not so good at—psychology, rhetoric, aesthetics. Why bring individuals back into the picture, then? There are several important reasons.

For one thing, it is important to remind ourselves that the relationship between social facts and linguistic facts is indirect. The ways individuals talk indubitably have something to do with how they are identified by others with social groups and how they identify themselves, or refuse to identify themselves, with social groups. Individuals' speech equally indubitably has something to do with shared linguistic and pragmatic conventions about how to create and interpret sentences and discourses. We would not be able to understand each other if this were not the case. But intervening between the social fact and the linguistic output is individual choice, in the service of self-expression.

This leads to another observation I think important: language is just as crucially self-expressive as it is referential or relationship-affirming, poetic or rhetorical. Among the many schemes linguists and rhetoricians have suggested for categorizing the functions of language, one I have found especially useful can be represented by juxtaposing Roman Jakobson's familiar charts as I have done in figure 7.1. To each of the elements of linguistic communication (in capital letters) corresponds one of the functions of language (in lower case). One or another function can be foregrounded in any given case: talk that is mainly about the context (the world) is referential, for example; talk mainly about the existence and quality of the contact between addresser and addressee is phatic; talk mainly about the code they are using is metalingual; and talk that focuses on the sounds, words and structures of the message itself is poetic. But talk always serves all these functions: all talk is always referential, phatic, metalingual, poetic, and all talk also has the two functions for which Jakobson's terms are confusing and, I think, too narrowly defined: "conative" and "emotive." By conative, or addressee-focused, Jakobson meant vocative or imperative. More broadly, however, all talk is addressee-focused, in the sense that it is aimed at enlisting the audience's participation in discourse and sometimes the audience's agreement or action, and accommodated in its design to addressers' expectations about their audiences. Thus the conative function might better be labeled "rhetorical." Jakobson's emotive function labels the ways speakers always express their attitudes about what they are saying as they say

CONTEXT
referential
MESSAGE
poetic

ADDRESSER .... ADDRESSEE

emotive   CONTACT   conative
(self-expressive)   phatic   (rhetorical)
CODE
metalingual

Figure 7.1   Functions of language; after Jakobson 1960, pp. 353, 357.

it. It would be better, I think, to call this function of language "self-expressive." As it does the other things it does—refer to situations in the world, affirm people's connectedness, comment on itself, claim assent and adherence—talk always also shows who speakers take themselves to be, how they align themselves with others and how they differentiate themselves from others. All talk displays its speaker's individual voice. This is necessary because self-expression is necessary: no matter how much a society may value conformity or define people in relationship to others, individuals must on some level express individuated selves.

In order to do this, speakers must do things with language that other speakers do not do. Each speaker must, quite literally, be idiosyncratic. As we have seen, linguistic idiosyncrasy can take many forms and can be found on many levels. We have seen examples of idiosyncratic ways of displaying attitude (my father's *aaahh*), idiosyncratic ways of dividing up stories (*and uh . . . uh* in the "Stormy Weather" story), idiosyncratic ways of carrying out predefined linguistic tasks (by the Texas Poll interviewers), and idiosyncratic approaches to the whole display of self in discourse (Barbara Jordan's remarkable consistency of style). What follows from the necessity of idiosyncrasy in discourse is the necessity of an approach to the interpretation of language that makes idiosyncrasy understandable: a pragmatics based on general cognitive procedures of contextualization (Gumperz 1982) or hypotheses about relevance (Sperber and Wilson 1986), rather than on fixed interpretive rules. Because speakers are, for a fundamental reason, unconventional, language use cannot be seen as fundamentally conventional—even if, as is the case, conventionality is far more often than not useful in structuring utterances and understanding them.

That language is self-expressive in this fundamental way also has implications for the study of variation. An approach to variationist socio-linguistics that considers individual choice and individual voice may have a great deal to say about the mechanisms of linguistic choice and change. Linguistic models associated with class, ethnicity, gender, region, and so on need to be seen as resources on which speakers draw as they construct individual ways of sounding. Some speakers are more resourceful than others; the fairly insular communities characterized by largely private interpersonal contacts that have been favored as research sites for socio-linguistics may in fact produce less resourceful speakers than do more heterogeneous communities with more public forms of influence. But everyone's speech varies, to a greater or lesser degree; all speakers, in other words, draw on multiple ways of sounding as they draw on the several or many ways of being and acting that are modeled in their environments. Recent work on sociolinguistic variation suggests that by now traditional explanatory variables such as socioeconomic class, gender, and level of self-consciousness need to be supplemented with work on whom people associate with (Milroy 1987), how they express momentary or lasting identification with the groups their interlocutors belong to (LePage and Tabouret-Keller 1985), and how they feel about where they live (Bailey 1991). Sociolinguistic inquiry carried out from the perspective of the individual, based on case studies of particular people choosing ways to speak and act, could provide another source of illumination.

Finally, I have argued, both explicitly and by example, for a linguistic methodology based on close reading. I do not mean to suggest that all linguists drop what they are doing and start emulating literary critics. I do suggest, though, that the kind of close attention to real examples of language use that is traditionally the focus of criticism, illuminated by an awareness of the importance of creativity and self-expression supplementing linguistics' traditional disciplinary awareness of the importance of convention, formulaicity, and rule, can help linguists to see things about how language works that are usually obscured. The task of linguistics, that of understanding language in its entirety, is much larger than the task of literary criticism, which describes and evaluates only one of the uses of language. Accordingly, linguists must continue to bring many resources to the job. What people do when they talk has a great deal to do with knowledge that can be modeled with rules and conventions. It has a great deal to do with the need for unambiguous referentiality. Intuitive work and quantitative analyses of large corpora of data have important roles to play. But the linguistics of language cannot be fully explanatory without a linguistics of the individual speaker.

Notes

1. Becker attributes the term "new philology" to Ortega y Gasset (1957, 1959). I discuss Becker's approach in greater depth in what follows; see Becker 1975, 1979a, 1979b, 1981, 1982a, 1982b, 1984a, 1984b, 1986, 1988, 1994.

2. Claims for conceptions of person like that of the Balinese have also been made by Read (1955) for the Gahuku-Gama of New Guinea and by Dumont (1970) for Asian Indians. Shweder and Bourne (1984) report on a questionnaire study of concepts of person in India.

3. Young adults are best at identifying voices, and women are slightly better than men under laboratory conditions. Blind people do significantly better than sighted ones. See Bull and Clifford (1984) for details of experimental studies of "ear"-witnessing.

4. See Ladefoged 1975, pp. 187–191, for a more thorough basic account of acoustic differences in voice quality and Laver 1979 for bibliographic information about research in the area.

5. Graddol and Swann (1989, pp. 12–40) provide a thorough discussion of the social aspects of the physical voice. See also Pittam 1994 for recent work on voice and social interaction.

6. Holdcroft (1991) argues that Saussure was not as thoroughgoing a social realist as some have taken him to be. He points out that Saussure's emphasis on *langue* as a social phenomenon was in reaction not to individualists but to linguists such as August Schleicher, who thought of language as analogous to a biological organism. Furthermore, Saussure's conception of *parole* includes a great deal more than is commonly assumed, including, for example, sentence formation, which Saussure saw as entirely a matter of individual choice. But whatever Saussure's actual position was, work based on his conception of language subsequently focused almost entirely on the social aspects of his model,

becoming increasingly likely to see *langue* as an entity existing independent of individual competences.

7. See Heller and Wellbery 1986 for a discussion of the incompatibility of "classical" individualism with the social theory of the late nineteenth century and the poststructuralist "crisis of individualism."

8. Changes of this sort, involving language-learning ability and strategy, typically occur at the beginning of adolescence, not at the end, so this seems an ad hoc way to account for the twin findings.

9. I am grateful to Jill Brody for making this connection for me.

10. I do not intend to provide a complete overview of discourse analysis here. For that, see Brown and Yule 1983; Schiffrin 1994.

11. Discourse analysts do not always or even usually choose to focus on what is individual, of course. Some use discourse analysis for precisely the opposite purpose; Fairclough (1985) and other "critical" discourse analysts argue that the autonomy of the individual is an illusion.

Chapter 2

1. We are still far from being able to do this, of course; language is still mostly mysterious, which is why linguists continue to find it fascinating. To be able to model language, discourse, and cognition in such a way as to enable a machine to speak like a person to a person is the elusive goal of research in artificial intelligence.

2. Names in the stories have been changed, as have the tellers' names.

3. Parentheses enclose material that was impossible or difficult to make out on the tape. Words in parentheses are best guesses.

4. Karen Bruce gave me the idea of transcribing speech this way.

5. On "episodes" in discourse, see van Dijk 1981. I use the term as van Dijk does; an episode is part of a text that is set off from what precedes and follows in some thematic way, by being about a different set of events or a different place or character or by being told from a different point of view.

6. Not all instances of *so* are, of course, markers of new episodes. This one, like the one in "**So** Doc got his gun," seem to function mainly to link story events causally. I discuss the multifunctionality of words like *so* in chapter 3; the authoritative discussion of the issue is Schiffrin 1987.

7. See Tannen 1989, pp. 98–133, on the functions of dialogue in conversation.

8. Each *rr* represents a long (almost one second), heavily retroflexed liquid, which modulates in pitch and loudness from soft and low to loud and high and back to soft and low.

9. On functions of repetition in conversation, see Tannen 1987a, 1987b, 1989; Norrick 1987; and Johnstone 1994.

10. On senses of *carry*, see the *Dictionary of American Regional English*, vol. 1, p. 550.

11. Some sociolinguists—e.g., Labov 1972a; Macaulay 1991—have suggested that lower-class speakers are more creative language users than middle-class speakers because they have the resources of more varieties available to them and because they are less bound by the conservative conventions fostered by literacy. Bernstein (1970) suggests the opposite, that lower-class speakers speak a "restricted code." I prefer to avoid making either claim, on the grounds that creativity is notoriously hard to measure and that every speaker, due to the nature of language, is resourceful.

Chapter 3

1. Irvine (1978) describes a similar phenomenon among speakers of Wolof. High-status speakers deliberately make grammatical mistakes as a way of differentiating themselves from people of lower castes.

2. Learning to write self-expressively is thought by some to be a necessary step in the cognitive development of a writer (Britton et al. 1975).

3. In literary criticism the term "voice" has several meanings. Some writers use it to refer to the trace of the author in a text, some to the persona of the narrator; it is also used to refer to literary genres, periods, and trends, as in "the voice of the Southwest" or "the voice of the nineteenth century." Current literary theory tends to disregard authorial voice, in accordance with the move toward minimizing the importance of authors' intentions. Voices, or "discourses," are thought to appertain to groups rather than to individuals, and responsibility for creating meaning is instead placed on readers.

4. Research in psycholinguistics has measured "fluency" by number of syllables produced, speech rate, and number of filled and unfilled pauses. As children grow up, for example, their stories come to have more syllables; more syllables per second; fewer, shorter unfilled pauses; fewer false starts and repeats; and more "fillers" such as *you know* or *like*. O'Connell (1988, pp. 181–212) reviews such studies. I take a different approach here but would not be surprised if the speakers I identify as articulate were also "fluent" in these ways.

5. Some sources refer to "nominal relative" clauses, a subset of nominal clauses consisting of nominal clauses introduced with *wh-* elements (Quirk and Greenbaum 1973, p. 319). I classify these with nominal clauses rather than with relative clauses, a category I restrict to include only noun-modifying clauses. I do not include "sentential relatives" such as "He admires Mrs. Brown, which surprises me" (ibid., p. 383), of which there are none in the data in any case. See Fox and Thompson 1990 and sources they cite on the structure and semantics of relative clauses in English.

6. See Thompson 1984, 1987; Tomlin 1985.

7. Schiffrin (1987, pp. 217–227) suggests that uses of *so* like these serve to mark transitions or potential transitions in the "participation framework" of the discourse: chances for a hearer to complete an idea or take the floor. But *so* is often a boundary marker in monologue, marking breaks between episodes without thereby giving hearers a chance to take over responsibility for the discourse (Johnstone 1990a, p. 52; see also the discussion in chapter 2 of the function of *so* in Mattie Blair's story). I do not have enough relevant data to resolve this issue, but I suspect that *so* may serve a general function as a signal of potential boundary and that its specific function may vary with speaker and situation. In Bryant's speech, *so* in fact often prefaces the last sentence in a turn, but in Stoller's speech it tends to mark turn-internal boundaries at which others do not take over.

8. Perelman and Olbrechts-Tyteca (1969, pp. 193–260) call arguments like these "quasi-logical." One of their examples of such an argument is the one we often use, explicitly or implicitly, in planning parties: "John is a friend of mine, and Sue is a friend of mine, so John and Sue ought to get along." This argument echoes transitive proofs such as

$$A = B$$
$$B = C$$
$$\therefore A = C,$$

except that friendship, unlike numerical equivalence, is not a transitive relationship.

9. Little research has been done on gender differences in persuasive style. Tannen (1990, pp. 91–92) cites a study by Roberts and Jupp (1985) of a faculty meeting at which women's arguments were not accepted by men because the women made reference to personal experience to support claims. My suggestion that logical modes of proof sound more masculine than nonlogical modes is conjecture based on the fact that traditional Western models for speech such as Aristotelian rhetoric (as well as traditional models for other modes of behavior) tend most often to be based on the actual behavior of men rather than women.

Chapter 4

1. With the help of the director of the Texas A&M Public Policy Resources Laboratory, James Dyer, the sociolinguist Guy Bailey arranged for the Texas Poll run of January 1989 to be taped for the initial purpose of collecting data about phonological variation in the state. That part of the project, as well as some of the transcription, were funded by United States National Science Foundation grant BNS-8812552 to Bailey. I am grateful to Bailey for letting me use the tapes and to the student volunteers who provided first-draft transcriptions of many of them. A longer and somewhat different version of the section of this chapter on interviewers has appeared as Johnstone 1991.

2. This system does not always work the way it is supposed to. Callees often appear to misunderstand the directions, summoning the oldest or the youngest adult rather than the one whose birthday was most recent. In one of the thirty-six interviews we look at here, the callee simply refused to summon the appropriate respondent, saying "she wouldn't want to talk to you," and the interviewer interviewed him instead.

3. On the whole, anaphora and other sorts of links to previous talk were rare in the interviews. Respondents tended not to connect answers with previous ones and did not object to being asked at the end of the interview for demographic information they may already have supplied in its course. This is an interesting feature of this speech event, though not one I will pursue here.

4. It is not easy to refuse to be interviewed by the Texas Poll. Because the reputation of a polling service depends on its producing truly representative samples, targeted respondents who decline to be interviewed are called back up to three times, the final time by a senior staff member who specializes in getting people to cooperate.

5. Although the numbers are small, Strauss and Schatzman's findings about class appear to be only partially borne out in the Texas Poll data. Well-educated, middle-aged women seemed to be the most businesslike about the survey, adding minimal syntax to their answers and providing least justification. Of the three respondents whose interviews diverged most from what is expected by being extremely conversational, so much so that the interviewer was drawn into the conversation, two were retired men, one a lawyer and one a laborer.

6. While respondents' ethnicity may have been clear from their voices in some cases, in many cases it probably was not. Research by Bailey and Maynor (1989) and Haley (1990) has shown that people cannot reliably distinguish Southern whites' voices from those of Blacks, especially when the speakers are older.

7. Tannen's (1989) notion of "involvement," developed from Lakoff's (1973) work on politeness, captures the same facts about how interlocutors must always simultaneously respect each other's needs for independence and for connection.

8. Johnstone, Ferrara, and Bean (1992) list fifteen techniques for discourse task management employed by the interviewers.

9. On individualism in the thought and writing of Emerson, Thoreau, Adams, and James, see Hansen 1990.

10. Gonnaud (1987) discusses Emerson's individualism in depth.

11. Philipsen (1992) contrasts this mainstream view, "the ideology of dignity," with the view held by residents of a working-class ethnic enclave in Chicago, for whom "the person is fundamentally a persona, a bundle of social identities" (p. 15).

12. This example is from Johnstone et al. (1994, p. 10).

13. The value of individual uniqueness is alluded to even when Americans are being asked to conform. A direct-mail clothing catalogue, for example,

urges women to "express your individuality with uniquely designed Aztec Separates." The goal of the ad is, of course, to get as many women as possible to order identical "unique" sweaters and shirts.

Chapter 5

1. In the facetious words of the columnist Molly Ivins (1993), Jordan "can't help sounding like God Almighty."

2. More than any other stylistic feature, the use of long words is traditionally associated with education. It is thus an obvious resource for someone wanting to express an educated self. Her education is an important part of Jordan's claim to personal authority, and she mentions it often.

3. DuBois (1986) speaks of statements like the ones I describe here as "ritual utterances." A ritual utterances is one "the evidence (or authority) for [which] is found in the utterance itself" (pp. 322–323). Such utterances sound like (though they are not always) analytic statements, in which the truth of the statement is established by the meaning of the words, as in "All bachelors are unmarried." Though Jordan's talk is not ritual in most of the ways DuBois has in mind, her use of copular *be* does help to make her claims seem self-evident in this way.

4. Note that this way of calculating consistency yields figures that could be the same for one speaker all of whose talk is relatively formal and another whose language is always informal. It simply displays how much difference there is between texts.

Chapter 6

1. Like the story by Lon Bauer discussed in chapter 1, these stories are part of a corpus of personal experience narrative collected in and around Fort Wayne, Indiana, in the early 1980s. Johnstone 1990a discusses the forms and functions of the Fort Wayne stories in general, and the story about singing "Stormy Weather" in particular (pp. 49–52).

References

Abrahams, Roger D. 1976. *Talking black*. Rowley, MA: Newbury.

Angelo, Bonnie. 1991, June 3. An ethical guru monitors morality. *Time*, pp. 9–10.

Arieli, Yehoshua. 1964. *Individualism and nationalism in American ideology*. Cambridge, MA: Harvard UP.

Ash, Sharon. 1988. Speaker identification in sociolinguistics and criminal law. In Kathleen Ferrara, Becky Brown, Keith Walters, and John Baugh, eds., *Linguistic change and contact* (Proceedings of N-WAV XVI), pp. 25–33. Austin: Department of Linguistics, U of Texas.

Bailey, Guy. 1991. Directions of change in Texas English. *Journal of American Culture* 14: 125–134.

Bailey, Guy, and Natalie Maynor. 1989. The divergence controversy. *American Speech* 64: 12–39.

Balester, Valerie. 1993. *Cultural divide: A study of African-American college-level writers*. Portsmouth, NH: Boynton/Cook-Heinemann.

Bates, Elizabeth, Inge Bretherton, and Lynn Snyder. 1988. *From first words to grammar: Individual differences and dissociable mechanisms*. Cambridge: Cambridge UP.

Bauman, Richard. 1977. *Verbal art as performance*. Rowley, MA: Newbury House. (Rpt. 1984, Prospect Heights, IL: Waveland).

Bauman, Richard, and Joel Sherzer, eds. 1974. *Explorations in the ethnography of speaking*. Cambridge: Cambridge UP.

Bean, Judith Mattson. 1992. Margaret Fuller's legacy: Gender, voice, and authority. Doctoral dissertation, Texas A&M U.

Bean, Judith Mattson, and Barbara Johnstone. 1994. Workplace reasons for saying you're sorry: Discourse management and apology in telephone interviews. *Discourse Processes* 17: 59–81.

Becker, A. L. 1975. A linguistic image of nature: The Burmese numerative classifier system. *International Journal of the Sociology of Language* 5: 109–121.

195

Becker, A. L. 1979a. The figure a sentence makes: An interpretation of a classical Malay sentence. In Talmy Givón, ed., *Syntax and semantics*, vol. 12, *Discourse and syntax*, pp. 243–259. New York: Academic P.

Becker, A. L. 1979b. Text-building, epistemology and aesthetics in Javanese shadow theater. In A. L. Becker and Aram Yengoyan, eds., *The imagination of reality: Essays in Southeast Asian coherence systems*, pp. 211–244. Norwood, NJ: Ablex.

Becker, A. L. 1981. On Emerson on language. In Deborah Tannen, ed., *Georgetown University round table on languages and linguistics 1981*, pp. 1–11. Washington, D.C.: Georgetown UP.

Becker, A. L. 1982a. Beyond translation: Esthetics and language description. In Heidi Byrnes, ed., *Georgetown University round table on languages and linguistics 1982*, pp. 124–138. Washington, D.C.: Georgetown UP.

Becker, A. L. 1982b. Binding wild words: Cohesion in Old Javanese prose. In Harimurti Kridalaksana and Anton Moeliono, eds., *Pelangi Bahasa: A collection of essays for J. W. M. Verhaar, S.J.*, pp. 19–35. Jakarta: Bhratara P.

Becker, A. L. 1984a. Biography of a sentence: A Burmese proverb. In Edward M. Bruner, ed., *Text, play, and story: The construction and reconstruction of self and society* (1983 Proceedings of the American Ethnological Society, Stuart Plattner, proceedings ed.), pp. 135–155. Washington, D.C.: American Ethnological Society.

Becker, A. L. 1984b. The linguistics of particularity: Interpreting superordination in a Javanese text. In Claudia Brugman and Monica Macaulay, eds., with Amy Dahlstrom, Michele Emanatian, Birch Moonwomon, and Catherine O'Connor, *Proceedings of the Berkeley Linguistics Society, Tenth annual meeting*, pp. 425–436. Berkeley, CA: Berkeley Linguistics Society.

Becker, A. L. 1986. The figure a classifier makes: Describing a particular Burmese classifier. In Colette Craig, ed., *Noun classes and categorization* (Typological Studies in Language 7). Amsterdam: John Benjamins.

Becker, A. L. 1988. Language in particular: A lecture. In Deborah Tannen, ed., *Linguistics in context: Connecting observation and understanding*, pp. 17–35. Norwood, NJ: Ablex.

Becker, A. L. 1994. Repetition and otherness: An essay. In Barbara Johnstone, ed., *Repetition in discourse: Interdisciplinary perspectives*, vol. 2, pp. 162–175. Norwood, NJ: Ablex.

Bellah, Robert N., Richard Madsen, William M. Sullivan, Ann Swidler, and Steven M. Tipton. 1985. *Habits of the heart: Individualism and commitment in American life*. Berkeley: U of California P.

Bernstein, Basil. 1970. *Class, codes and control, vol. 1: Theoretical studies towards a sociology of language*. London: Routledge & Kegan Paul.

Bernstein, Cynthia. 1993. Measuring social causes of phonological variation in Texas. *American Speech* 68: 227–240.

Biber, Douglas. 1988. *Variation across speech and writing.* Cambridge: Cambridge UP.

Biber, Douglas, and Edward Finegan. 1989. Styles of stance in English: Lexical and grammatical marking of evidentiality and affect. *Text* 9: 93–124.

Bickerton, Derek. 1990. *Language and species.* Chicago: U of Chicago P.

Bloch, Maurice. 1971. Symbols, song, dance and features of articulation. *European Journal of Sociology* 15: 55–81.

Brenner, Michael. 1981. Aspects of conversational structure in the research interview. In Paul Werth, ed., *Conversation and discourse: Structure and interpretation,* pp. 19–40. London: Croom Helm.

Briggs, Charles L. 1986. *Learning how to ask: A sociolinguistic appraisal of the role of the interview in social science research* (Studies in the Social and Cultural Foundations of Language 1). Cambridge: Cambridge UP.

Britton, J., T. Burgess, N. Martin, A. McLeod, and H. Rosen. 1975. *The development of writing abilities 11–18.* Urbana, IL: National Council of Teachers of English.

Brown, Gillian. 1990. Domestic individualism: Imagining self in nineteenth-century America. Berkeley: U of California P.

Brown, Gillian, and George Yule. 1983. *Discourse analysis.* Cambridge: Cambridge UP.

Brown, Penelope, and Stephen C. Levinson. 1987. *Politeness: Some universals in language usage.* Cambridge: Cambridge UP. (First published 1978 in Esther Goody, ed., *Questions and Politeness.*)

Bull, Ray, and Brian R. Clifford. 1984. Earwitness voice recognition accuracy. In Gary L. Wells and Elizabeth F. Loftus, eds., *Eyewitness testimony: Psychological perspectives,* pp. 92–123. Cambridge: Cambridge UP.

Callow, Kathleen, and John C. Callow. 1992. Text as purposive action: A meaning-based analysis. In William C. Mann and Sandra A. Thompson, eds., *Discourse description: Diverse linguistic analyses of a fund-raising text,* pp. 5–37. Amsterdam and Philadelphia: John Benjamins.

Carden, Guy. 1970. A note on conflicting idiolects. *Linguistic Inquiry* 1: 281–290.

Carpenter, Liz. 1985, April. On my mind: Barbara Jordan talks about ethics, optimism, and hard choices in government. *Ms.* 13: 75–76, 112.

Chafe, Wallace. 1980. The deployment of consciousness in the production of a narrative. In Wallace Chafe, ed., *The pear stories: Cognitive, cultural, and linguistic aspects of narrative production,* pp. 1–50. Norwood, NJ: Ablex.

Chafe, Wallace. 1986. Cognitive constraints on information flow. In Russell Tomlin, ed., *Coherence and grounding in discourse,* pp. 21–51. Amsterdam: John Benjamins.

Chafe, Wallace. 1994. *Discourse, consciousness, and time: The flow and displacement of conscious experience in speaking and writing.* Chicago: U of Chicago P.

Chambers, J. K., and Peter Trudgill. 1980. *Dialectology.* Cambridge: Cambridge UP.

Cheepen, Christine. 1988. *The predictability of informal conversation*. London and New York: Pinter Publishers.

Chomsky, Noam. 1986. *Knowledge of language*. New York: Praeger.

Cicourel, Aaron. 1964. *Method and measurement in sociology*. New York: Free Press.

Coleridge, Samuel Taylor. 1907. *Biographia Literaria*. London: Oxford UP.

Coulmas, Florian, ed. 1981. A Festschrift for the native speaker. The Hague: Mouton.

Coulthard, Malcolm. 1985. *An introduction to discourse analysis*, new ed. London: Longman.

Craig, Colette G. 1979. Jacaltec: Fieldwork in Guatemala. In Timothy Shopen, ed., *Languages and their speakers*, pp. 2–57. Philadephia: U of Pennsylvania P.

Crystal, David, and Paul Fletcher. 1979. Profile analysis of language disability. In Charles J. Fillmore, Daniel Kempler, and William S.-Y. Wang, eds., *Individual differences in language ability and language behavior*, pp. 167–188. New York: Academic P.

Dorian, Nancy. 1994. Varieties of variation in a very small place: Social homogeneity, prestige norms, and linguistic variation. *Language* 70: 631–696.

DuBois, John W. 1986. Self-evidence and ritual speech. In Wallace Chafe and Johanna Nichols, eds., *Evidentiality: The linguistic encoding of epistemology*, pp. 313–336. Norwood, NJ: Ablex.

Dumont, Louis. 1970. *Homo hierarchicus*. Chicago: U of Chicago P.

Dumont, Louis. 1985. A modified view of our origins: The Christian beginnings of modern individualism. In Michael Carrithers, Steven Collins, and Steven Lukes, eds., *The category of the person: Anthropology, philosophy, history*, pp. 93–122. Cambridge: Cambridge UP.

Ehrlich, Susan. 1994. Repetition and point of view in represented speech and thought. In Barbara Johnstone, ed., *Repetition in discourse: Interdisciplinary perspectives*, vol. 1, pp. 86–97. Norwood, NJ: Ablex.

Emerson, Ralph Waldo. 1990. *Essays: First and second series*. New York: Vintage Books/Library of America.

Epstein, E. L. 1978. *Language and style*. London: Methuen.

Fairclough, Norman L. 1985. Critical and descriptive goals in discourse analysis. *Journal of Pragmatics* 9: 739–763.

Ferguson, Charles. 1979. Phonology as an individual access system: Some data from language acquisition. In Charles J. Fillmore, Daniel Kempler, and William S.-Y. Wang, eds., *Individual differences in language ability and language behavior*, pp. 189–201. New York: Academic P.

Ferrara, Kathleen. 1994. Repetition as rejoinder in therapeutic discourse: Echoing and mirroring. In Barbara Johnstone, ed., *Repetition in discourse: Interdisciplinary perspectives*, vol. 2, pp. 66–83. Norwood, NJ: Ablex.

Finnegan, Ruth H. 1977. Oral poetry: Its nature, significance, and social context. Cambridge: Cambridge UP.

Fox, Barbara A., and Sandra A. Thompson. 1990. A discourse explanation of the grammar of relative clauses in English conversation. *Language* 66: 297–316.

Fraser, Bruce. 1981. On apologizing. In Florian Coulmas, ed., *Conversational routine*, pp. 259–271. The Hague: Mouton.

Friedlander, B. 1970. Receptive language development: Issues and problems. *Merrill-Palmer Quarterly of Behavior and Development* 16: 7–15.

Friedrich, Paul. 1986. *The language parallax*. Austin: U of Texas P.

Friedrich, Paul, and James Redfield. 1979. Speech as a personality symbol: The case of Achilles. In Anwar S. Dil, ed., *Language, context, and the imagination: Essays by Paul Friedrich*, pp. 402–440. Stanford, CA: Stanford UP. (Orig. pub. in *Language* 54 (1978): 263–288.)

Geertz, Clifford. 1980. Blurred genres: The refiguration of social thought. *American Scholar* 49(2): 165–179.

Geertz, Clifford. 1984. "From the native's point of view": On the nature of anthropological understanding. In Richard A. Shweder and Robert A. LeVine, eds., *Culture theory: Essays on mind, self, and emotion*, pp. 123–136. Cambridge: Cambridge UP.

Goffman, Erving. 1959. *The presentation of self in everyday life*. New York: Doubleday.

Gonnaud, Maurice. 1987. An uneasy solitude: Individual and society in the work of Ralph Waldo Emerson. Princeton: Princeton UP.

Gottlieb, Marvin. 1986. *Interview*. White Plains, NY: Longman.

Graddol, David, and Joan Swann. 1989. *Gender voices*. Oxford: Basil Blackwell.

Greenblatt, Stephen Jay. 1980. *Renaissance self-fashioning: From More to Shakespeare*. Chicago: U of Chicago P.

Grice, H. P. 1975. Logic and conversation. In P. Cole and J. L. Morgan, eds., *Syntax and semantics*, vol. 3, *Speech acts*, pp. 41–58. New York: Academic P.

Grimes, Joseph E. 1975. *The thread of discourse*. Berlin, New York, Amsterdam: Mouton.

Grimshaw, Allen D. 1969. Language as data and obstacle in sociological research. *Items* 23: 17–21.

Gumperz, John J. 1982. *Discourse strategies*. Cambridge: Cambridge UP.

Gumperz, John J., and Deborah Tannen. 1979. Individual and social differences in language use. In Charles J. Fillmore, Daniel Kempler, and William S.-Y. Wang, eds., *Individual differences in language ability and language behavior*, pp. 305–325. New York: Academic P.

Guy, Gregory R. 1980. Variation in the group and the individual: The case of final stop deletion. In William Labov, ed., *Locating language in time and space*, pp. 1–36. New York: Academic P.

Haley, Ken. 1990. Some complexities in speech identification. *SECOL Review* 14: 101–113.

Hallowell, A. I. 1955. The self and its behavioral environment. In A. I. Hallowell, ed., *Culture and experience*, pp. 75–110. Philadelphia: U of Pennsylvania P.

Hansen, Olaf. 1990. *Aesthetic individualism and practical intellect: American allegory in Emerson, Thoreau, Adams, and James*. Princeton: Princeton UP.

Harris, Zellig. 1952. Discourse analysis. *Language* 28: 1–30.

Heller, Thomas C., and David E. Wellbery. 1986. Introduction. In Thomas C. Heller, Morton Sosna, and David E. Wellbery, eds., *Reconstructing individualism: Autonomy, individuality and the self in Western thought*, pp. 1–15. Stanford, CA: Stanford UP.

Hockett, C. F. 1987. *Refurbishing our foundations: Elementary linguistics from an advanced point of view*. Amsterdam: John Benjamins.

Hoinville, Gerald, and Roger Jowell, in association with Colin Airey, Lindsay Brook, Gillian Courtenay, Barry Hedges, Graham Kalton, Jean Morton-Williams, David Walker, and Douglas Wood. 1978. *Survey research practice*. London: Heinemann Educational Books.

Holdcroft, David. 1991. *Saussure: Signs, system, and arbitrariness*. Cambridge: Cambridge UP.

Hollien, Harry. 1990. *The acoustics of crime: The new science of forensic phonetics*. New York: Plenum P.

Holmes, Janet. 1989. Sex differences and apologies: One aspect of communicative competence. *Applied Linguistics* 10: 194–213.

Hopper, Paul. 1988. Emergent grammar and the a priori grammar postulate. In Deborah Tannen, ed., *Linguistics in context: Connecting observation and understanding*, pp. 117–134. Norwood, NJ: Ablex.

Hopper, Paul J., and Sandra A. Thompson. 1993. Language universals, discourse pragmatics, and semantics. *Language Sciences* 15: 357–376.

Hopper, Robert. 1990. Speech errors and the poetics of conversation. Paper presented at Speech Communication Association Annual Meeting, Chicago.

Hopper, Robert, and Philip Glenn. 1994. Repetition and play in conversation. In Barbara Johnstone, ed., *Repetition in discourse: Interdisciplinary perspectives*, vol. 2, pp. 29–40. Norwood, NJ: Ablex.

Hudson, R. A. 1980. *Sociolinguistics*. Cambridge: Cambridge UP.

Hyman, H., et al. 1954. *Interviewing in social research*. Chicago: U of Chicago P.

Hymes, Dell. 1972. Models of the interaction of language and social life. In John J. Gumperz and Dell Hymes, eds., *Directions in sociolinguistics: The ethnography of communication*, pp. 35–71. New York: Holt, Rinehart and Winston.

Hymes, Dell. 1974. *Foundations in sociolinguistics: An ethnographic approach*. Philadelphia: U of Pennsylvania P.

Hymes, Dell. 1979. Sapir, competence, voices. In Charles J. Fillmore, Daniel Kempler, and William S.-Y. Wang, eds., *Individual differences in language ability and language behavior*, pp. 33–45. New York: Academic P.

Hymes, Dell. 1981. *In vain I tried to tell you: Essays in native American ethnopoetics*. Philadelphia: U of Pennsylvania P.

Irvine, Judith. 1978. Wolof noun classification: The social setting of divergent change. *Language in Society* 7: 37–64.

Ivins, Molly. 1993, August 25. If the Lord comes callin', ask for some ID. *Bryan College Station Eagle*, p. A6.

Jakobson, Roman. 1960. Concluding statement: Linguistics and poetics. In Thomas A. Sebeok, ed., *Style in language*, pp. 350–377. Cambridge, MA: MIT P.

Johnstone, Barbara. 1987a. "He says . . . so I said": Verb tense alternation and narrative depictions of authority in American English. *Linguistics* 25: 33–52.

Johnstone, Barbara. 1987b. Linguistic strategies and cultural styles for persuasive discourse. In Stella Ting-Toomey and Felipe Korzenny, eds., *Language, communication, and culture: Current directions* (International and Intercultural Communication Annual, vol. 13), pp. 139–156. Beverly Hills: Sage Publications.

Johnstone, Barbara. 1987c. Perspectives on repetition. *Text* 7, no. 3 (special issue).

Johnstone, Barbara. 1990a. *Stories, community and place: Narratives from middle America*. Bloomington: Indiana UP.

Johnstone, Barbara. 1990b. "Orality" and discourse structure in Modern Standard Arabic. In Mushira Eid, ed., *New perspectives on Arabic linguistics*, vol. 1, pp. 215–233. Philadelphia: John Benjamins.

Johnstone, Barbara. 1990c. Variation in discourse: Midwestern narrative style. *American Speech* 63: 195–214.

Johnstone, Barbara. 1991. Individual style in an American public-opinion survey: Personal performance and the ideology of referentiality. *Language in Society* 20: 557–576.

Johnstone, Barbara. 1993. Community and contest: Midwestern men and women creating their worlds in conversational storytelling. In Deborah Tannen, ed., *Gender and conversational interaction*, pp. 62–80. Oxford: Oxford UP.

Johnstone, Barbara, ed.. 1994. *Repetition in discourse: Interdisciplinary perspectives*, vol. 1 and 2. Norwood, NJ: Ablex.

Johnstone, Barbara, et al. 1994. Repetition in discourse: A dialogue. In Barbara Johnstone, ed., *Repetition in discourse: Interdisciplinary perspectives*, vol. 1, pp. 1–20. Norwood, NJ: Ablex.

Johnstone, Barbara, Judith Mattson Bean, and Delma McLeod-Porter. forthcoming. Ethnography and discourse analysis in dialectology: Methods of a study of language, region, and personal identity in Texas. In *Proceedings of Methods VIII International Conference on Dialectology, 1993*.

Johnstone, Barbara, Kathleen Ferrara, and Judith Mattson Bean. 1992. Gender, politeness, and discourse management in same-sex and cross-sex opinion-poll interviews. *Journal of Pragmatics* 18: 145–170.

Jordan, Barbara. 1992. Interview by Delma McLeod-Porter, Judith Mattson Bean, and Barbara Johnstone, Austin, TX, February 12.

Keenan, Elinor Ochs. 1973. A sliding sense of obligatoriness: The polystructure of Malagasy oratory. *Language in Society* 2: 225–243.

Keenan, Elinor Ochs. 1974. Norm-makers, norm-breakers: Uses of speech by men and women in a Malagasy community. In Richard Bauman and Joel Sherzer, eds., *Explorations in the ethnography of speaking*, pp. 125–143. Cambridge: Cambridge UP.

Knox, Laurie. 1994. Repetition and relevance: Self-repetition as a strategy for initiating cooperation in non-native/native speaker conversations. In Barbara Johnstone, ed., *Repetition in discourse: Interdisciplinary perspectives*, vol. 1, pp. 195–206. Norwood, NJ: Ablex.

Koch, Barbara Johnstone. 1983a. Presentation as proof: The language of Arabic rhetoric. *Anthropological Linguistics* 25: 47–60.

Koch, Barbara Johnstone. 1983b. Arabic lexical couplets and the evolution of synonymy. *General Linguistics* 23: 51–61.

Koch, Barbara Johnstone. 1984. Repeating yourself: Discourse paraphrase and the generation of language. *Proceedings of the first Eastern States Conference on Linguistics*, pp. 250–259. Columbus: Ohio State U.

Kosinski, Jerzy N. 1972. *Being there*. New York: Bantam.

Kunsmann, P. 1976. Reduplication as a strategy for language acquisition. Paper presented at Linguistic Society of America Summer Meeting, Oswego, NY.

Labov, William. 1972a. *Sociolinguistic patterns*. Philadelphia: U of Pennsylvania P.

Labov, William. 1972b. The logic of nonstandard English. In William Labov, *Language in the inner city*, pp. 201–240. Philadelphia: U of Pennsylvania P.

Labov, William. 1972c. The transformation of experience in narrative syntax. In William Labov, *Language in the inner city*, pp. 354–396. Philadelphia: U of Pennsylvania P.

Labov, William. 1979. Locating the frontier between social and psychological factors in linguistic variation. In Charles J. Fillmore, Daniel Kempler, and William S.-Y. Wang, eds., *Individual differences in language ability and language behavior*, pp. 327–340. New York: Academic P.

Ladefoged, Peter. 1975. *A course in phonetics*. New York: Harcourt Brace Jovanovich.

Lakoff, Robin. 1973. The logic of politeness, or minding your p's and q's. In Claudia Corum, T. Cedric Smith-Stark, and Ann Wiser, eds., *Papers from the ninth regional meeting of the Chicago Linguistic Society*, pp. 292–305. Chicago: Chicago Linguistic Society.

Laver, John. 1979. *Voice quality: A classified research bibliography*. Amsterdam: John Benjamins.

Leech, Geoffrey N. 1983. *Principles of pragmatics*. London: Longman.

LePage, R. B., and Andrée Tabouret-Keller. 1985. *Acts of identity: Creole-based approaches to language and ethnicity*. Cambridge: Cambridge UP.

Levinson, Steven C. 1983. *Pragmatics*. Cambridge: Cambridge UP.

Linde, Charlotte. 1993. *Life stories: The creation of coherence.* Oxford: Oxford UP.

Longacre, Robert E. 1976. *An anatomy of speech notions.* Lisse: Peter de Ridder.

Lord, Albert B. 1960. *The singer of tales.* Harvard Studies in Comparative Literature, Vol, 24. Cambridge, MA: Harvard UP.

Love, Nigel. 1990. The locus of language in a redefined linguistics. In Hayley G. Davis and Talbot J. Taylor, eds., *Redefining linguistics*, pp. 53–117. New York: Routledge.

Macaulay, Ronald K. S. 1991. *Locating dialect in discourse: The language of honest men and bonnie lassies in Ayr.* New York: Oxford UP.

Majewski, W., H. Hollien, and J. Zalewski. 1972. Speaking fundamental frequencies of Polish adult males. *Phonetica* 25: 119–125.

Mauss, Marcel. 1938. Une catégorie de l'esprit humain: La notion de personne, celle de "moi". In *Journal of the Royal Anthropological Institute* 68. (A category of the human mind: The notion of person; the notion of self, trans. H. D. Wells. In Carrithers, Michael, Steven Collins, and Steven Lukes, eds. 1985. *The category of the person: Anthropology, philosophy, history*, pp. 1–25. Cambridge: Cambridge UP.)

Mehler, J., J. Bertoncini, M. Barriere, and D. Jassik-Gerschenfeld. 1978. Infant recognition of mother's voice. *Perception* 7: 491–497.

Merritt, Marilyn. 1994. Repetition in situated discourse: Exploring its forms and functions. In Barbara Johnstone, ed., *Repetition in discourse: Interdisciplinary perspectives*, vol. 1, pp. 23–36. Norwood, NJ: Ablex.

Milroy, James. 1992. *Linguistic variation and change.* Oxford and Cambridge, MA: Blackwell.

Milroy, Lesley. 1987. *Language and social networks.* Oxford: Basil Blackwell.

Morris, Colin. 1987. *The discovery of the individual, 1050–1200.* Toronto and Buffalo: U of Toronto P in association with the Medieval Academy of America.

Murchland, Bernard. 1987. *Voices in America: Bicentennial conversations.* Ann Arbor, MI: Prakken Publications.

Nash, Sunny. 1986, Dec. 28. On being black in Houston: The story of Sanko, a city-born man with a food cart. *Houston Post Magazine*, pp. 6–8.

Nash, Sunny. 1992a, Sept. 10. Blacks in focus: Photos reveal slave descendants' story. *Bryan College Station Eagle*, p. B4.

Nash, Sunny. 1992b, Oct. 8. From slave to citizen: The founding of a people. *Bryan College Station Eagle*, p. B3.

Nash, Sunny. 1992c. Kwanzaa, an African American celebration. *Legacy* 1: 6.

Nash, Sunny. 1993a, February 4. Gymnastics a hit in Bryan in the '50s. *Bryan College Station Eagle*, p. B2.

Nash, Sunny. 1993b, Mar. 4. Hudge, the traveling fiddler. *Bryan College Station Eagle*, p. B3.

Nathan, Harriet. 1986. *Critical choices in interviews: Conduct, use, and research role.* Berkeley: Institute of Governmental Studies, University of California, Berkeley.

Norrick, Neal R. 1987. Functions of repetition in conversation. *Text* 7: 245–264.

O'Barr, William, and Bowman K. Atkins. 1980. "Women's language" or "powerless language"? In Sally McConnell-Ginet, Ruth Borker, and Nelly Furman, eds., *Women and language in literature and society*, pp. 93–110. New York: Praeger.

O'Connell, Daniel C. 1988. *Critical essays on language use and psychology*. New York: Springer-Verlag.

Ochs, Elinor. 1979. Planned and unplanned discourse. In Talmy Givón, ed., *Syntax and semantics*, vol. 12, *Discourse and syntax*, pp. 51–80. New York: Academic P.

Ong, Walter. 1982. *Orality and literacy*. London and New York: Methuen.

Ortega y Gasset, José. 1957. *Man and people*. New York: Norton.

Ortega y Gasset, José. 1959. The difficulty of reading. *Diogenes* 28:1–17.

Paul, Hermann. 1889. *Principles of the history of language*, trans. H. A. Strong. New York: Macmillan.

Payne, Arvilla. 1980. Factors controlling the acquisition of the Philadelphia dialect by out-of-state children. In William Labov, ed., *Locating language in time and space*, pp. 143–178. New York: Academic P.

Perelman, Chaim, and L. Olbrechts-Tyteca. 1969. *The new rhetoric: A treatise on argumentation*, trans. John Wilkenson and Purcell Weaver. Notre Dame, IN: U of Notre Dame P.

Philipsen, Gerry. 1992. *Speaking culturally: Explorations in social communication*. Albany: State U of New York P.

Pike, Kenneth L. 1967. *Language in relation to a unified theory of the structure of human behavior*. The Hague: Mouton.

Pittam, Jeffery, ed. 1994. *Voice in social interaction: An interdisciplinary approach*. Thousand Oaks, CA: Sage.

Polanyi, Livia. 1979. So what's the point? *Semiotica* 25: 207–241.

Polanyi, Livia. 1985. *Telling the American story: A structural and cultural analysis of conversational storytelling*. Norwood, NJ: Ablex.

Preminger, Alex, ed. 1974. *Princeton encyclopedia of poetry and poetics*. Princeton, NJ: Princeton UP.

Quirk, Randolph, and Sidney Greenbaum. 1973. *A concise grammar of contemporary English*. New York: Harcourt Brace Jovanovich.

Read, K. E. 1955. Morality and the concept of the person among the Gahuku-Gama. *Oceania* 25: 233–282.

Reisman, David, with Nathan Glazer and Reuel Denney. 1950. *The lonely crowd: A study of the changing American character*. New Haven: Yale UP.

Roberts, Celia, and Tom Jupp. 1985. Informal presentation on men's and women's talk in an academic meeting, Linguistic Society of America Summer Institute, Georgetown University.

Robins, R. H. 1979. *A short history of linguistics*. London: Longman.

Rosaldo, Michelle Z. 1984. Toward an anthropology of self and feeling. In Richard A. Shweder and Robert A. LeVine, eds., *Culture theory: Essays on mind, self, and emotion*, pp. 137–157. Cambridge: Cambridge UP.

Rosen, Harold. 1988. The autobiographical impulse. In Deborah Tannen, ed., *Linguistics in context: Connecting observation and understanding*, pp. 69–88. Norwood, NJ: Ablex.

Ross, John Robert. 1979. Where's English? In Charles J. Fillmore, Daniel Kempler, and William S.-Y. Wang, eds., *Individual differences in language ability and language behavior*, pp. 127–163. New York: Academic P.

Sachs, Jacqueline, Philip Lieberman, and Donna Erickson. 1973. Anatomical and cultural determinants of male and female speech. In Roger W. Shuy and Ralph Fasold, eds., *Language attitudes: Current trends and prospects*, pp. 74–84. Washington, D.C.: Georgetown UP.

Sacks, Harvey, Emanuel A. Schegloff, and Gail Jefferson. 1974. A simplest systematics for the organization of turntaking for conversation. *Language* 50: 696–735.

Sapir, Edward. 1921. *Language*. New York: Harcourt, Brace, and World.

Sapir, Edward. 1949. *Selected writings of Edward Sapir in language, culture, and personality*, ed. David G. Mandelbaum. Berkeley: U of California P.

Saussure, Ferdinand de. 1966. *A course in general linguistics*, ed. Charles Bally and Albert Sechehaye; trans. Wade Baskin. New York: McGraw Hill. (Original work published 1916.)

Saville-Troike, Muriel. 1982. *The ethnography of communication: An introduction*. Oxford: Basil Blackwell.

Schafer, Roy. 1981. Narration in the psychoanalytic dialogue. In W. J. T. Mitchell, ed., *On narrative*, pp. 25–49. Chicago: U of Chicago P.

Schiffer, S. R. 1972. *Meaning*. Oxford: Clarendon P.

Schiffrin, Deborah. 1981. Tense variation in narrative. *Language* 57: 45–62.

Schiffrin, Deborah. 1987. *Discourse markers*. Cambridge: Cambridge UP.

Schiffrin, Deborah. 1994. *Approaches to discourse*. Cambridge USA: Blackwell.

Schnebly, Cynthia. 1994. Repetition and failed conversation in the Theater of the Absurd. In Barbara Johnstone, ed., *Repetition in discourse: Interdisciplinary perspectives*, vol. 1, pp. 98–112. Norwood, NJ: Ablex.

Scollon, Ron. 1982. The rhythmic integration of ordinary talk. In Deborah Tannen, ed., *Georgetown University round table on languages and linguistics 1981*, pp. 335–49. Washington, D.C.: Georgetown UP.

Scollon, Ron. 1995. Plagiarism and ideology: Identity in intercultural discourse. *Language in Society* 24: 1–28.

Sherzer, Joel. 1975. Semantic systems, discourse structures, and the ecology of language. In Ralph W. Fasold and Roger W. Shuy, eds., *Studies in language variation*, pp. 283–293. Washington, D.C.: Georgetown UP.

Sherzer, Joel. 1982. Poetic structuring of Kuna discourse: The line. *Language in Society* 11: 371–390.

Shweder, Richard A., and Edmund J. Bourne. 1984. Does the concept of the self vary cross-culturally? In Richard A. Shweder and Robert LeVine, eds., *Culture theory: Essays on mind, self, and emotion*, pp. 158–199. Cambridge: Cambridge UP.

Sperber, Dan, and Dierdre Wilson. 1986. *Relevance: Communication and cognition*. Cambridge, MA: Harvard UP.

Stano, Michael E., and N. L. Reinsch Jr. 1982. *Communication in interviews*. Englewood Cliffs, NJ: Prentice-Hall.

Steiner, George. 1989. *Real presences*. Chicago: U of Chicago P.

Strauss, Anselm, and Leonard Schatzman. 1955. Cross-class interviewing: An analysis of interaction and communicative styles. *Human Organization* 14: 28–31.

Tannen, Deborah. 1984. *Conversational style: Analyzing talk among friends*. Norwood, NJ: Ablex.

Tannen, Deborah. 1987a. Repetition in conversation: Toward a poetics of talk. *Language* 63: 574–605.

Tannen, Deborah. 1987b. Repetition in conversation as spontaneous formulaicity. *Text* 7: 215–243.

Tannen, Deborah. 1989. *Talking voices: Repetition, dialogue, and imagery in conversational discourse*. Cambridge: Cambridge UP.

Tannen, Deborah. 1990. *You just don't understand: Women and men in conversation*. New York: William Morrow.

Taylor, Charles. 1989. *Sources of the self: The making of modern identity*. Cambridge, MA: Harvard UP.

Thompson, Sandra A. 1984. "Subordination" in formal and informal discourse. In Deborah Schiffrin, ed., *Georgetown University round table on languages and linguistics 1984*, pp. 85–94. Washington, D.C.: Georgetown UP.

Thompson, Sandra A. 1987. "Subordination" and narrative event structure. In Russell S. Tomlin, ed., *Coherence and grounding in discourse*, pp. 435–454. Philadelphia: John Benjamins.

Tocqueville, Alexis de. 1960. *Journey to America*, trans. George Lawrence; ed. J. P. Mayer. New Haven: Yale UP.

Tocqueville, Alexis de. 1966. *Democracy in America*, trans. George Lawrence; ed. J. P. Mayer & Max Lerner. New York: Harper and Row.

Tomlin, Russell R. 1985. Foreground-background information and the syntax of subordination. *Text* 5: 85–122.

Tomlin, Russell. 1994. Repetition in second language acquisition. In Barbara Johnstone, ed., *Repetition in discourse: Interdisciplinary perspectives*, vol. 1, pp. 172–194. Norwood, NJ: Ablex.

Trudgill, Peter. 1986. *Dialects in contact*. New York: Basil Blackwell.

Urban, Greg. 1994. Repetition and cultural replication: Three examples from Shokleng. In Barbara Johnstone, ed., *Repetition in discourse: Interdisciplinary perspectives*, vol. 2, pp. 145–161. Norwood, NJ: Ablex.

van Dijk, Teun A. 1981. Episodes as units of discourse analysis. In Deborah Tannen, ed., *Georgetown University round table on languages and linguistics 1981*, pp. 177–195. Washington, D.C.: Georgetown UP.

Varenne, Hervé. 1977. *Americans together: Structured diversity in a midwestern town*. New York: Teachers College P.

Warren, James Perrin. 1990. *Walt Whitman's language experiment*. University Park, PA: Pennsylvania State UP.

Whitman, Walt. 1966. *Leaves of Grass, and selected prose*, ed. Sculley Bradley. New York: Holt, Rinehart, and Winston.

Whitman, Walt. 1987. *An American primer*, ed. Horace Traubel. Stevens Point, WI: Holy Cow! P.

Wilson, Bob, and Ann M. Peters. 1988. What are you cookin' on a hot? *Language* 64: 249–273.

Wolfson, Nessa. 1976. Speech events and natural speech: Some implications for sociolinguistic methodology. *Language in Society* 5: 188–209.

Wolfson, Nessa. 1982. CHP: *The conversational historical present in American English narrative*. Dordrecht: Foris.

Young, Katharine Galloway. 1987. *Taleworlds and storyrealms*. Boston: Martinus Nijhoff.

Index

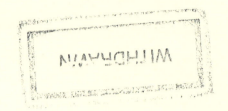